ADONIS

Selections from

L'ADONE

of Giambattista Marino

Giambattista Marino

(Frontispiece from first edition of *L'Adone,* Paris, 1623)

ADONIS

Selections from

L'ADONE

of Giambattista Marino

Translated with an Introduction by

Harold Martin Priest

Cornell University Press

ITHACA, NEW YORK

CORNELL UNIVERSITY PRESS

First published 1967

Library of Congress Catalog Card Number: 67–13467

PRINTED IN THE UNITED STATES OF AMERICA
BY KINGSPORT PRESS, INC.

Acknowledgments

I SHOULD like to express my gratitude to Margaret Datz for the drawings she has made for this volume.

The portrait of Marino facing the title page is a reproduction of the frontispiece in the first edition of *L'Adone* (Paris, Oliviero di Varano, 1623).

To present the reader with a comprehensive view of the poem of which this work offers selected passages, I have translated the summaries of cantos from *Marino e i Marinisti*, edited by Giuseppe Guido Ferrero, Volume 37 in "La letteratura italiana —Storia e testi" (Milan and Naples, Ricciardi, 1954). This material has been included with the kind permission of the publisher.

I am deeply indebted to Professor John Freccero of The Johns Hopkins University for his careful checking of the accuracy of my translation as well as for general advice and encouragement. His corrections and emendations have been invaluable in my rendering of scores of intricate passages, and his criticism of my introductory essay has served well in points of scholarship and criticism.

I also owe particular thanks to Dr. Carlo Moscovici and Dr. Giovannella Moscovici for their generous help over several years in unraveling complex passages in the Italian text.

Among the numerous colleagues, students, and friends who have read parts of my manuscript and given me valuable suggestions, I wish to express my special appreciation for their critical examination of the introduction to Professors Gunnar

Boklund and Russell Porter. Mrs. Alberta Weare has read the entire manuscript with a sharp eye for inconsistencies of diction and meter.

Officials of the University of Denver who have been generous in their practical assistance as well as encouragement are Chancellor Chester M. Alter, Dean James E. Perdue (now president of State University of New York, College of Oswego), and Gerald W. Chapman, Chairman of the Department of English.

The participation of my wife, Willa, in this work is difficult to assess. One large, tangible contribution has been the typing of the manuscript in its numerous stages. Beyond that her sound judgment and good taste have been of great help to me time and again. Finally her understanding, patience, and forbearance during the long periods of my affair with *L'Adone* merit special acknowledgment.

HAROLD MARTIN PRIEST

Denver, Colorado
September 1966

Contents

Introduction

WITHOUT doubt the most spectacular event in the European publishing world in 1623 was the appearance of the Paris edition of Marino's long-awaited *L'Adone* ("Adonis"). And despite its inordinate length, the poem was republished in at least eleven editions during the next fifty years, a fact that leaves little doubt of its enthusiastic reception. That *L'Adone* has been so largely forgotten serves to point a moral, especially when one remembers another publication of 1623, the first folio of Shakespeare's plays. A recent listing in a bookseller's catalogue of a first edition of *L'Adone* for $130.00 underscored this lesson of the vagaries of fame. A Shakespeare first folio would bring several hundred times that amount. As the goddess Fortune declares to Adonis, speaking of the globe she holds:

> "Thus does this rolling orb keep changing moods,
> 'tis only constant in inconstancy."   [*L'Adone* I, 50]

The value of a Shakespeare first folio is not a matter for argument. As to the merits of Marino's book, there is general agreement that its reputation was inflated in its time; but surely its almost complete neglect through two and a half centuries was also undeserved, as critics are gradually coming to recognize. It is hoped that this book will make a contribution toward the renewal of appreciation for Marino's masterpiece "this side idolatry."

MARINO

The most commonly accepted form of the poet's name seems to have been Giambattista Marino, though the more formal Giovanni Battista and Giovan Battista are also familiar; and an alternate spelling of the surname, Marini, is frequently found in bibliographies. On the title page of his works, however, he favored the use of "Il Cavalier Marino."

The career of Marino, viewed in broad perspective, appears to have been a series of spectacular successes, though closer inquiry reveals a few periods of reversal and depression. He was first and last a poet, not like so many of his contemporaries a soldier-poet, or a diplomat, painter, explorer, or bishop with the avocation of poet. And in an epoch of patronage, he was most fortunate in his patrons, who included a cardinal, a duke of Savoy, a queen regent of France, and finally a king of France. He was first and last a court poet, spending almost his entire career in some of the most cultivated European courts of the first quarter of the seventeenth century.

Marino's career was clearly patterned by the cities in which he lived for extended periods: Naples, Rome, Ravenna, Turin, and Paris.

Naples, 1569–1600

A Neapolitan by birth and temperament, Giambattista was born in 1569. His father was something of a literary dilettante but was determined that the young man should become a lawyer. The high-spirited son developed a violent distaste for the law and at the same time an intense interest in literature. Finally abandoning his legal studies, he was expelled from his father's house and was then free to amuse himself with a gay and reckless band of young Neapolitans and to devote his talents and energies to literary pursuits. His rising reputation as a writer of amorous verse is signaled by his participation in the academy of the Svegliati, his reception in several aristocratic houses, and his appointment as secretary at the court of the

Prince of Conca, where he enjoyed his first taste of elegant court life.

As a young blade he became involved in several reckless affairs and was twice sentenced to prison. He was first condemned because a girl he seduced died following an abortion. Subsequently he was accused of involvement in forging credentials to represent a friend as a priest. He managed to escape from prison and made a hasty departure from Naples. Thus, in 1600, at the age of thirty-one, he left his native city in disgrace, not to return until the last year of his life.

Rome and Ravenna, 1600–1608

Marino was well received in Rome where he was able to cultivate numerous literary associations, notably through the Accademia degli Umoristi, and he was again fortunate in receiving excellent patronage. First he was given employment under Monsignor Melchiorre Crescenzio, a powerful figure at the papal court, and subsequently under Cardinal Pietro Aldobrandini, a nephew of Pope Clement VIII.

In 1602 he made a trip to Venice to supervise the publication of his first volume of lyrics, which he entitled simply *Rime*. This collection furnished the nucleus for the several expanded and revised selections of his abundant lyric output, upon which his early celebrity was founded.

During his residence in Rome no more is heard of trouble with the police. He was devoting considerable attention to the Scriptures and patristic literature, and the fruits of this study appear in his later religious poetry and especially in his prose treatises, *Dicerie Sacre* ("Sacred Discourses").

In 1605, after the death of Clement VIII and the election of a new pope, Cardinal Aldobrandini left Rome to take up residence in Ravenna and took his poet-secretary with him. Life in Ravenna seemed comparatively dull for Marino after his years in Rome, but he got some diversion from various missions to Venice, Rimini, Mantua, Modena, and Ferrara, where he found more colorful court circles and where he was well received because of his considerable reputation as a poet.

Turin, 1608–1615

Marino accompanied the cardinal on a visit to Turin for the double wedding of two daughters of the reigning duke, Carlo Emanuele I. The court life at Turin, the "Rome of the North," charmed Marino, and he contrived to stay there on one pretext or another until he was finally granted the cardinal's permission to remain permanently.

In addition to the wedding hymns which he wrote for the grand nuptials, he composed a panegyric honoring the illustrious duke. The duke in his turn awarded Marino a knighthood in recognition of his literary attainments. Ever after, Marino used his title with understandable pride, Il Cavalier Marino.

His spectacular rise at the court of Savoy brought him added honors but inevitably stirred bitter enmities as well, especially among literary figures whom he displaced in favor. A feud developed between Marino and one Gaspare Murtola, and an exchange of satirical sonnets developed into a scandal of vituperation. At the climax of this feud, Murtola's fury provoked him to try to shoot his enemy; but, evidently as inept with a pistol as with his pen, he missed his man and wounded Marino's companion instead. Murtola was sentenced to death for his rash deed but was pardoned at the request of Marino.

The poet's enviable fortune at the court of Turin was, however, abruptly reversed, apparently because of some offense to the duke, whether real or imagined. Marino again found himself in a dismal prison; and there he remained for fourteen months despite the intervention of several influential pleaders. One of his letters gives a vivid if perhaps exaggerated picture of the wild life sharing his cell.

As soon as the sun has taken a plunge, the rats come out and perform a wild caper for me; and because they are of such a gigantic race, they appear to be the Sons of Earth who would batter down the heaven of my bedstead. . . . As for the bugs, I don't wish to speak of them, because they are so beastly elephantine that whoever would strip them of their hide could make a great profit by making boots from it. [Letter of 10 February 1612]

After his release from prison, though the gilt of the court life was sadly tarnished for him, he was obliged by his patron to remain in Turin for nearly three years.

The seven-year period in Turin was one of great literary activity, and yet we do not date the publication of many works from these years, chiefly because he was working on several long poems which he was unable to finish during that period. In 1608, the year of his coming to Turin, he had published a revised edition of the *Rime* under the title of *La Lira,* parts I and II. In 1614 he published *La Lira,* part III, by far the best selection of his short poems and the last volume of lyrics to be published under his supervision. The second important publication of the Turin period was his prose work, *Dicerie Sacre.* This work, also published in 1614, contained three long treatises or sermons based on elaborate metaphors worked around the subjects of Painting, Music, and Heaven.

Paris, 1615–1623

In the spring of 1615 Marino set out on a trip to Paris with the intention of staying for about a year. Marie de Medici, who was established as regent after the death of her husband, Henry IV, and during the minority of her son, Louis XIII, had for several years urged Marino to visit Paris. It was a fortunate time for Italians in Paris, for not only was the queen regent Italian, but her chief minister and favorite was the Italian Concini; consequently, the whole atmosphere of the court was Italianate.

Marino came to Paris armed with a glowing panegyric to the queen entitled *Il Tempio* ("The Temple"). Soon he added to his laurels by a marriage hymn on the occasion of a double royal wedding between Louis XIII and Anne of Austria, and Louis' sister Elizabeth and Prince Philip of Spain, afterward Philip IV. Marino's letters to friends in Italy reported that he was "honored, esteemed, and caressed." "I am alive, thanks be to God, healthy and (what is worse) rich as an ass. Here my affairs prosper exceedingly."

In the turbulent years that followed, the Queen Mother was temporarily deposed and Concini murdered. Still Marino's position appears to have remained secure if not quite so exalted. By 1620 he was confiding to his friends his wish to return to Italy, but he stayed on in Paris until 1623, presumably because of the advantages of publishing his major works in France where censorship was less stringent than in Italy.

In the Paris years he published *Epithalami,* 1616, a collection of ten wedding hymns; *La Galeria,* 1619, a collection of 600 poems describing and praising works of art and their artists; *La Sampogna* ("The Shepherd's Pipe"), 1620, a collection of idylls, part mythological and part pastoral; and finally *L'Adone,* 1623. Of these works only *La Galeria* was originally published in Italy. Actually it was the difficult and protracted publication of his enormous *L'Adone* which held him in Paris so long. This was the work for which he had the greatest concern with respect to censorship. A second edition appeared in Venice only a few months after the first edition in Paris, and in the second edition we do find evidence of some retouching of several passages but not, in all probability, to the extent that Marino had feared.

One question concerning Marino's life in Paris inevitably arises: What was his association with the famous literary circle which gathered in the home of the Marquise de Rambouillet? That celebrated coterie, later to develop the cult of *préciosité,* had much in common with Marino in their aims for refinement of language, elegance of manners, and extravagance of metaphor; and it has been traditional to represent Marino as the center of attention and admiration in the *chambre bleue.* No positive evidence has been discovered, however, to support this hypothetical relationship.

Rome and Naples, 1623–1625

The wanderer's return to Italy was a veritable triumph, a reception such as few men of letters have ever been accorded.

Clearly he was regarded as the greatest living Italian poet. In Rome the senators held a banquet in his honor. He was elected "prince" of the academy of Umoristi. And whenever he made a public appearance crowds flocked to hear him. In Naples his welcome was that of a conquering hero. He stood on intimate terms with the Spanish viceroy, and a bitter feud arose between two literary academies over which should have the honor of naming him its prince.

The enjoyment of this extraordinary celebrity was somewhat marred by literary squabbles between his admirers and his detractors over such questions as the relative merits of Tasso and Marino. In 1624 he received the depressing news that *L'Adone* had been placed on the Index. He was now tired, yet he was under great pressure for public appearances. Furthermore, he was trying to bring to completion his biblical epic, *La Strage degl'Innocenti* ("The Slaughter of the Innocents"), which he did not live to see in print.

Marino died in March of 1625 and was accorded a spectacular funeral. Most Italians and many Europeans believed him to be one of the world's greatest poets.

L'ADONE

Scope and Variety

During the later decades of the sixteenth century and the first half of the seventeenth, the subjects for heroic poetry which had dominated Renaissance literature were being forsaken for other types of story matter. The theme of Christian knights in Christian wars, their military and amorous adventures, as typified by the poems of Ariosto, Tasso, Camoëns, and Spenser, had evidently run its course.

The prevalent new subjects for narrative verse show a division into two contrasting schools: mythological or Ovidian on the one hand, and biblical on the other. The popularity of the biblical epic is illustrated by Du Bartas' *La Semaine,* Tasso's *Il Mondo Creato,* Giles Fletcher's *Christ's Victory and Triumph,* and Milton's *Paradise Lost* and *Paradise Regained*. Marino himself made an important contribution to this poetic tradition with his *La Strage degl'Innocenti*. The other new vein for narrative poetry, important as an index of the ambivalence of the late sixteenth and early seventeenth centuries, was based on erotic classical story materials and was conveniently designated the "Ovidian school." The first and best examples which will come to mind for English readers are *Hero and Leander,* as treated by Marlowe and Chapman, and Shakespeare's version of *Venus and Adonis*. Scores of writers, both Continental and English, explored this vein; and if the results were not often distinguished, at least there was a flourishing vogue. Gongora's *Polifemo y Galatea* was one of the best poems to come out of this movement. This renewed cultivation of classical material was in the air when Marino commenced writing his *L'Adone* and *La Sampogna*.

"The new Ovid" was a title often applied to Marino, and for good reasons. In addition to the obvious fact of his having related many of the myths from the *Metamorphoses,* he had acquired a reputation for racy erotic poetry; and furthermore, like Ovid, he lived in, and to a certain extent spoke for, a silver age of his nation's literature.

The love story of Venus and Adonis appears in Ovid's *Metamorphoses* [Bk. X, ll. 503–59, 705–39] in a version containing fewer than one hundred lines. During the Renaissance, following the popular practice of the "Ovidian school," the story was retold, with varying degrees of embellishment, by poets of several nationalities. Shakespeare's famous version is expanded to 1200 lines, partly by means of long conversations between the lovers and partly by reporting the lament of Venus after the death of Adonis. Not only is Shakespeare's version of the story much longer than Ovid's, it is also different in spirit. Venus is smitten with love for young Adonis but cannot lure him into amorous play. All he wants to do is go hunting. The cherished myth is thus refashioned in a somewhat comic vein.

The purpose of rehearsing ancient myths, as practiced by the

"Ovidians," was to demonstrate one's sensibility and taste in the interpretation and to exercise one's ingenuity in expanding the bare narrative with new incidents as well as descriptive, dramatic, and reflective passages and with whatever decorations imagination could invent. This practice of expansion of the story was referred to by the term *copia*. And it was in no small measure his skillful application of *copia* which brought fame to Marino and his version of Venus and Adonis, for he built his poem to 41,000 lines. Marino's poem is longer than the *Faerie Queene* or *Orlando Furioso,* and more than twice as long as the *Iliad, Odyssey, Divine Comedy,* or *Jerusalem Delivered.* It is four times the length of *Paradise Lost.*

To comprehend Marino's *modus operandi* we need to examine some of the principal means employed in developing his elaborate epic. The single most productive method of expanding his basic plot is by introducing other classical myths of love. He does this so frequently that we can see *L'Adone* as a minor encyclopedia of classical lore. For example, after giving the story of Venus and Adonis a fair start in Canto I, he devotes virtually the entire second canto to Clizio's lengthy recounting of the tale of the Judgment of Paris. The story of Venus and Adonis is resumed in Canto III, but Canto IV is devoted to the romance of Cupid and Psyche. In Canto V there are five more lovers' tales reported, this time in the space of a hundred stanzas. Canto VII introduces the myth of Venus and Mars being trapped in a net by Vulcan and exposed in shame before the Olympian gods. Marino then abandons this rehearsing of classical myths almost entirely until he reaches Canto XIX where, in connection with the mourning for Adonis, six more myths of love and death are recounted. Altogether the material in this category, the story within the story, accounts for between seven and eight thousand lines of the poem.

In addition to the myths retold, scores of other subjects are introduced, the presence of which can be justified only by the most liberal approach to the question of unity. At one point the author tells his life story. A game of chess takes up 400 lines.

There is a detailed account of a splendid entertainment in a theater equipped with a revolving stage. Adonis is escorted on a flight into the heavens, which takes him to the spheres of the Moon, Mercury, and Venus. There is time for eloquent panegyrics to various noble and royal dynasties to which Marino was indebted or with which he hoped to ingratiate himself. There is a long section on the history of poetry, and a fantastic account of a musical duel between a lute player and a nightingale.

These colorful interpolations are representative of the numerous portions of the poem which might be classed as digressions. Certainly they could be deleted without damage to the central plot. One might accuse Marino of merely padding his tale, but a more sympathetic interpretation would classify the digressions as *copia*. One thing is certain: several of the passages in question are among the most famous in the whole work, and they are also the ones that the reader will remember and the anthologist will select. This practice of introducing diverse subject matter should tell us something about the essential character of the poem.

Another element which contributes to the bulk of the poem is the descriptive matter. For a narrative poem *L'Adone* has an extraordinarily high proportion of lines devoted to description. Examples might be drawn from portraits of individual characters as well as allegorical figures, but far more prominent are the woodland scenes and the many pictures of splendid palaces, fountains, and gardens, which Marino elaborated with such evident pleasure and such display of art.

In the category of descriptive-narrative *divertimenti*, with numerous prominent episodes, much the longest passage is the celebrated account of the Garden of Pleasure. The episode comprises Cantos VI through VIII, a section of nearly 5,000 lines, and could very well be published as an independent poem. The Garden of Pleasure is divided into five sections: the Eye, the Nose, the Ear, the Mouth, and the Touch. In these gardens we encounter scenes, characters, and festivities of the most wonder-

ful variety. Here Marino earned his reputation for ingenuity
and fertility of imagination, and here too he gained the title of
"Poet of the Five Senses," with all that the title implies in terms
of credit and deprecation.

L'Adone can be catalogued, superficially, as an extended version of a classical myth. The setting is prehistoric Greece. The
cast of characters includes—in addition to Venus and Adonis—
Cupid, Apollo, Mercury, Mars, and a few more Olympian deities, as well as sea nymphs, wood nymphs, satyrs, and bacchantes.
There is also the wicked witch Falsirena, who seems a bit of a
foreigner in that company. We find few mortals with names to
remember. The shepherd Clizio is one. A scene in Canto XVI
includes a score of human characters, contenders for the crown
of Cyprus and judges at the "election," but these characters appear only once and are quickly forgotten.

The time, the setting, and the characters of the poem are
purely classical; and more than that, classical allusions are introduced on almost every page. We must not only be impressed
with Marino's extensive knowledge of this field of learning, but
we must also recognize a similar familiarity and keenness on the
part of his contemporary readers; for many of the allusions are
brief and indirect, demanding that the reader exercise his wit
as well as draw upon a ready store of classical learning. Not
many readers now are sufficiently grounded in the lore of antiquity to cope with all the references and allusions found here;
hence footnotes appear to be in order for a modern edition. It
is only reasonable, however, in our total assessment of the poem,
to recognize that the fund of knowledge and the form of wit
demanded constitute one of the important elements of the
poetics of the age.

Even with L'Adone's obviously classical setting, it can hardly
escape the reader that Marino's enthusiasm for the splendors of
the court life in his own time—the pomp, elegance, and lavish-
ness of Baroque art and entertainment—has made its way into
the poem. At certain points in the story one visualizes a scene

of Arcadian simplicity, but other passages conjure up pictures of the most elaborate Baroque palaces, theaters, fountains, and formal gardens in which Marino's contemporaries took their pleasure. The presentation of these Baroque scenes constitutes one of Marino's major successes. When these passages are compared with descriptions of similar subjects by other poets we must appreciate their attention to concrete features and their effectiveness in capturing the style of contemporary decor. Poets long before Marino had mentioned fountains often enough, but their references were almost always perfunctory; actual description seldom went beyond "crystal depths," though there were a few more elaborate ones, for instance in Tasso and Spenser. With Marino such a description as that of the four fountains in the courtyard of the Palace of Love, dwelling as it does upon the rich materials and fantastic sculptured figures, creates an image which is reminiscent of Baroque fountains in the Bernini style and which is, moreover, quite new to poetic literature.

It must be recognized, then, that the world of *L'Adone* is compounded of the sylvan grace and charm of the golden world of Greece and the magnificence of the Baroque ambience, a combination of elements which might well have resulted in a distressing ambivalence. As Marino handles his material, however, the reader is never struck with any feeling of incongruity, because the splendid palaces and gardens described are represented as the earthly dwellings and playgrounds of the gods. Indeed the fusion of diverse elements contributes greatly to the interest and the entertainment of the poem. One is inevitably reminded of the ladies and gentlemen of the Court of Versailles who divided their time between attendance at elegant, formal functions at the palace and playing at shepherd and shepherdess with Marie Antoinette in the gardens.

The appellation "Poet of the Five Senses," which has been attached to Marino, can be interpreted in either a laudatory or pejorative sense. By some it has been employed to impute a serious limitation in the scope of Marino's poetry, particularly of *L'Adone*, suggesting that Marino's whole interest lay in sensory pleasure. Calcaterra would have it that although Marino claimed to be soaring in the empyrean of sensation and myth, transforming semblance and quality, "in reality, if one observes well, he was the poet of a single chord: the sensual and erotic." [1] Other critics, however, who have found matter for praise in the poem, have invariably exhibited their greatest admiration for passages concerned with the sensuous, stating that this is what made Marino a poet. After all sensory experience is acknowledged to be a prime essential of poetry. The question then is whether the poet works this vein to the exclusion of everything else or abuses it by merely pandering to sensations of purely animalistic nature. What must be recognized is that for Marino the world of sensory delights encompasses the worlds of music, painting, architecture, and gardening, as well as the refined and sensitive responses to the simplest forms of beauty in nature. And if indeed Marino elevates sensation to a position out of proportion to its true philosophical worth, his devotion to it assuredly results in passages of warmth and insight that strip "the veil of familiarity from the world, and [lay] bare the naked and sleeping beauty which is the spirit of its forms."

The examination of *L'Adone* for evidence of seriousness of purpose is rewarded to a degree, despite the traditional opinion to the contrary. Marino's philosophy—or if that is too elevated a term, his view of life—lays heavy emphasis on the enjoyment of life; and in his scheme the highest form of pleasure is love, love that is primarily pagan and sensuous. The love Marino talks about involves the enjoyment of beauty and of the union of bodies. Nevertheless, we are not allowed to forget that love represents the life principle. In several key passages Marino associates Venus with divine procreation, and we discover that the frivolous play on the terms *living, dying, living again*—terms which are often repeated in such

---

[1] Carlo Calcaterra, *Il Parnaso in Rivolta* (Bologna, Mulino, 1961), p. 17. (Translations from the Italian are mine—H.M.P.)

passages as the "Song of Kisses"—is at times related to the cosmic treatment of the life-death-rebirth cycle which from primitive times has been associated with the myth of Adonis. In the elaborate hymn to Venus, the universal mother, we perceive something of this aim to represent love as the primal life force, as may be judged from the following brief excerpt:

> *"Commessura d'amor, virtù ch'innesti*
> *Con saldi groppi di concordi amplessi*
> *E le cose terrene e le celesti,*
> *E supponi al tuo fren gli abissi istessi;*
> *Per cui con fertil copula contesti*
> *Vicendevol desio stringe i duo sessi,*
> *Sì che mentre l'un dona e l'altro prende*
> *Il cambio del piacer si toglie e rende."*   [VII, 80]

> "O binding force of love, a power that links
> with firmest knots of mutual embrace
> both things celestial and terrestrial
> and even subjugates the dark abyss;
> through whose control, reciprocal desires
> impel both sexes, coupling fertilely,
> so that while one gives and the other takes,
> exchange of joys is rendered and received."

Certainly this association of love with the life principle is not new, but its frequent recurrence in *L'Adone* is evidence of a desire on the part of Marino to endow his poem with some degree of depth and dignity. And a further sign of his seriousness of purpose is exhibited in his development of the microcosm-macrocosm concept in connection with his praise of the human body. Coming at the beginning of the key section of the work, the Gardens of the Five Senses, this concept is afforded an appropriate emphasis. The idea that man is "a little world made cunningly" to correspond point by point with the order of the great world, the universe, is one of the favorite doctrines of the philosophers of the period and one which is echoed often

among poets of a philosophical turn. The following excerpt
will serve as a key to the elaborate passage treating the theme:

> *"Quasi in angusta mappa immensa sfera,*
> *Fu l'universo epilogato in esso.* . . .*

> *"È distinto in tre parti il maggior mondo,*
> *L'una è de' sommi dei, che 'n alto stassi.*
> *De le sfere rotanti hanno il secondo*
> *Loco le belle e ben disposte classi.*
> *Ritien l'ultimo sito e più profondo*
> *La region de gli elementi bassi;*
> *E quest'altro minor, ch'ha spirti e sensi,*
> *Ben di proporzion seco conviensi.*

> *"Sostien la vece del sovran motore*
> *Nel capo eccelso la virtù, che 'ntende;*
> *Stassi a guisa di sol nel mezzo il core,*
> *Lo qual per tutto il suo calor distende.*
> *Il ventre ne la sede inferiore*
> *Qual corpo sublunar varia vicende;*
> *Così in governo e nutrimento e vita*
> *Questa casa animata è tripartita.* . . .*"   [VI, 11, 12, 13]

"Like some great sphere drawn on a narrow map,
the universe was epilogued in it [the body]. . . .

"The major world [2] is portioned in three parts,
the one of the great gods, which stands on high.
The several orders of the rolling spheres,
so fair and well disposed, have second place.
The last and lowest site of all contains
the region of the lowest elements;
to these this other, lesser world [3] conforms,
which is with senses and with spirits blessed.

"The power of understanding, in the head,
retains the role of sovereign governor;

[2] The macrocosm, or the universe.
[3] The microcosm, or the human body.

midway, holding the sun's place, stands the heart,
which spreads its gentle warmth to all the rest.
The belly, in the lower, corporal seat,
like a sublunar body, fosters change;
in government, in nourishment, in life,
this animated house is tripartite. . . ."

L'Adone, an exceedingly long poem, which is represented in the following translation by only 1,000 stanzas (one-fifth of the entire poem), has occasional weaknesses. It is at times tiresome, tasteless, overblown, and repetitious. But it contains many fine and beautiful passages. The rich variety of scenes and incidents offers an abundance of interesting and charming entertainment. The subject matter of the poem was naturally dictated by the particular tastes and interests of the author, which evidently reflected accurately the tastes and interests of his generation. As one cannot ignore the voices of the metaphysical poets and the Jacobean dramatists if he hopes to understand the early seventeenth century, by the same token one cannot ignore the voice of Marino in *L'Adone,* particularly for that facet of the age which is designated as Baroque. In *L'Adone* a passionate devotion to the world of classical antiquity, so all-pervasive in those times, is combined with a proud representation of the spectacle of court splendors which Marino drew from the palaces, gardens, and fountains of that age of magnificence.

The Marinistic Style

Heretofore attention has been fixed on those aspects of Marino's invention which allowed him to build his poem to such amazing length and delightful variety. The other aspect of his poetry that has always attracted special attention, whether for praise or criticism, is his style. In his own day it was this style more than anything else that established his prodigious reputation. To say it was an ornate style is not enough. The goal

he aimed for was an effect of grandeur; and his concept of
beauty, like that of his age generally, was one of decoration—
decoration that was both elaborate and rich. The structure of
Baroque architecture, balanced and skillfully proportioned, is
basically classical. The outlines, however, are largely concealed
by a heavy incrustation of elaborate carvings, and the interiors of
palaces and churches alike dazzle the eye with yet more sculpture, colored marble, and quantities of gleaming gold and
silver. Organic design is thus almost forgotten in the presence of
the overpowering surface ornament. The same devotion to the
ornamental aspects of poetry is eminently characteristic of
Marino's verse, and it was on this basis that his age assessed the
virtues of a poet's work. That this was a prevailing current of
taste and that Marino was a virtuoso in linguistic decoration
goes far to explain his phenomenal contemporary success. A
study of the European literary scene of Marino's time reveals
euphuism, Gongorism, *préciosité*, and the metaphysical school,
none of which are quite identical with Marinismo but all of
which lean heavily on excessive ornateness of style.

Marino's particular brand of ornateness is far from simple;
yet its distinguishing qualities can be isolated and identified
with as much clarity as is ever possible in matters of this
nature. First, he employs the entire canon of the figures of
classical rhetoric, and his employment of figures is not only
varied but frequent. Out of the great variety of devices, however,
a few can be recognized as favorites, and by far the most
important in both quantity and quality is the metaphor, which
serves as the real key to the Marino style. In his metaphors
readers discovered the particular genius of Marino and some
critics discovered the basis for a new aesthetic for poetry.

Many early seventeenth-century artists and poets, sensing
the futility of competing with the Renaissance masters by
imitating established modes, instituted a desperate search for
new means to attain distinction: new vocabulary, new perspec-
tives, new this, new that. For poets the watchwords were novelty,
ingenuity, wit, conceit, *acutezza*, *pointe*. And it was precisely

for his ingenuity in the treatment of metaphors and conceits that Marino became an idol for the hour.

An often quoted declaration, originally intended ironically, serves admirably as a credo for Marino and his school:

> È del poeta il fin la meraviglia
> (Parlo de l'eccellente e non del goffo) :
> Chi non sa far stupir, vada alla striglia!   [Murtoleide, XXXIII]

> The aim of the poet is the marvelous
> (I speak of the excellent, not the dull one) :
> who knows not how to astonish [stupefy], go to the stable!

His constant aim for new conceits is plainly pronounced in one of the sectional invocations in *L'Adone*. Addressing Urania, he pleads:

> Movi la penna mia tu, che'l ciel movi,
> E detta a novo stil concetti novi.   [X, 2]

> Guide thou my pen, O thou who movest heavens,
> and to a new style dictate new conceits.

To present in reasonably brief space a comprehensive impression of the style of *L'Adone*, the discussion will be concerned chiefly with three salient features: irregularities of syntax, verbal patterns for sound effects, and metaphors. Other features will be mentioned or discussed only briefly.

The extraordinary irregularities of sentence arrangement constitute a noteworthy if not a major stylistic feature of the poem. Even if allowance is made for the freedom of most Italian poets in this respect, Marino must be singled out for a syntax that is highly unnatural. One is tempted to say he is Miltonic, but he goes far beyond Milton in his leaps and turns. The nearest comparable patterns are those found in Latin or Anglo-Saxon poetry.

This feature, known in the terminology of classical rhetoric as *hyperbaton*, is defined as the placing of essential grammatical elements in unnatural location: subject delayed, verb delayed, verb and subject inverted or widely separated, substantive and modifier separated. To understand the extent of the distortion the reader would need to make a detailed examination of passages in the original. The syntax of the translation is frequently distorted as well, but not to the extent that the original is, and not necessarily in the identical manner or in the same passages. The translator, who has had to find his way through a thousand stanzas, could not fail to be deeply impressed with this aspect of the style. It is a rare occurrence when in unraveling the construction of a stanza one can start with the first line.

Playing games with language, Marino enjoyed using the various figures involving words of similar sound in juxtaposition or in balanced constructions. He delighted in phrases such as:

> *O mia dorata ed adorata dea.*

> O my golden [haired] and adored goddess.

A more elaborate development of this type of figure is shown in this often quoted passage:

> *Con tai lusinghe il lusinghiero amante*
> *La lusinghiera dea lusinga e prega.*   [III, 151]

> With such seductions the seductive dame
> prays and seduces the seductive youth.

This is an extravagant example exhibiting a tasteless display of cleverness, as Marino's detractors are quick to point out. It may be said in Marino's defense that this was a kind of disease of the age, and that, as Symonds remarks, even Shakespeare sometimes adopted the style:

> Take all my loves, my love, yea take them all;
> What hast thou then more than thou hadst before?
> No love, my love, that thou may'st true love call:
> All mine was thine, before thou hadst this more. . . .
> [Sonnet XL]

Let it further be remarked in Marino's defense that the extravagant passage from his work quoted above is by no means typical. His more characteristic practice with *adnominatio* and similar schemes of word repetition is skillful and pleasing. Unfortunately many of these figures, like puns, are necessarily lost in translation.

Word play is only one phase of the concern for sound effects. Mirollo observes:

Manipulating words as though they were sounds alone, Marino revels in alliteration, assonance, and consonance in line after line. When words as they stand do not satisfy his zeal for harmony, he lavishly employs their diminutives. He is easily tempted . . . by rhyming feats and difficult rhythmic effects; and he cannot resist continually decorating the structure of his thought with both.[4]

One word more before we leave the subject of the poet's interest in sound. We have observed how concern for the oral effects of his verse is demonstrated through the studied use of various artful devices, but this does not sufficiently emphasize his constant attention to the melodic quality of his poetry. A memorable passage in the seventh canto of *L'Adone* presents Poesy and Music as twin goddesses, and it is evident to anyone reading the poem in Italian that a concern for a musical quality was fundamental to Marino's poetic credo. Here again the translator must confess inadequacy. Even if occasionally the translation produces a passage that falls pleasantly on the ear, it is certain that the effects produced are not the same in English as those of the Italian. The difference in the language makes this impossible.

One of the most surprising discoveries concerning the figurative patterns of *L'Adone* is the scarcity of similes. One often

[4] James V. Mirollo, *The Poet of the Marvelous, Giambattista Marino* (New York and London, Columbia University Press, 1963), p. 139. This work contains a section on Marino's style which fills almost one hundred pages. It is not only the most comprehensive and most fully illustrated study of the subject but also, in my opinion, the most judicious. I am indebted to this work for both information and interpretation in a good many points in this introduction.

reads for ten or twenty pages without encountering a single
one. The explanation is that Marino was intensely committed
to the development of metaphors as a principal tool for poetic
expression. The proportion of metaphors to similes is probably
fifty to one.

The similes, when he does introduce them, are only moder-
ately successful. The shorter ones tend toward the conventional,
as does this one:

> *Gli tinge il viso in quel rossor, che suole*
> *Prender la rosa infra l'aurora e'l sole.*   [I, 42]

> which tinged his face with such a gentle blush
> as roses wear between the dawn and day.

Even this has a pleasing freshness: the blush is not merely like
a rose but the color of the rose *infra l'aurora e'l sole.*

Those similes which Marino obviously meant to be impres-
sive are of the longer, "Homeric" variety. They often constitute
charming vignettes, but in some instances they are not entirely
successful in clarifying the passage with which they are
associated.

In one passionate scene when Venus wishes to restrain the
eager Adonis temporarily, we read:

> *Come a fiero talor veltro d' Irlanda*
> *Buon cacciator, che 'nfuriato il veda,*
> *Benchè venga a passar da la sua banda*
> *Vicina assai la desiata preda,*
> *La libertà però che gli dimanda*
> *Non così tosto avien che gli conceda,*
> *Anzi fermo e tenace ad ogni crollo*
> *Tira il cordon, che gl' imprigiona il collo;*
>
> *Così nè men, per più scaldar l'affetto*
> *Nel difficil goder l'amante accorta,*
> *Mentr'ei volea del suo maggior diletto*
> *Con la chiave amorosa aprir la porta,*

Di quel primo appetito al giovinetto
L'impeto affrena e'l bacia e'l riconforta.   [VIII, 70, 71]

As sometimes with a savage Irish hound
a skillful hunter, seeing him on fire,
although, perchance, the hunted prey has passed
within close range of all the restless pack,
and though the hound is straining to be free,
he will not yet release him for pursuit;
at every tug he holds tenaciously,
he grips the leash and keeps the collar fast;

just so did Venus manage, clever dame,
to add heat to his passion by her art;
while he was fain to open wide the door
of that supreme delight with amorous key,
she checks the force of that first appetite
of youth with kisses and with blandishments.

A long passage—fifty stanzas—describing a game of chess
opens with a simile: "Now here . . . as on the battlefield . . ."
and extends the analogy throughout the entire account of the
game. The idea of the parallel between war and chess was
readily provided by the names for the chess pieces, including
even the pawns, which were represented as infantry, and the
archers, which in the modern chess sets are bishops. Still
Marino must be credited with a masterful execution of the
whole analogy by describing with exaggerated vigor and
solemnity the conflict on the board and creating a spirited
burlesque akin to Pope's famous account of the game of ombre
in "The Rape of the Lock."

Among the rhetorical devices which we know were especially
popular with Marino and many of his contemporaries and
indeed with many long before them, we recognize paradox and
the related oxymoron: i.e., the combining of contradictory
terms. One passage should serve for illustration, as anyone
acquainted with Renaissance poets will surely recall similar

examples. The following series of paradoxes represents one stanza of the fifteen that Marino devotes to a characterization of Love.

> *Lince privo di lume, Argo bendato,*
> *Vecchio lattante e pargoletto antico,*
> *Ignorante erudito, ignudo armato,*
> *Mutolo parlator, ricco mendìco;*
> *Dilettevole error, dolor bramato,*
> *Ferita cruda di pietoso amico,*
> *Pace guerriera e tempestosa calma;*
> *La sente il core e non l'intende l'alma.*   [VI, 173]

> A sightless lynx, an Argus blindfolded,
> an ancient suckling, playful aged sire,
> an ignorant sage, a naked man-at-arms,
> a silent talker, wealthy mendicant;
> delightful error, and appealing grief,
> a cruel wound come from a piteous friend,
> a warlike peace, tempestuous calm; that which
> the heart feels but the soul knows not.

The pathetic fallacy is another artifice which captured the fancy of the whole Marinistic school. One striking example occurs in a scene where Venus is hiding herself in the woods.

> *Videsi di dolcezza ancora il faggio,*
> *Il faggio, onde pendean l'arco e la veste,*
> *Non potendo capir quasi in sè stesso,*
> *Fa più germogli e divenir più spesso.*   [VIII, 45]

> Even the beech tree shows its sympathy—
> that beech on which the bow and garments hang—
> although not comprehending in itself
> how it put forth more buds and grew more dense.

The broad term conceit is commonly applied to a variety of specific figures, especially to extended similes and metaphors. There are, however, certain passages that cannot be readily classified but which develop some kind of novelty in the concept presented, and certainly these can reasonably be labeled conceits. Let us select one instance for illustration. The author speculates on what caused the freckles on the face of an otherwise handsome youth:

> Che fan con poche macchie ingiuria al resto
> Spruzzate di lentigini le gote.
> Fu forse opra d'Amor, ch'accinto e presto
> A temprar le saette in su la cote,
> Mentre l'oro affinava a le faville,
> Gliene sparse in su 'l volto alquante stille.   [XVI, 95]

> that some few freckles on his cheek are found
> which trifling blemishes cause injury.
> Perhaps 'twas Cupid's work, as he prepared
> to whet his arrows on the grinding stone,
> and while he was refining the gold tips
> he let some sparks fly in the young lad's face.

Of all the features of the Marinistic style, the one that has drawn the greatest attention is the metaphor. Marino has often been associated with his contemporary John Donne because both men were distinguished for originality and ability to surprise and amaze, especially through their use of metaphors; but an important distinction separates the two, a distinction which goes to the heart of the poetic system of each. The poet who aims for novelty through his metaphorical development must resort to one of two methods: either he will base the metaphors on traditional elements but treat them in some new and unexpected fashion, or he will introduce new elements, subjects not previously considered suitable poetic material. Donne, archrebel, earned his reputation as innovator especially for the latter treatment. Introducing a wholly new body of materials, he startled his reader with figures involving worms and fleas and mechanical objects as well as with the terminology of merchants and lawyers. Marino, in deliberately choosing the other course, adopted a practice which presumably

requires less daring but which, at the same time, places greater
demands upon the ingenuity of the author. In Marino's
metaphors one discovers a preponderance of the traditional
elements of poetry: fire and ice; flowers, birds, and stars;
silver, gold, and gems.

Among the distinguishing features of Marino's style of
metaphor is the abandonment of the sixteenth-century
doctrine that the figure should establish "a difficult equi-
librium between pleasure and morality on the one hand,
artifice and truth on the other." [5] Instead Marino and his
associates accepted the doctrine that a metaphor might be
purely decorative (artificial), with the sole purpose of pleasing
the audience. According to the analysis of Tesauro,[6] whose work
was a major source for the examination and illustration of the
Marinistic style, poetic speech is not dependent on ordinary
logic but on *ingegno* (which may be translated as "ingenuity,"
"wit," or "the genius of creativity"); and it achieves an
interpenetration of objects one with another. Modern critics
who are rediscovering Marino's merits after the long depression
of his fame, are indebted to Tesauro for having recognized that
Marino's poetry is not merely ornamental but that it contains
a metaphorical creativity of a new and high order. Donato
points out:

It becomes apparent that his [Tesauro's] poetic principles do not constitute a denial of the criterion of truth in poetry, but that poetical
truth exists on a plane quite apart, where this criterion can no longer
be applied, inasmuch as the function of poetry is to transform the
world into a spectacle. This spectacle is primarily organized by the
poet who remains sole master of the universe.[7]

The new significance of the metaphor as it became divorced

---

[5] Eugenio Donato, "Tesauro's Poetics: Through the Looking Glass," *Modern Language Notes*, Vol. 78 (1963), p. 15. I have made extensive use of this
excellent interpretation of the work of Tesauro.

[6] Emanuele Tesauro, *Il cannocchiale aristotelico* (Venice, Paolo Baglione,
1663).

[7] Donato, *loc. cit.*, p. 26.

from the realms of everyday reality to create and explore a
new reality is expressed by another modern critic in this
passage:

The metaphor, in effect, in the use which Baroque writers made of it,
does not seem reducible to a plain and extrinsic rhetorical fact, rather
it appears to respond to the expressive necessity of a mode of feeling
and of manifesting things, as an element of a complex game of allusions and illusions, as an ideal possibility for the translation of all
terms of the knowable into a vision of reality in which things seem to
lose their static and well-defined nature to wander carried away in a
universal transport which alters outlines and significances. The metaphor, rather than a rhetorical fact, seems in the Baroque age a vision
of life; [whence] for this culture one could speak positively of a universal "metaphorism" and a "metamorphism" as of essential modes of
noting and expressing reality.[8]

A conventional treatment of figures of comparison (similes
and metaphors) in their simplest form employs objects in a
comparison according to their dominant trait; e.g., for
whiteness compare milk, lilies, ivory, or snow. "Her hands
were white as snow." Such a figure, often repeated, is in danger
of losing its effectiveness, of becoming a dead image. But
that same familiarity can condition the mind for ready response
to a metaphorical substitution, whereupon a new effect is
available. The snow or milk stands for the fair white hand,
red flames for rubies, and rubies for lips or drops of blood;
blond tresses, of course, are gold. Here for example is Marino's
description of a girl with a ruby ring on her finger:

> E de la bianca man, ch'ad arte stende,
> D' indiche fiamme il vivo latte accende.   [VIII, 33]

On her white hand, which coyly she extends,
the living milk is lit with orient flame.

And here Venus, bending over the dying Adonis, wipes away
the blood with her hair:

[8] Giovanni Getto, "La polemica del Barocco," *Letteratura Italiana: Le
Correnti* (Milan, Marzorati, 1956), pp. 469–470.

È del costato i tepidi rubini
Terge con l'or de' dissipati crini.   [XVIII, 152]

and with her unbound tresses of bright gold
she wipes the tepid rubies from his chest.

In a similar passage Venus ministers to Adonis, who has just returned from the hunt, tired, breathless, and perspiring. She wipes away the drops of sweat with her hair.

L'or biondo e crespo, il terso avorio e bianco
Tre volte e quattro a rasciugar gli riede.   [VIII, 108]

The blond and curly gold three times or four
returns to dry the clear white ivory.

In one of these passages, it will be observed, the white hand is first mentioned and then later referred to as "the living milk," but in another passage "the clear white ivory" stands alone, and the reader's understanding depends on his familiarity with the metaphoric convention. This might be called the first grade in Marino metaphors. More startling perhaps, because it is more remote, is the designation of the ruby ring as orient flames. Here flame is introduced for its redness, which is definitely a secondary characteristic, the dominant characteristic being heat. In the last of the passages quoted above, drops of blood are called rubies, which is orthodox enough, but the expression "tepid rubies" makes a striking transfer of the warmth of the blood to the rubies. When the figure is based on some physical property other than the dominant trait of the object concerned, we are in a psychological zone which Marino cultivated zealously.

In the following stanza the conventional association of pearls with dewdrops or tears is interwoven in a fanciful description of Cupid weeping at daybreak.

Pianse al pianger d'Amor la mattutina
Del re de' lumi ambasciadrice stella,
E di pioggia argentata e cristallina

Rigò la faccia rugiadosa e bella,
Onde di vive perle accolte in brina
Potè l'urna colmar l'alba novella,
L'alba che l'asciugò col vel vermiglio
L'umido raggio al lagrimoso ciglio.   [I, 22]

The Morning Star shed tears for weeping Love,
ambassadress unto the king of light,
and streaked her lovely, dewy countenance
with showers silvery and crystalline,
whence Dawn drank from the overflowing urn
the living pearls commingled with hoarfrost,
and with a bright vermilion veil he dried
the humid sparkles from his tear-stained lids.

Marino gives a special display of extravagant fancy when
Adonis looks in wonder at the wounded foot of Venus.

Il ciel d'amor dal cristallino giro
Di sanguigne rugiade un nembo piove.
Quando tra gli alabastri unqua s'udiro
Nascer cinabri in cotal guisa o dove?
Da fonte eburneo uscir rivi vermigli,
Da le nevi coralli, ostri dai gigli?   [III, 117]

The heaven of love, from out its crystalline
abode, rains down a cloud of sanguine dew.
When have I ever heard that cinnabar
was born from alabaster in this wise,
that ivory fountain poured vermilion drops,
that red from lilies came, coral from snow?

At moments which seem to the author to demand special
fanfare, he may resort to the device of listing alternate
metaphors. As if in answer to the unspoken question: "What
is . . . ?" or "How can we describe . . . ?" the poet offers a
series of strikingly varied attributes. Most familiar to English
readers is the passage from *Macbeth* which characterizes
sleep:

. . . sleep,—the innocent sleep:
Sleep that knits up the ravell'd sleave of care,
The death of each day's life, sore labour's bath,
Balm to hurt minds, great nature's second course,
Chief nourisher in life's feast.

Marino has Venus lavish praise upon the mouth of Adonis in
a burst of epithets.

"*Quella bocca mi porgi. O cara bocca,*
De la reggia del Riso uscio gemmato,
Siepe di rose, in cui saetta e scocca
Viperetta amorosa arabo fiato,
Arca di perle, ond'ogni ben trabocca,
Cameretta purpurea, antro odorato,
Ove rifugge, ove s'asconde Amore
Poic' ha rubata un'alma, ucciso un core."   [VIII, 122]

"Grant me that mouth. O dear, beloved mouth,
the jeweled exit of the realm of Smiles,
a hedge of roses, whence a little viper
amorously exhales a scented breath,
coffer of pearls, whence blessings overflow,
a crimson chamber, cavern odorous,
a refuge where Love steals away and hides
when he has robbed a soul or stabbed a heart."

Probably the most celebrated and certainly the most quoted
example of this artifice is this passage in praise of the
nightingale:

Chi crederà . . .
O ch' altro sia che la liev' aura mossa
Una voce pennuta, un suon volante?
E vestito di penne un vivo fiato,
Una piuma canora, un canto alato?   [VII, 37]

Who would believe . . .
that it is other than the vibrant air,
a feathered voice, a flying sound perhaps,

indeed a living breath in feathers dressed,
or a canorous plume, a winged song?

The extraordinary variety of metaphoric figures in *L'Adone*
can only be suggested in an essay of this type, but a few more
samples may be useful to illustrate some of the direction of
the author's imagination. In appraising the features of a lad
who is an aspirant in the masculine beauty contest, one judge
finds fault with the rather large mouth:

Di quello spazio investigando il vero
Ch'al bel fonte del riso è sponda e margo. . . .   [XVI, 85]

examining the measure of that space
which is the margin of the fount of smiles. . . .

The description of the seacoast in terms of barking dogs was
certainly not a new concept with Marino, but its treatment
as metaphor is effective in these lines:

Lunge di là, dov'a morir va l'onda,
E con roco latrar morde la sponda.   [I, 56]

far, far from where the waves depart to die,
and where, with barking hoarse, they gnaw the beach.

Finally, there is a curious phrasing where a wolf is pictured
stealing back into the woods after having raided a flock of
sheep. Literally the line reads:

Serra al ventre la coda e si rimbosca.   [XVIII, 101]

presses tail to belly and reforests himself.

The development of a passage of figures within a figure makes
for new complexity and added refinements. A simile comparing
a youth parading before the public in the beauty contest to a
strutting peacock, extending over two stanzas, includes four
separate figures within it, two of them involved similes and
two of them metaphors.

Tanti non ha l'ambizioso augello
Ne le penne rosate occhi dintorno,
Quando quasi un aprile o un ciel novello,
Di cento fior, di cento stelle adorno,
De l'ampia rota sua superbo e bello
Apre il ricco teatro al novo giorno,
E 'l tesor vagheggiando, ond'ella è piena,
A sè medesmo è spettatore e scena;

Quanti pien di vaghezza e di baldanza
Il garzonetto intorno a sè n'accolse. . . .   [XVI, 83-84]

Not so many eyes the pompous bird
has in his roseate feathers spread about,
when as an April or an evening sky,
with hundred flowers or hundred stars adorned
he opes the wheel of that rich theater,
proud and beautiful, to a new day,
and showing off its treasures to the full,
is for himself the spectator and scene;

as, filled with pleasure and with pride, the youth
attracted all the glances of the crowd. . . .

Marino, of course, held no monopoly on the kind of
metaphor that created its startling effect through reference
to a single attribute of an object despite incongruities which
other properties of the object might bring to mind in the
comparison. A good many poets adopted the system, and some
—Gongora and Crashaw, for instance—carried it to greater
extremes than did Marino. Crashaw's "The Weeper" contains
numerous metaphorical extravagances which may challenge
all competition in the field.

The term *ingegno,* about which so much was written in the
seventeenth century, and upon which Tesauro founded his
theory of the new school of poetry, signifies the creative faculty
of imagination which produces metaphors. This they held to be
the highest faculty of man, the faculty through which he most
closely resembles God the creator. Tesauro writes:

Just as God from what is not produces what is, so *ingegno* of non-entity forms entity: it makes the lion become a man and the eagle a city. It joins a woman onto a fish and fabricates a siren for a symbol of the adulator. It couples the bust of a goat with the posterior of a serpent and forms the chimera as a hieroglyph of madness. Whence it was that among certain ancient philosophers *ingegno* was called a particle of the divine mind.[9]

In a final word regarding the virtue of the Marinistic style and of Baroque poetry in general, Flora insists that the school must be credited with having established a

principle which the moderns, through various paths, have received and professed strictly in art: the allusive, which is a major force in expression. The allusiveness of the seventeenth century was often the old and contorted allegory, but it was also sometimes a joy of analogical relationships in which palpitated the new panic sense. . . . The fact is that the poetic medium of the Baroque age is full of germs and ferments; thus it is more inventive and unrestrained than even that of the golden age of the sixteenth century.[10]

So much attention has been given to the Marinistic rhetoric here and in all discussions of Marino that the reader may be led to expect stylistic pyrotechnics in such quantity that the story is largely obscured and that the resultant effect is purely ornamental. Such is not the case, however, as an examination of the poem will demonstrate. There are many passages of comparatively straightforward narrative or descriptive matter in which a degree of judgment and restraint must be recognized. It is primarily at points in the work which excite the poet that he develops his stylish exhibitions, but these passages, it must be admitted, are sufficiently numerous to earn the poem the designation of Baroque.

Notes on the Translation

Marino's verse form is *ottava rima*, the traditional pattern used by most of the major Italian poets writing long narrative

[9] Tesauro, *op. cit.*, p. 76.
[10] Francesco Flora, *Storia della letteratura italiana* (Milan, Mondadori, 1950), III, 673, 677.

poems, notably Boccaccio, Boiardo, Ariosto, and Tasso. The
lines contain eleven syllables (hendecasyllabic), without any
fixed number or regular arrangement of accents such as we are
accustomed to find in traditional English verse. The stanzas
have eight lines, which rhyme *a b a b a b c c*.

Because of the involved, ornate style, the abundant use of
recherché and archaic or Latinate vocabulary, and the extreme
wrenching of syntax, much of the poem is difficult to read in
comparison with such works as *Orlando Furioso* and *Jerusalem
Delivered*.

The present translation adopts a verse form which is
essentially different from the Italian but which is familiar
and widely accepted in English poetry, namely blank verse.
This represents a compromise between two extremes in translation: one, to use rhymed English verse adhering to the
scheme of the original, the other, to use prose. Attempting to
conform to the original verse form where rhyme is employed
often forces drastic sacrifices of meaning, as anyone knows who
has experimented with rhyme in translation. The other course,
producing a literal prose translation, certainly offers the greatest
accuracy of meaning, but the reader inevitably loses much of
the sense of reading a poem.

The style of the translation is marked by the acceptance of
certain tricks of phrasing and archaisms—for example, "thee"
and "thou," "his lady fair"—which are generally frowned upon
by contemporary poets. The language of Marino's English
contemporaries—of Shakespeare, Spenser, and the King James
Version of the Bible—seems, however, to match the tone of
Marino's archaic poetic diction admirably. It is interesting to
note in this connection that Italians who read Spenser are often
struck with his resemblance to Marino.

There is no doubt that translating an Italian poem into
rhymed English verse requires far more frequent and more
violent distortions of original meaning than does translating
into unrhymed English verse. But it is only fair to warn the
reader that even blank verse requires a certain amount
of freedom in translation. Much of the translation falls fairly

readily into a line-for-line equivalent, but it frequently occurs that the most natural English equivalent of an Italian line demands some adjustment before it can be expressed in iambic pentameter. Sometimes there are syllables to spare in the English version and sometimes there are too few syllables. Curiously enough there is no great preponderance of one situation or the other. In these instances obviously the translator has to add or subtract material to produce a metrical line.

These problems can be easily illustrated by two short passages. In the scene from the Judgment of Paris where the three goddesses appear before Paris in all their naked glory, we read:

> *Tacea, se non che gli arbori felici*
> *Allievi de la prossima palude,*
> *Mossi talor da venticelli amici*
> *Bisbigliavano sol ch' erano ignude.* [II, 130]

A literal translation of these lines gives us:

> It [the woods] was silent, save that the happy trees,
> pupils of the nearby marsh,
> moved sometimes by friendly little winds,
> only whispered that they were nude.

The syllable count of these four lines of English is respectively: 10, 7, 9, 8. A few lines later Paris addresses the contestants:

> *"O Dei," dicea, "che meraviglie veggio?*
> *Chi de l'ottimo a trar m'insegna il meglio?*
> *Son prodigi del ciel? sogno o vaneggio?*
> *Qual di lor lascio? o qual fra l'altre sceglio?"* [II, 133]

Literally this would read:

> "O goddesses," he said, "what marvels do I see?
> Who will teach me to draw the best from the ultimate?
> Are they prodigies from heaven? Am I asleep or in a trance?
> Which of them shall I leave, or which choose from the others?"

These lines of English contain 12, 13, 16, 13 syllables respectively.

From this brief sampling the reader may gain some impression of the problems confronted in rendering a translation in blank verse that attempts to maintain a high degree of fidelity with respect to sense and style.

The other problem arises when faithful English rendering of the Italian line does not conform to the accent pattern of iambic pentameter, even making liberal allowance for the widely accepted variations to be found in good English versification. To adjust such irregularities in accent to the demands of meter, many passages have made compromises with literal accuracy, but never, it is hoped, to the point of serious distortion of either the sense or the spirit of Marino's Italian.

The matter of syntactical distortion is common enough in all schools of poetry, and in Italian poetry it is generally treated more loosely than in English; but Marino's intricate treatment of syntax is extravagant even by Italian standards. It can only be compared to the syntax of classical Latin verse. Obviously a faithful, literal rendering of the Italian word order would produce pure gibberish in some passages. The English version is necessarily unfaithful at times in this respect.

The attempt to render certain Italian words in English often leaves one with a sense of frustration. For example, *bel* (*bella, bello*) can be translated as "beautiful," "fair," "lovely," or "handsome." The selection of the best English equivalent should depend upon the nature or sex of the object described and on the context of the passage. Instead, the demands of prosody often tip the scales in favor of a one-, two-, or three-syllable word.

One kind of problem in translation can be seen in the rendering of *cinghiale,* "wild boar"—a word that is, of course, a key term in this story. The Italian word is pronounced *chingyahleh,* and has a character and a ring that is perhaps a little too noble or poetic for the creature it describes but that is poorly rendered by "wild boar," "hog," or "swine," which are all that English has to offer.

Most of the puns and other forms of wordplay and *double-*

entendre are inevitably lost through translation. The best we can do under the circumstances is to call this phenomenon to the attention of the reader and offer a few examples. In a passage about Music and Poesy, the poet employs several terms which in Italian carry one meaning for everyday usage and yet have technical significance in the vocabulary of the musician. For example:

> *Con la cara gemella è sì connessa,*
> *Che i ritmi apprende a* misurar *da lei*
> *E da lei, che le cede e le vien dietro,*
> *Prende le* fughe *e le* posate *al* metro.   [VII, 67]

> yet with her twin she [Poesy] is so close entwined
> she learns to measure rhythms from that mate,
> from her, who yields and follows after her,
> she imitates the measures, flights and rests.

Fughe (sing. *fuga*) has the double meaning of "flights" and "fugues" in Italian, both of them implied in this passage. Unless there happens to be an English word matching the double meaning, the translator is forced to make a choice. Here "flight" is selected as the primary meaning for the passage because the sisters are engaged in a dance. There is a temptation in such cases to call attention to the entertaining word-play in a footnote, but there are too many of them.

Prominent among the host of *double-entendres* are those with erotic overtones. Here there is only a chance that English terms can be found to suggest both meanings. Where Marino says

> *L'alma mia con la tua copula il bacio,*   [VIII, 128]

we say

> my soul couples with thine.

Obviously the force of *copula* is lost in "couples," except for readers who are familiar with Shakespeare's vocabulary.

Sometimes the erotic innuendos do not depend on the

double meaning of particular words in a passage but simply on rather familiar underlying ambiguities treated with more or less subtlety. There are, for instance, frequent references to love that causes one to die a happy death but will restore one to life—to die again. Such passages give the translator less difficulty because they do not ordinarily depend on such precision and subtlety of diction as the puns referred to above. A typical example of the life-death-resurrection theme is found in the following speech in which Venus is instructing Adonis in matters of love.

> *"Così dolce a morir l'anima impara,*
> *Esca fatta a l'ardor, segno a lo strale,*
> *E sente in fiamma dolcemente amara*
> *Per ferita mortal morte immortale.*
> *Morte, ch'al cor salubre, ai sensi cara,*
> *Non è morte, anzi è vita, anzi è natale:*
> *Amor, che la saetta e che l'incende,*
> *Per più farla morir, vita le rende. . . ."*   [VIII, 118]

"Thus sweetly can the spirit learn to die,
tinder to flame, a target for the dart,
can feel within the sweetly bitter flame
and from a mortal wound immortal death.
A death that pleases both the heart and sense
no death is, rather it is life, is birth;
and Love that burns and pierces her, the more
he makes her die, the more he renders life. . . ."

For a less familiar type of figurative innuendo, we may observe Adonis' declaration to Venus:

> *"Tosto ch'a dolce guerra Amor protervo*
> *Mi venne oggi a sfidar con tanti vezzi,*
> *Tesi anch'io l'arco, ed or già temo il nervo*
> *Per soverchio rigor non mi si spezzi.*
> *Non posso più; de l'umil vostro servo*
> *Il troppo ardir non si schernisca o sprezzi,*
> *Che vorria pur, come veder potete,*
> *De la gloria toccar l'ultime mete."*   [VIII, 67]

"No sooner did that haughty Cupid come
to challenge me with all these subtle charms,
I drew my bow, and now I fear the cord
will break from the extremity of strain.
I can endure no more. No longer scorn
the too great ardor of your humble slave,
for I indeed would, as you well can see,
attain the glory of the final goal."

The foregoing remarks on the general problems of translation and the more specific problems of translating Marino's poetry into English blank verse are introduced not so much as a defense of the present work but rather as a notice to the reader of some of the important differences which are inevitable consequences of this kind of undertaking, however skillfully and conscientiously performed.

Basis for the Selection of Passages

The present work offers approximately one thousand stanzas from a poem of slightly over five thousand. The selection of passages for such a presentation has been based on a number of considerations. Naturally the favorite passages, as indicated by recent Italian editions, and the passages most frequently discussed by historians and critics have been included. There are three comparatively recent Italian works presenting extensive selections of *L'Adone*. Carlo Culcasi's 1930 "reduction"[11] comprises 1042 stanzas, including some representation from all of the twenty cantos of the epic. His system was to choose a great number of short passages, many of them only five or ten stanzas in length, and some even shorter. Ferrero's representation[12] for *L'Adone* includes 870 stanzas with fewer but generally longer passages. He has drawn his material from thirteen of the cantos. Getto's

---

[11] *L'Adone*, selections, edited and annotated by Carlo Culcasi (Milan, Sonzogno, 1930).

[12] *Marino e i marinisti*, edited by Giuseppe G. Ferrero (Milan and Naples, Ricciardi, 1954).

edition [13] represents a radically different system of selection. He has chosen a single long passage including all of Cantos V, VI, and VII—a section of 607 stanzas.

A number of passages that are not represented at all or at best only briefly in the previous anthologies are presented in this selection because of claims of interest which seemed valid to the translator and to the associates and students with whom he has consulted.

Marino's original outline according to one of his earliest references to a plan for the treatment of the Adonis story—then plotted in three cantos—was to present the matter as follows: first, the meeting of the goddess and the youth and their falling in love; second, their enjoyment of their love; and third, the hunt, the death of Adonis, and the grief of Venus. These aspects of the basic story are represented here almost in their entirety.

One other important consideration in planning the selection has been to illustrate the extraordinary variety of the material which Marino added to the simple plot, since the character of the poem is strongly marked by this strange and wondrous panorama. In addition to such well-known myths as the judgment of Paris, there are curiosities and *divertimenti* such as the chess game, the invention of the telescope, the boar hunt, the theatrical extravaganza, and the woodland concert of the lute player and the nightingale. With these samplings and the summary of the entire story which is also provided, the reader should be able to gain a reasonably accurate impression of the work as a whole.

[13] *Opere scelte di Giovan Battista Marino e dei marinisti,* edited by Giovanni Getto (Turin, Unione Tipografico-Editrice Torinese, 1954).

Outline of the
Story of L'Adone[1]

Canto I. THE DESTINY. *Subject of the work and dedication* [2]
(1–10). *Infant Cupid, having been spanked by his mother,*
wishes to avenge himself: On the advice of Apollo, he de-
cides he will cause Venus to fall in love with the youthful
Adonis (11–40). *Adonis is overtaken by a storm at sea*
(41–58). Vulcan forges an arrow for Cupid with which he
will wound his mother (59–87). Cupid visits the palace of
Neptune: Through his prayers *the god of the sea stirs up*
a tempest which drives Adonis' ship to the coast of Cyprus,
realm of Venus (88–132). *There Adonis meets a young*
shepherd, Clizio, custodian of the garden of Venus; Clizio
prophesies that Adonis will reign in that land; and with a
drugged potion of food and wine disposes him to love
(133–170).

Canto II. THE PALACE OF LOVE. *The palace of Venus described:*
the storied entrance (1–32). The tree of the golden apples

---

[1] This digest of the poem is translated from the summaries of cantos in
Marino e i marinisti, edited by Giuseppe Guido Ferrero, Volume 37 in "La
letteratura italiana—Storia e testi" (Milan and Naples, Ricciardi, 1954). This
material is used with the kind permission of the publisher, Riccardo Ricciardi
Editore.

[2] Italics in the outline indicate those sections of the poem that have been
translated either in their entirety or in a slightly abbreviated form.

*by six doves, rises to heaven with the goddess of love and
with Mercury* (1–23). *The moon and its spots* (24–42).
The telescope. Eulogy to Galileo (43–48). The grotto of
Nature (49–86). The isle and the city of dreams (87–
107). The flight to the heaven of Mercury. The Palace of
Art: the arts and sciences, the inventors, the library (108–
167). The sphere (168–184), and the war between France
and Italy reflected therein (185–287).

Canto XI. THE BEAUTIES. In the heaven of Venus: the spirits of
the most famous and beautiful ladies, ancient and modern.
Eulogy on Maria de' Medici (1–170). From the disposition
of the heavens which accompanied the birth of Adonis,
Mercury casts the horoscope of his future and of his early
death (171–183). Venus urges Adonis not to credit the
falsehoods of the threatening astrology (184–214).

Canto XII. THE FLIGHT. Jealousy, an infernal fury, pricks the
heart of Mars (1–60). Through fear of the wrath of the
god, Venus urges Adonis to flee (61–81); then she exerts
herself to placate the anger of Mars (82–94). Adonis in
the realm of Falsirena: He rejects the love of the enchantress and departs (95–261), but he again falls into Falsirena's
hands and is thrown into prison (262–292).

Canto XIII. THE PRISON. The sorcery practiced by Falsirena to
make Adonis fall in love with her (1–21). She calls up
from inferno the spirit of the dead warrior, and comes to
learn that Adonis is the lover of Venus (22–82). The sufferings of Adonis in prison, the devices of Falsirena (83–
155). Adonis, transformed into a bird through the effects
of a magic philter, flies from the prison, arrives in the Garden of Touch, and there is a pained witness to the love
transports of Venus and Mars and to the games of the
"little loves" (156–209). Through the instruction of Mercury, immersing himself in the fountain of the garden of
Falsirena, he resumes his human form (210–235); he enters the treasure chamber and there retrieves the ring that

Venus had given him, takes with him the bow and quiver of Meleager, and escapes (236–252). The anger and complaints of Falsirena, who sends Orgonte to pursue Adonis (253–266).

Canto XIV. THE ERRORS. To avoid recognition, Adonis dons feminine attire, is captured by Malagorre, a bandit chief, and held prisoner together with two youths, Filauro and Filora (1–42). Malagorre and his band are put to flight by Orgonte. Malagorre wounds Filora but is then killed by Orgonte (43–139). The death of Orgonte (140–154). Filauro kills himself for love of Adonis, whom he believes to be a girl (155–172). To the fugitive Adonis, Sidonio recounts the unhappy vicissitudes of his love for Dorisbe (173–313). Adonis, abducted by a savage, is freed by Sidonio, who kills the savage (314–341). Happy ending of the history of Sidonio's love for Dorisbe (342–407).

Canto XV. THE RETURN. Exordium (1–7). Spring (8–14). Adonis encounters Venus, who has assumed the disguise of a gypsy expert in palmistry. Venus reveals herself to him, and the two lovers return to the Palace of Love (15–118). *The game of chess* (119–172). *The nymph Galania transformed into a tortoise* (173–182). A contest between Cupid and Mercury judged by Venus (183–202). Venus promises Adonis that he will be elected King of Cyprus (203–237).

Canto XVI. THE CROWN. The beauty contest for the election of the King of Cyprus (1–76). *The candidates* (77–186). *Adonis is about to win the contest when Tricane arrives, whom Falsirena has transformed by magic into a beautiful youth, but in the presence of Venus the Anubis resumes his disgusting and deformed appearance and is driven away in derision* (187–228). Adonis is acclaimed the King of Cyprus (229–269).

Canto XVII. THE DEPARTURE. To go to the festival of Cythera, Venus is obliged to leave Cyprus and Adonis (1–48). Adonis asks to hunt in the enclosed park of Cyprus. Venus

grants her consent against her will, and she urges him to
be cautious (49–64). Venus dresses and adorns herself with
great care (65–82), and departs accompanied by the band
of Cupids (83–94). She crosses the sea on Triton's back.
Gloomy prophecy of Proteus—the death of Adonis (95–
129). Triton relates the story of Glaucus, and Venus
searches in vain for Glaucus through all the sea, then has
herself transported to Cythera (130–186).

Canto XVIII. THE DEATH. Through the instigation and bribes
of Falsirena, Aurilla, handmaiden of Venus, reports to
Mars the love of Venus and Adonis and kindles his jealousy (1–16). The anger and grief of Mars. Together with
Diana he plots revenge (17–42). *The hunt. The wild boar
is smitten with love for Adonis. Adonis mortally wounded
by the tusk of the beast* (43–101). *Adonis appears to Venus
in a dream and announces his death to her* (102–131). *The
complaint of the nymphs and the lament of Venus for the
death of Adonis* (132–192). The grief and anger of Cupid
(193–225). The amorous but murderous wild boar is
dragged by cupids before Venus and excusing himself for
his blunder obtains her pardon (226–241). Aurilla, con-
scious of her guilt, commits suicide, and is turned into a
vagrant breeze (242–253).

Canto XIX. THE SEPULCHER. Ceres, Thetis, Apollo, and Bacchus pay visits of condolence to Venus for the death of
Adonis (1–19). Stories of love and death: Apollo tells of
Hyacinth (20–62); Bacchus, of Pampinus (63–123); Cybele, of Acis, Galatea, and Polyphemus; Thetis, of Camil-
lus and Carpo, of Leander, and of Achilles (124–325). The
tomb of Adonis is built (326–347). *The pompous obsequies.
The epitaph* (348–405). *Venus transforms the heart of
Adonis into a flower, an anenome* (407–424).

Canto XX. THE SPECTACLES. The funeral games. The first day:
the archery contest (1–61); the ballet (62–94); the dance
of Terpsichore (95–114). The second day: the wrestling
match (115–194); the fencing (195–249). The third day:

the jousting (250–333); the trained knights (334–348).
The tourney: eulogy for the princes and gentlemen of Italy
(349–376). The strange tension between Austria and the
"Golden Flame" (the two grand monarchies: Spain and
France) (377–484). Eulogy for Louis XIII (485–515).

ADONIS

Selections from

L'ADONE

of Giambattista Marino

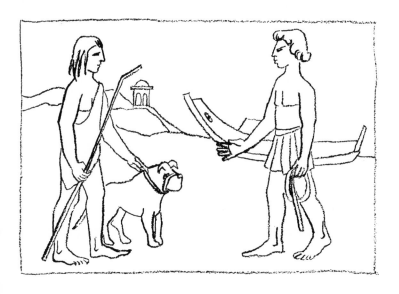

CANTO I

The Destiny

[The scale and tone of the entire poem are clearly established in the opening cantos. In discovering that the lovers will not meet until the middle of the third canto, we recognize that there is ample time for every embellishment which ingenuity can devise. The story line is briefly introduced with the spanking of Cupid by Venus and his subsequent visit to Apollo, who spitefully proposes a scheme for the infant god to gain revenge against his mother. But with the frail narrative—at times almost forgotten—we encounter every conceivable classical ornament and all manner of deities of every rank. At morn we behold the gates of the east opening and Phoebus reining the chargers of his fiery chariot; fickle Fortune enters with her elusive forelock and her turning wheel; a raging storm at sea is stirred by father Neptune; the simple country life is revealed in terms of Arcadian charm and purity. And so the glories of the golden age are unfolded before us in their richest colors.]

INVOCATION

1. I call on thee, by whom that most benign
   and gentle sphere of heaven is moved and ruled,
   the holy mother of Love,[1] daughter of Jove,
   adored in Cyprus' and Cythera's shrines;
   O thou whose star, whence every grace rains down,
   is the fair messenger of night and day;
   whose gracious rays, so lucid and fecund,
   make calm the heavens, enamor all the world.

2. 'Tis thou alone on mortals canst bestow
   serene enjoyment in a peaceful life.
   For thee, placated, Janus locks his shrine,[2]
   and Furor, softened, holds his ire in check;
   wherefore the mighty god of arms and war
   is wont to languish prisoner on thy breast,
   and with the arms of joy and of delight
   makes war in peace, his battlefield the bed.

3. Wilt thou relate to me of that loved youth
   the trials and the glories high and proud;
   how first he dwelt with thee and thence what fate
   destroyed him, staining with his blood the grass.
   Wilt thou instruct me to report the pains
   both sharp and bitter of thy wounded heart,
   the gentle quarrels and the soft complaints;
   and sue for me in singing of thy swans.

4. While I attempt, O gracious deity,
   to spin a web, defiant of the years,
   striving to tell the flame that kindled thee,
   the torments first so sweet and then so grave;
   may Love, with grace to equal my offense,
   lend me light wings for such a daring flight;

---

[1] Cupid, commonly referred to by Marino as Love (*Amore*).

[2] Janus' temple stood open in time of war, was closed in time of peace.

and, though I am unworthy, with his torch
bring fire to my heart, light to my mind.

5. And thou, great Louis,[3] who surpasseth far
   Adonis bright for splendor and for grace;
   and, yet a youth, full well dost imitate
   the model of thy dead progenitor,[4]
   for whom Vulcanus sweats, for whom 'tis meet
   that Paris gather palms, carve effigies;
   I pray thee heed and succor me, that I
   thy lily [5] with my laurel may entwine.

6. If to this lofty theme I bring my pen,
   which by itself could never hope to soar,
   I do it to obtain both wind and wings
   for this great theme from thy sustaining grace.
   Deprived of this, my feeble intellect,
   which to thy heaven of honors ne'er could fly,
   has fears that in the heat of so bright sphere
   my bold, audacious wax must surely melt.[6]

7. But when that zeal, which now exceeds thy years,
   unfurling thy paternal ensign free,
   surpasses with its valor others' hopes,
   by conquering the puissance and the pride
   of cruel tyrant who in Asia reigns,
   and when that flower attains its fullest bloom,
   then one with sword at side and one with lyre,
   you will be Mars, Apollo I shall be.

8. The goddess [7] of the laurel ever green,
   immortal governess of names and styles,
   for all my labors spin my thread of life
   on golden distaff adamantine strong,

[3] Louis XIII, age 22 when *L'Adone* was published.   [4] Henry IV.
[5] The golden lily of the royal house of France.
[6] Allusion to the myth of Icarus.
[7] One of the muses, presumably Calliope.

and grant to this my humble work the fame
to live among the precious pagan books,
as will befall when, thundering in war,
my songs are heard amid your clashing arms.

9. The royal Lady [8] named for that same sea
where sprang the goddess whom I celebrate
in verses, one who much resembles her,
bore a new Cupid by another Mars;
she, whose fair face reveals as much of power
as he of hardiness and skill in arms,
perhaps will harken, nor disdain my song
because I write of tender dalliance.

10. The true Parnassus shades and ne'er reveals
its mysteries to the simple or profane,
but under a deceptive crust conceals,
as in a rude Silenus,[9] secret gods.
Hence, from the veil which my invention weaves
in wanton verses, fanciful and vain,
this deeper meaning others may perceive:
immoderate pleasure terminates in grief.

CUPID SPANKED

11. Cupid, that cruel infant, not long hence
had kindled Jove anew with flames of love.
His jealous spouse [10] first burned with wrath, then chilled;
her heart was swollen with most bitter gall,
and 'gainst the imp, with querulous complaint,
she bore her injury to Cytherea; [11]

---

[8] Maria de' Medici, the Queen Mother.

[9] A fat, old drunkard, companion of Bacchus. Reference here is to a Greek practice of placing images of other divinities in hollow statues of Silenus.

[10] Juno.

[11] Venus, so called because her birthplace was near the Island of Cythera.

for which the lad, clever beyond his age,
spanked by maternal hand, wept bitterly.

12. "Alas! Is't possible," Venus exclaimed,
"that I will ne'er have peace on thy account?
What horned serpent do the sands of Nile
nurture more malicious or malign?
What Fury mad, what sanguinary fiend
in Stygian cave has such a rabid mind?
Tell me, thou asp of heaven, whence dost thou
extract that venom to infect all hearts?

13. "For Juno wouldst thou still contaminate
legitimate enjoyment, chaste embrace?
Shall I still hear of thee these same complaints,
a minister of follies, cause of woes,
a breeder of confusion, worm of griefs,
disease of senses, drunkenness of hearts,
begot by fraud, by devilish fury nursed,
slayer of judgment, cursed appetite?

14. "My anger makes me want to break those strings
and bow which strike so many ghastly wounds,
nor do I know why I do not destroy
those many treacherous nets that thou dost set,
or why I drive thee not from heaven at once,
and why I send thee not to long exile
on the Hyrcanian peaks 'mid Caspian wilds,
rash archer, there to shoot at savage beasts.

15. "I needs must be content in spite of all,
that thou spread sufferings and ills below
among the frail and languid mortal race,
whose cries and sad laments are heard each hour;
but shall I grant thee leave to shoot thy darts
in heaven, not sparing the immortal gods?
Shall I permit that even the gods sustain
thy wicked torments, serpent proud and sly?

16. "What more? This mischief maker boasts to goad
    e'en the almighty ruler of the stars,[12]
    and oft to such a state reduces him
    that now a bull he lows, now swims a swan.[13]
    An evil-breeding monster, reft of sight,
    shall he display such brazenness with us?
    Shall one whose tongue is coated still with milk
    make such affront?" This said, she spanked the lad.

17. With switch of twisted branches of a rose,
    bristling with thorny briars, she punished him,
    and on those dainty limbs, with cruel strokes,
    she turned their vivid pink a deeper red.
    The twin poles trembled, and the starry court
    was greatly stirred at the shrill infant's cry.
    All heaven was moved, for more it fears the wrath
    of infant Cupid than Typheus [14] bold.

18. From the maternal palace parts the son
    and off he goes with much the same disdain
    with which the trampled Afric viper glides
    with hissing sound along the sandy shore,
    or as the grizzly bear, when wounded sore,
    comes lunging from his stony den and goes
    with trembling steps to hide in horrid depths
    of valleys dim and black Lucanian rocks.

19. Thus, whipped and smarting sore with spiteful grief,
    he weeping fled up to the neighboring sphere,[15]
    where robed in shining crimson vestments sits
    enthroned the monarch of the hours, the Sun.
    And at the entrance of the golden gate

[12] Jupiter.

[13] References to disguises assumed by him when he fell in love with Europa (as a bull) and Leda (as a swan).

[14] A fierce giant buried under Mt. Aetna.

[15] Sphere of Apollo, the Sun God, which was adjacent to that of Venus.

he met fair Lucifer,[16] herald of dawn,
the star that in the east was opening
the lucent portals with a golden key.

20. With him the Dawn by gradual degrees
set out along the luminous highway,
upon a steed of fire tenebrous,
the reins all dappled with ambrosial dew,
forerunner of the morn, strewing the road
with lilies fresh and living crocuses,
his whip adorned with rose and violet,
he sped along the path before the Sun.

21. The glorious lamp, that at the golden portal
anticipates the Sun's first coming forth,
was Cytherea's minister and guide,
with streaming locks in splendor all aglow.
Already had the chariot been dispatched
to drive away the shadows ere her hour,
and waited the arrival of the goddess
when the proud infant, weeping, came in view.

22. The Morning Star shed tears for weeping Love,
ambassadress unto the king of light,
and streaked her lovely, dewy countenance
with showers silvery and crystalline,
whence Dawn drank from the overflowing urn
the living pearls commingled with hoarfrost,
and with a bright vermilion veil he dried
the humid sparkles from his tear-stained lids.

23. When Cupid came for refuge to that inn,
he found the Prince of Hours [17] ready girt
for a new course, gem-studded whip in hand,
his eager chargers harnessed, bit in mouth;
those fiery coursers panting, full of zeal,
their haughty manes seemed burning on their necks,

[16] The morning star.   [17] Phoebus: Apollo: the Sun.

and, scornful of delay, they struck the ground
with stomping, while their neighing drowned the wind.

24.   There also stands the Year, with wings outspread,
who always binds the end with the beginning,
and like a serpent ringed and coiled, he bites
the extremity of his voluted tail;
and like Anteus,[18] fallen and revived,
he seeks new substances on which to gnaw.
With him he has the train of months and days,
the long, the short, the fervid and the chill.

25.   Time's daughters four, the Seasons, proffer him
a golden crown from which day scintillates.
Two groups of winged handmaidens he had,
twelve darkly clad and twelve vermilion-hued.
While these accompanied the car adorned
with gilded yoke and bridle rose-entwined,
the Sun god turned his flaming eyes and saw
the grief of Love, who languishing drew near.

26.   Apollo was at enmity with Venus
and ever nursed a hatred in his breast,
since he exposed the wanton spectacle
of her adultery of long ago,[19]
the time he charged the stealthy predator [20]
before the sooty smith,[21] and spitefully,
to their eternal shame among the gods,
drew back the veil on those embraces sweet.

APOLLO'S SCHEME

27.   Now when the injured Cupid bares his wrongs,
"What foolish plaints are these?" Apollo cries.

[18] The giant who, by touching the earth, his mother, was restored with new vigor.

[19] Reference to the episode of Vulcan (at the instigation of Apollo) spying on the embraces of Venus and Mars, trapping them in a net, and exposing them to the heavenly court.

[20] Mars.   [21] Vulcan, the husband of Venus.

"Art thou not he who by the Peneus' shore
'gainst me strove for the palm in rivalry?
Thou, thou, mind of the world and soul of souls,
victor of mortals, yea immortals too;
now with thy pointed darts and flaming brand,
canst thou not find a vengeance for such hurt?

28. "How much better it would be, instead
of bathing that sweet face with childish tears,
to turn thy grief to ire, and whet thy dart
upon the injury for which thou moan'st.
Bring it to pass that she for whom thou weep'st,
her breast transfixed, shall weep because of thee;
for if thou wouldst thou canst achieve renown
and satisfaction too; now hear the means.

29. "Yonder in the rich and happy realm
of Araby alone Adonis dwells;
for beauty he without an equal stands,
a fitting rival for the Phoenix he.
Adonis, born of her [22] whose nurse connived
to join with her own father in one bed;
of her who, changed into a tree,[23] distills
her griefs even yet in odors lachrymose.

30. "Deceived, the king reviled the wicked girl,
whose heart was kindled with such foul desire;
whence he, discovering the outrage vile,
burned with disdain as much as she with love.
So she was forced to seek a lonely spot
there to expose that pledge so ill conceived,
that furtive pledge of love whose mother then
was sister too, whose sire was his grandsire.

---

[22] Myrrha was enamored of her father. With her nurse she arranged a secret rendezvous with her father, Cinyras, without his knowledge of her identity. Adonis was the offspring of this incestuous union. Cf. Ovid, *Met.* X, 298 ff.

[23] Myrrha was transformed into a myrrh tree.

31. "My shining eyes have never yet beheld
     a face so lordly-featured and so fair.
     Unlucky child, to whom the stars displayed
     their rigor even e'er they showed their light.
     Against him miser heaven marshalled force
     both dire and cruel, not yet seen by him;
     while one arose another had its setting,
     since at the mother's death the son was born.

32. "What trophy more renowned? What other prize
     dost thou aspire to, richer or more proud,
     than that thou pierce her heart with bitter wound
     for him, who is about to plough the waves?
     Sweet would be the wounds but so profound
     no power of stone or herb would bring a cure.
     Let this be worthy vengeance for thy hurt;
     prophetic voices tell me it shall be."

                         .   .   .   .   .

37. Like bellows were those efficacious words,
     which puffed with pride the listener's foolish heart,
     whereon, excited, Cupid quickly left
     Phoebus' flaming throne without a word;
     and plunging down from the ethereal sphere
     toward the shores of his maternal seat,[24]
     drove with the beating of his ardent wings
     on windy paths, and lighter than the wind.

38. And like a comet threatening prodigies,
     its countenance alight with flame and sparks,
     though horrible yet beautiful and bright,
     the traveler cleaves the spacious fields of air;
     the pilots from this shore and that behold
     with what bright purple feet he prints the clouds,
     and with what golden pen he writes and signs
     downfall to kingdoms and the deaths of kings;

     [24] Cyprus.

39. so while brave Love, descended from the sky,
goes scouring the lower realms of air,
bearing his torch and holding firm his bow,
he leaves a trace of splendor trailing him.
With burning track and bright with golden flame,
he everywhere strikes beams among the clouds,
and marks his course through heaven with long lines,
streaks and bands of light, imprints of fire.

40. He plunges downward, anger goading him,
and sharply plummeting, he nears the sea.
He skims the shore like some swift waterfowl,
and with his wings creates a whirring sound.
No ravenous falcon, when he snatches up
with his fierce talons simple, harmless dove,
is half so joyous as the peevish god
when fair Adonis comes within his view.

41. Adonis then was in the age which feels
the spark of love most vigorous and keen,
and had a disposition apt to face
new trials of tempestuous years ahead.
Nor on the roses of his lovely cheeks
had blossomed any bud of gold as yet;
or if there showed some shadow of light hair,
it seemed like flower in field or star in heaven.

42. All comely tossed and curling was his hair
in blond and wispy ringlets of bright gold,
under which there sprang the candid band
of ample brow in smiling majesty.
A sweet vermilion, gently burning flame,
mingled with the milk and living frost,
which tinged his face with such a gentle blush
as roses wear between the dawn and day.

43. But who can well portray those two bright eyes,
serenest stars, beneath those arching brows?

Who can tell the scarlet of those lips,
that are so ripe and full of glowing treasure?
What ivory's whiteness or what lily fair
can match that throat, which raises and sustains,
like marble column, all the heaven of grace
united in that handsome countenance?

44. When as a doughty hunter, bearing bow,
and armed with quiver and with piercing darts,
handsome yet fierce, he drives the fleeing beast,
or bides his onrush, standing at the break,
and in a graceful pose, a warlike hunter,
he bends his bow, delivering swift death,
he then resembles Cupid save in this:
Adonis lacks the blindfold and the wings.

45. In him are joined such treasures of both love
and nature that he holds them little worth;
he strives to mask the sun of his fair brow,
and dim the April of his lovely face.
But though he practices fierce menacings,
his nature knows of nought but gentle ways;
however rude and scornfully he frowns,
he casts a charm on others, spite of all.

46. Now while through forests of Arabia,
where he was born and passed his early years,
he was pursuing through the rugged brush
the winding tracks of timid, gentle beasts,
some error, or celestial destiny
drew him from desert country toward the coast,
where Palestine upon its outmost reach
provides a border to the western sea.

47. Having reached the glorious, sacred coast,
illustrious for its fair Idumean palms,
and having tired his feet, as was his wont,
in following a swiftly fleeing stag,

he there discovered, drawn up on the sand
amid the spray, without a guard or pilot,
a little bark, left by the fishermen,
but stored with necessary sailing gear.

48. And, lo, he sees approaching on the waves
a lady,[25] changeable in face and garb,
who has her blond hair gathered in a knot
upon her brow, and what is bald she hides.[26]
Her flowing vestments, snowy white and red,
the breezes toss with light and trembling breath.
Her skirt is slithery and, like empty air,
ever escapes the hand that grasps at it.

49. In her right hand she bears a turning globe,
a cornucopia in her ample lap.
Often she flees, then speedily returns,
on liquid pathways floating playfully.
Winged are her feet, and lighter than a leaf
she wheels about and dances in the wind;
and while she moves swift footed in the dance,
she lifts her voice thus in accompaniment:

50. "Whoever wishes to be blessed on earth,
enjoy its treasures and possess its realms,
let him reach out to grasp this golden lock,
and ne'er delay the seizing of his joys;
for, once the time and circumstances change,
he may not hope to capture his lost good.
Thus does this rolling orb keep changing moods,
'tis ever constant in inconstancy."

51. Thus she sang; then, breaking off her song,
she cast a favoring smile upon the youth,
and swiftly drawing toward the shore, she launched

---

[25] Fortune.
[26] The back of her head was bald, hence the expression, "Seize Fortune by the forelock."

the little vessel, seated at the helm.
"Adonis, follow me," she said, "and learn
what kindly stars have promised at thy birth.
Grasp now the golden lock I offer thee,
and do not fear to come where I shall lead.

52. "Although of old by folk I was esteemed
to be an idol false, a shadow vain,
and some say I'm unstable, nay, insane,
the enemy of virtue, stupid, blind,
and others call me tyrant impotent,
sometimes by human prudence overcome,
yet am I a magician, goddess, queen;
nature obeys me, heaven to me bows down.

53. "Who sets himself to follow Love or Mars
is well advised to call upon my name.
Whoever ploughs the wave or cleaves the ground,
whoever longs for honor or for fame,
must offer vows and prayers before my throne,
for I dispense all scepters and all realms.
My judgment rules all things beneath the sun,
and, at a nod, I grant or snatch away.

54. "Me then adore, and to the highest point
upon my wheel thou quickly wilt ascend.
Through me thou wilt be guided to a throne
which cursed mother's error snatched from thee; [27]
but have a care that thou retain that place
to which the fates have elevated thee;
for often when a peril is foreseen,
a prudent course averts catastrophe."

55. She ceases; he now fascinated longs
to venture out and sail along the coast,
and entering the slender craft for sport,
begins to launch it and to ply the oars.

[27] He should have been heir to the throne of Cyprus.

Lo, with a gentle breath of favoring wind
the sandy shore now gradually retreats,
yet as he glances backward from the sea,
he seems to be still cruising that same shore.

56. Pleasantly he glides along the coast,
the sandy beach lies smooth and silver bright,
and by slow stages he blots out the bank
where he departed from his native land.
Hence he entrusts himself to faithless floods
and to the mercy of the treacherous winds,
far, far from where the waves depart to die,
and where, with barking hoarse, they gnaw the beach.

57. So clear and bright the wave-washed shores appear,
the traveler can number one by one
the conches in the deep and humid caves
in the profoundest entrails of the beach.
Gentle zephyrs shake the sails in flight,
caressing airs, but these are soon cut short;
the sea is altered and the sky breaks faith.
How ill advised is he who trusts in winds.

58. O thou, as rash as thou wert diligent,
thou first bold maker of the reckless wood,
who dared to violate the ancient peace
of the tempestuous kingdom of the deep; [28]
thou hadst a heart more firm than rocky reef,
a mind more bold than the voracious sea,
when thou, disdaining ocean's mighty force,
went out defying death in fragile pine.

THE STORM

118. So speaks Neptune, and as he speaks he shakes
his triple-pointed spear and cleaves the sea.

[28] The theme of the courage of the first man who made a boat and
sailed far out on the sea is reminiscent of the famous "Aes triplex"
passage in Horace, *Carmine* I, 3.

From the cerulean bed a mighty heap
of spumy alps arises toward the stars.
The winds now clash in menacing aspect,
the horrid spirits of the hollow clouds;
and it appears the sky, dissolved in hail
and shattered, means to plunge into the sea.

119. Boreas [29] with warlike trumpeting
provokes the tempest into combat wild.
The archer Iris bends her painted bow,
but fires, instead of arrows, darts of flame.
The proud Orion, constellation grim,
brandishes his weapon, fierce and bloody,
menaces the heavens and opens veins
of clouds, swollen with water and with fire.

120. Out from its fixed confines the tumid sea
ascends on high and swells with monstrous pride.
Ruinous the rain pours in the sea,
the sea with sky, the sky with sea is joined.
In a new mode and unaccustomed style
birds learn to swim and fishes learn to fly.
Elements to elements oppose,
and clouds to clouds, waves, waves, and winds to winds.

121. So high the flood did mount the sky, well nigh
the Dog Star there could quench his summer thirst,
the vessel Argus,[30] not yet safe in heaven,
was threatened by an even fiercer storm.
And you, O frigid Bear,[31] against all laws,
and e'en in spite of Juno's jealousy,
you freely bathed in the forbidden sea
the gleaming fringes of your starry coat.

[29] The stormy north wind.

[30] The ship of the Argonauts was turned into a constellation by
Minerva.

[31] Calisto, a maiden loved by Jupiter, was changed into a bear by the
jealous Juno, whereupon Jupiter transformed the bear into a constellation, Ursa Major.

122. What wilt thou do, Adonis, wretched youth,
far from thy home and at the helm unskilled?
A puerile desire has gradually
so drawn thy ill-maneuvered little skiff
that all in vain thou sighest for thy home,
confused and overwhelmed by such great risks.
Too late thou dost repent, pale and dismayed,
and dost commence now to despair of port.

123. Now, now, the timid pilot must perforce
resign himself to the caprice of chance.
The raucous thunder shakes the turbid gloom
of heaven mid the jagged lightning streaks;
and he, the haughty ruler of the seas,
to shriek of Auster,[32] howl of Aquilon,[33]
with sharp-toothed lightning emulates high Jove,
upheaving ocean and tormenting earth.

124. The little vessel speeds, and swift and light
the sea's strong current bears it on its back.
The gunwale sometimes dips and drinks the wave,
and seems about to be engulfed in it.
Adonis turns more pale and chill than snow,
for he no longer sees his escort by,
and vast before him death's grim face appears,
confounds his sight and fills his breast with fear.

125. The while deprived of any earthly aid,
the tossing skiff veers wildly right and left,
its sides sore battered and its canvas ripped,
amid that wavy and tempestuous war;
and when the lad considered all hope lost,
lo, suddenly the little boat is beached,
is vomited out of the sea through reeds
onto the sand, and there it checks its course.

[32] The north wind.   [33] The south wind.

ADONIS' LANDING ON CYPRUS
AND INTRODUCTION
TO LIFE ON THE ISLAND

126. Beyond the Aegean, where arises first
      that major planet, usher of the day,
      under a climate temperate and benign
      a most delightful island spreads its hems.[34]
      Nearby the Taurian mountains lift their peaks,
      nearby the famous Nile divides the sands.
      Opposite lie Rhodes and Sorio
      and fertile confines of Cilicia.

127. This is the land which to the goddess great,
      who sprang miraculously from a wave,[35]
      was so delightful, so beloved of yore,
      that oft, despising her divine abode,
      she here enjoyed a heaven more beautiful
      mid streams and shades, while others envied her;
      and for a symbol of her sacred self
      she had erected altars and a shrine.

128. Here the youth alights, on dry land safe,
      yet dubious still of his precarious state,
      for still he seems to see the broad abyss
      of threatening torrents gaping horribly.
      He casts his eyes about and sees himself
      surrounded by the waters, desert, woods.
      But so delightful is that solitude
      which he beholds, he asks no other joys.

129. The air unfolds in sweet serenity,
      in every season always warm and clear,
      which never in a grey and blustery spring
      is marred by rain or darkened o'er by storms;
      but shunning equally the injuries

[34] Cyprus.   [35] Venus.

from the extremes of cold, extremes of heat,
in happy smiles it varies not its ways,
eternal April ever young and green.

130. Love makes discordant creatures live in peace,
none grieving for another's cruelty.
The eagle nests companion to the swan,
the falcon dwells beside the turtledove.
Nor has the simple chicken cause to fear
the clever slights of the conniving fox.
The wolf, forsooth, keeps faith with gentle lamb,
and timid hind roams freely, safe from hound.

131. O'er the soft fields, whose panoply of flowers
a living vein of liquid nourishes,
the greedy air enfolds a fragrant blend
of mingled odors as it takes its flight—
air which not only lightly sports among
the branches by the shore, a fleeting sprite,
but even far out on the waters wafts
its fragrance to the passing mariners.

132. Adonis ventures forth, and everywhere
hears Procne's warbled notes or Philomel's;
the forest rings with sounds of shrill bagpipe,
the swineherd's raucous horn; the fields resound
with rustic sordine[36] and with flageolet,
with woodland pipes and shepherds' oaten reeds;
and alternately from the various parts,
the lowing and the bleating beasts are heard.

133. He spies a solitary youth,[37] who, weary,
is resting in a laurel's shade nearby.
A bow lies at his feet, and by his side

[36] Musical instrument like a spinet muted.
[37] The shepherd Clizio, who is identified in the "allegory" of *L'Adone* with a gentleman-poet of Genoa, Giovanni Vincenzo Imperiali, author of a poem called *Stato Rustico*.

rests a strange quiver of the hide of lynx.
The spotted hide of lynx all black and white
he wears, and in his hand he holds a lyre.
Sweetly to the lowing of the kine
he blends the melodies of sylvan love.

134. With gilded buskins he has clad his feet,
an ivory horn hangs by a sash of green,
his lips are smiling, with a ruddy hue,
a serene sparkle kindles his calm eyes.
His hair is flowing, cheeks are flowery,
and flowery the age which makes him fair.
All decked with flowers from head to feet is he,
flowers in his hand, his hair, his breast.

135. There curled beside his flank Adonis saw
a formidable mastiff lying prone,
which, spying him, rushed forward to attack
with fury and with wild, ferocious din.
But having laid his plectrum on the ground,
the courteous youth rose quickly to his feet;
and to arrest the savage beast, with word
he checked and struck him with his staff.

136. The savage one obeys and rests his head
beside his master's feet, his tail dropped low.
At that the master fastens round his neck
a silken collar with a sturdy leash.
He then invites and prays the royal youth
advance secure, who willingly complies.
He comes to where in rustic shepherds' fold
abides a humble, pastoral family.

137. One shepherd rests upon a flowery bank
beside a fountain, fresh and crystalline.
Another in the oak's thick summer shade
treacherously traps the greedy birds.

One, all alone, carves on the beech's trunk
verses on love's fuel and its fire.
Another tracks his nymph in hot pursuit,
one leaps, one calmly sits, another sleeps.

138. This one with love songs sweetens all the air,
attuned to wanton crystal's murmuring.
This one with sound of syrinx teaches rams
and bulls a kind of dance which they perform.
This one weaves baskets, while another weaves
garlands of flowers, purple, yellow, pink.
This plies the udders of the fertile ewe,
this fills with milk the pitchers and the jars.

139. With his fair guest the shepherd sits beneath
a pergola of myrtle's spreading shade.
Adonis first recounts his former trials,
then asks about the country and his host.
And while that one responds, Adonis hangs
upon his speech, which wounds his heart with love.
"O gentle pilgrim, strange," says Clizio,
"almost beyond belief thy fortunes seem!

140. "But calm thy brow and do not be displeased
to change thy native land for this fair spot;
for if as it appears thou lovest the hunt,
thou'lt find here harmless beasts having no claws.
'Tis my belief that not in vain the heavens
have brought thee out of mortal peril safe,
nor without cause has thy lost ship arrived
after so long a journey on these shores.

141. "Therefore, let friendly heaven fulfill thy vows
and favoring fortune second thy desires,
and as the moon with her cool steps doth glide
over the many regions here below,
sure she could not discover any realm

or zone more fitting for a form so fair.
Only such loveliness deserves to share
this reign with her who jointly rules with Love.

142.   "The isle where thou art come is Cyprus called,
       which lies amidst the Sea Panfilia.
       The palace of great Love, behold, is that
       which I am pointing toward on yon right hand.
       No profane foot may e'er approach the spot
       unless the fairest goddess grants consent.
       She oft descends from heaven to this realm,
       at other times the rich abode is closed.

143.   "She there has temples, altars, there with Love
       she has her statues, sacrifices, priests,
       and there as honors from the Greeks displayed
       a thousand of her votive offerings.
       The victims of the blindfold archer god
       present their ardent supplications here,
       and still the smoke of incense and the scent
       from garlands spread among the lights and pyres.

144.   "Here I, who once dwelt in Liguria,[38]
       did come to live by choice and not by chance.
       I pasture mid this fragrant greenery
       my wooly flocks; my name is Clizio.
       The custody of this her park to me
       the mother of the winged god has signed,
       where none save Venus is allowed to pass,
       and Diane, goddess of the woods and hunt.

145.   "Here I have found among these woods a port
       from all the bitter surge of human strife.
       Here in a safe asylum from the trials
       of civil turmoil heaven has guided me.
       My silken robes were ne'er so dear to me
       as these rude garments I am wearing now;

[38] Italian coastal region where Genoa is situated.

and I delight more in the fields and caves
than marble palaces and gilded domes.

146. "How much more pleasing is it now to hear
the murmurings of waters and of leaves
than from the forum, raucous and inane,
the clamor of the boistrous vulgar throng.
An herb, an apple, and a happy face,
how much more quietude is found in these
than in the sweat-stained bread a miser prince
dispenses at his mean, unsavory board.

147. "This simple, happy race of men, who roam
and pass the pleasant hours along with me,
enjoy the good which seldom worldly folk
experience save in their natal hour.
A life of liberty and innocence,
in whose estate nobility is nought;
for scorning wealth and caring nought for gold,
this is true wealth, this is the golden age.

148. "No viands rich, no sumptuous repast
bedecks and overloads my humble board.
Betimes a deer or goat provides us meat,
and always there are ripe, abundant fruits.
Sometimes I bid my woodland train rehearse
a simple ditty to the sound of pipes.
These folk I love as friends, not underlings;
this tumbled hut a palace in my eyes.

149. "Far from all vain, ambitious pageantries,
my scepter is a staff, my robes the fleece,
ambrosia here is milk, the goblet whence
I drink my hands, my nectar is the stream.
My statesmen plowmen, and my friends the dogs,
my servants oxen, courtiers the lambs;
musicians here are birds, the air, the stream;
our plumes the grasses, our pavilions boughs.

150. "The brightest light surrenders to these shades,
     melodious accents to their silence yield.
     Bright purple flames not here, nor glitters gold,
     of which the ornaments are blood and death.
     If flowers which the earth bestows bring not
     enough of fairest purple, brightest gold,
     Aurora with her magic splendor spreads
     her pomp of purple and the sun of gold.

151. "No other whisperer is tattling here
     except the whisper of the running brook.
     No adulator showers me with praise
     except its mirror, crystalline and bright.
     Livid envy, which can gnaw men's hearts,
     here finds no place, since hearts are free of it,
     except when in the branches here and there
     the birds in rivalry of song contend.

152. "Treason and calumny with all their snares
     make their abode amid the royal courts,
     by whose invidious teeth sweet innocence
     is put to death and faith is slashed and torn;
     here perfidy dwells not, and if perchance
     a bee should sting thee, yet the wound contains
     no venom, and in honey those same wounds
     are compensated for with usury.

153. "No cruel tyrant here is sucking blood,
     instead a farmer gently draws the milk.
     No miser hand here scars the hide or robs
     the substance from the poor, defenseless beasts,
     except for those who clip the wooly spoils
     from burdened sheep, who suffer not thereby.
     A sharp goad pricks the faithful oxen's flanks,
     but no immodest yearning pricks our breasts.

154. "With us there is no care for tempered iron
     of haughty Mars, the tools of blood and death;

the pitchfork and the plough of Ceres, yes,
by whose employment is our life sustained.
The savage furor and the blast of war
is never heard resounding through this land,
save only such as goats or bulls, enraged
by amorous combat, bellow to the sky.

155. "We wage no contests here with lance and sword
in this serene and blessed land of ours.
Sometimes, 'tis true, we brandish Bacchus' staff,
whence crimson wine, not blood, spills on the ground.
The only garrison that guards these fields
of ours consists of tender, verdant blades
which, springing up along the neighboring shores,
stand trembling to do battle with the waves.

156. "Boreas can never strike these woods
with horrid blast nor batter our retreat;
the violence of tempests does not plague
or shake our peaceful thoughts with anxious cares.
And if Jove sometimes sends his flaming darts
against the proud heads of the lofty oaks,
yet here the ire of great lords never comes
to strike us with their furious abuse.

157. "So in these green and solitary woods
I spend my quiet, pleasant days and years.
That sun, which drives off horrors sad and grim,
dispels afflictions, keeps my mind serene.
I fear no claw of bear or bite of snake
nor treachery from the rapacious wolf;
for this land harbors no wild beast or snake,
or if there be, they dwell in innocence.

158. "If there is any foreign element
to roil my calm, perturb my tranquil thoughts,
that thing is love alone. Alas, since first
I chanced the lovely Phyllis to behold,

for her I long, and for her sparkling eyes
I needs must burn with all-consuming heat;
and I could wish a single grave might hold
the ashes and the bones of that same fire.

159. "And yet so gentle are the darts of love,
its flame so easy and its chain so light,
that many cruel torments from her hand
are nought compared to one moment of bliss.
Thus even greedy for its suffering,
the soul drinks knowingly the poison cup;
and in those very eyes where dwells his grief
the heart a voluntary prisoner goes.

160. "Let him who likes choose luxury and ease,
I only prize the joys of country life;
I gladly change the palace for the bower,
and seek no greater prize than poverty.
Sated with charms that nurture treachery,
whose tempting bait conceals a fatal hook,
here I enjoy the winning of that joy
which everyone pursues and no one finds.

161. "Marvel not that simple, pastoral life
is so highly esteemed and praised by me,
for even on my native Janus' [39] shores
I sang of it with rustic harmony;
Apollo granted to my flageolet
immortal praise for harmony and wit,
whence those my verses, praised in Helicon,
resound along the whole Ligurian coast."

162. Amazed Adonis listened to the loves
of that apt lover, bent on his fair words.
Anon the speaker checked his loosened tongue,
then bade his servants speedily set forth
before them food, to which keen appetite
increased the flavor and the seasoning;

[39] A god associated with Genoa, home of the poet Imperiali.

the honey of delight, nectar of love,
sweet to the taste but poison to the heart.

163. Ne'er did the horrid juice of lotus flower
possess so much of secret potency;
never through magic incantation was
Circean brew concocted with such power,
but its supremacy it needs must yield
to this repast the shepherd served his guest:
insidious liquor, false, deceitful food,
sweet poison which can slay yet not displease.

164. In the Garden of Pleasure amorous Clizio
had picked the fruits from which the wine was pressed,
whence the intoxicated youth received
the subtle flames that burned within his breast.
He did not recognize them, felt no pain,
for until needed they would lie concealed,
as does the serpent in a chilly lair,
that shows no vigor until it is warmed.

165. He feels a new desire, which stirs his heart,
and like a serpent works through all his breast.
He loves, yet knows not love nor understands
the unfamiliar, sweet effect of love.
He wants to love but does not comprehend
what then should be the object of his love;
and e'er he learns this sickness to be love
he finds his heart to be consumed in fire.

166. Love, who raised the sail and plied the oars
when he was first transported to that land,
is hovering and fanning with his wings
the little flames, yet is not visible.
A courteous country fellow now has set
the final course before the eager guest;
Adonis, breaking his long fast, now eats,
drinks heartily, and while he feasts they talk.

167. "Sir, thou seest the sun, that aims its rays
     from midway in the bow whence day fires darts;
     wherefore thou wouldst be well advised, methinks,
     to rest with me till dawn of the new day.
     And heartily I promise thou wilt have
     a pleasant sojourn in this humble inn,
     and thou wilt find with rough bed, frugal meals,
     a courteous welcome and affection pure.

168. "As soon as I shall hear the morning breeze
     whisper in the myrtle and the beech,
     I will arise with thee and journey forth
     unto the house of Love, which is close by.
     In taking this new journey thou shalt find
     delights to compensate for all thy woes,
     since it is recognized thou art the true
     successor to the throne and empire here." [40]

169. Although Adonis does not fear the sun,
     having been bred to dangers and fatigues,
     the invitation of his gentle host
     he would not wish to spurn for courtesy.
     To gracious words he gracious words returns,
     agrees at once to make his harbor there;
     to destiny, which brought him, weary, worn,
     to such a blest abode, he offers thanks.

170. Soon Phoebus, dropping down to make his bed
     in ocean, leaving meadows pale with mist,
     and feeding to his fiery, foaming steeds
     celestial fodder in the heavenly stalls,
     who, damp and flecked with sweat and sparks of fire,
     now dip their heads in neighboring ocean's bath;
     thus, weary, two suns go to rest: mid flowers
     Adonis, Phoebus in the ocean's lap.

[40] Clizio believes that Adonis has been brought to Cyprus by fate and
is destined for the crown of the island.

CANTO II

The Palace of Love

[In the early stanzas Clizio conducts Adonis to the vicinity of
the Palace of Love with its gardens and surrounding wood.
A characteristic elaborate description shows us the view from
outside the walls and particularly the fantastically ornamented
gate. Further particulars of the architecture, the interior, and
the gardens are reserved for later sections of the poem.]

APPROACH TO THE PALACE

1. The young Alcides,[1] having reached the pass
   which stands as entrance to the road of life,
   doubtful, irresolute between two guides,
   he found the way divided in two roads.

---

[1] The Greek name for Hercules. The reference here is to Adonis in his
role as adventurer.

Easy and plain he sees the left-hand way,
all flower-decked with pleasures and delights;
the other one is marked with alpine crags,
with rugged boulders and with thorny briars.

2. A long time, hesitant and wavering,
between two pathways stood the unskilled youth;
at length, having considered well, he turned
his step far from the smooth and open road;
instead, that weary, steep one on the right
he chose, which toward true honor guided him,
whence through dire chances and strange enterprise
he mounted to the peak of glorious life.

3. And so goes he who with a judgment sound
pursues fair virtue's honorable track,
but anyone, who putting trust in vice,
seeks evil ways, which have the face of good,
at length across the smooth and spacious plain
arrives where thousand shackles bind his feet.
How many cunning snares, what hidden frauds,
the trickster variously can devise.

4. Through the arena of this mortal life,
the soul, a new Atalanta,[2] credulous,
goes rushing swiftly, and with nimble feet
hastens forward toward the journey's end.
But oft the senses, flatterers, can boast
to turn her[3] from her course, enticing her
with that most brilliant and appealing sphere,
the golden apple, which is called the world.

[2] A maiden very fleet of foot. To beat her in a race and win her for his bride, Hippomenes (Melanion in another version) carried three golden apples, which he tossed aside at intervals to delay her. She could not resist the temptation to turn off the course and pick them up, and she lost the race.

[3] Here and in the two succeeding stanzas "her" refers to "the soul" (*l'anima*) .

5. Let her escape the tempter, flee, despise
   the proffered sweets, delectable deceits,
   and though he flatters and caresses her,
   let her not waste in flowers the greening years.
   Ever with false charms, to lure her steps
   from worthy struggle, there are offered her
   a thousand amorous joys, delightful sports,
   which turn at last to ruin and to death.

6. Charmed by all such sweets, only to be
   made tinder for the flint, target for bow,
   she enters that fair mansion, lost, betrayed
   into enduring woes a thousand fold;
   cage without door, a prison without gate,
   sea without shore, a woods without a break,
   a treacherous labyrinth of error—such
   the palace is where Love has his retreat.

7. Lo, now the bird of morning beats his wings,
   preparing to announce the coming light,
   his head and feet appearing proudly decked
   with golden spurs and crest of crimson hue;
   the village clock, the trumpet of the day,
   with constant chiding he awakes the world,
   and with a diligence more than his wont,
   he bids the stars take leave, calls up the sun.

8. While from the place wherein he had reposed,
   roused from his pleasant sleep Adonis rises,
   wishing to see before the heat grows fierce
   if skies give forth good prospect for the hunt,
   the shepherd Clizio drives out his flock,
   accompanying it into a nearby wood,
   where to the music of the rustic pipes,
   he needs must lead it at midday for shade.

9. Should he perchance encounter on the way
   a doe or buck or any other beast

wandering through the shady brush, Adonis
thinks to bend the horned moon of his bow.
These arms he had—I know not how—retrieved
in safety from the fury of the storm;
nor do I know whether, in time of stress,
he rather would abandon these or life.

10. And thus while wandering, a foreigner,
he roams the ancient land, paternal realm,[4]
he furthers the sly archer god's design,[5]
and aids the plan of evil destiny.
But deeming that his way was blessed by fate,
since he escaped great peril in the skiff,
he hopes when he has sojourned there some days
that the lost scepter may return to him.

11. Perceiving how by such a strange advance
from out the odorous Arabian land
miraculously to the natal isle
heaven had escorted him in friendly wise,
and seeing that the scepter of the place
whence he had sprung was his by legal right,
in fortune's favor still he put his trust,
expecting it would smile on his affairs.

12. Just as the sun was lifting his clear brow
above the threshold of the golden door,
perhaps to spy if Love had carried out
as yet the counsel he had given him,
when, guided more by Love than by the swain,[6]
Adonis reached the glorious abode
of her whom the third sphere pays homage to,
who was still grieving for her errant son.

13. Although the lofty mansion's major gate
is closed as yet, as it is wont to be,

[4] Cinyras, father of Adonis, had ruled over Cyprus.
[5] Cupid, who is plotting against Venus and Adonis.   [6] Clizio.

the light of the exterior is such
Adonis is bedazzled by the gleam.
The famous palace of the sun itself
with its clear splendors, by comparison
would be but dim and poor, and so the youth
is overwhelmed, amazed in the extreme.

14. The palace where the goddess oft sojourns,
is circled by an adamantine wall.
Its cloisters and great galleries are cause
of scorn and envy to the Empyrean's court.
It has four fronts and four flanks round about,
four towers of custody, four portals fine;
and at the mid-point stands another tower,
which brings the number of the towers to five.

15. In its four corners the four towers are placed
according to the compass equally.
That in the middle, of the selfsame stone,
is broader and more soaring than the four.
One joins another, passage being made
by several bridges, gracefully designed,
and each of those four, with distinctive art,
is linked in graceful archway to the fifth.

16. So high, so delicate is every arch
which stretches out beneath each graceful bridge
that it appears the mighty, soaring weight
hangs in the air by some strange miracle.
The curve through which each bridge gives opening
sparkles with so many varied gems,
that by its light and color every arch
shows like a heavenly Iris here on earth.

17. The towers standing on the corner points
are square in shape and are of equal size;
only the principal one differing,
which is erected circular in form.

The lines are equidistant and are set
in rows with handsome architectural style,
and through each tower a garden is approached,
save that the large tower is embraced by one.

18. Neither with porphyry nor serpentine
did the shrewd master trim that edifice,
but made of finest oriental stone
pilaster, cornice, capital, and arch.
Instead of alabaster, marble fine
was interspersed with ruby and chrysolite;
and all the treasures of the Indian caves
and the Eritrean shores were emptied here.

19. From mines of Ganges the great builder chose
most precious and most lucent metal ores,
and from the rocks of Araby had dug
clear crystals and the purest diamonds,
with which he formed the lofty columns' trunks
in perfect measure and true intervals,
of which the base was jasper sound and bright,
the capitals were framed of emerald.

20. Between the columns, of most massive weight
enormous statues in the form of giants
and tall colossi with their heads bowed low
serve for supports in masterly device.
Each has been formed from one piece of green beryl
and has red eyes of burning garnet stones.
Each holds a wreath of varied tone and hew,
composed of sapphire, topaz, amethyst.

21. The major portal of that wondrous hall
gleams with the labor of the goldsmith's art.
The door, gold banded, turns on golden hinges,
its lock, bright and ornate, is likewise gold.
For the rich entrance calcedony choice
is the support and not mere ornament.

On the smooth treshold, trodden under foot,
almost as if despised, is balas [7] fine.

22. The middle part is silver, and in it
a thousand vivid forms are sharply etched;
their attitudes and faces clear and sharp
in the reliefs and the mosaics there.
Whoever holds his gaze intent thereon
will swear the feigned is real, exact and true.
The work, which though the work of art yet breathes
almost, nature admires as her own work.

23. Upon one panel of that noble door,
where every feature is displayed to life,
Vulcan has with his wondrous chisel carved
that goddess the inventor of first food.[8]
Aetna is seen to smoke, and Mongibello [9]
belches flame from out its snowy peaks.
Well could he imitate the fire and smoke
of home [10] with rubies and with carbuncles.

24. There she appears across the sunny fields,
all gaily dressed in new-blown buds and flowers;
she scatters purest gold with both her hands,
turning blonde the wavy fields of corn.
"O gentle rock," she, soundless, seems to say,
so well the words are silently expressed,
"be thy good earth faithful custodian
of the dear pledge I leave within thy breast."

25. Lo there, with many chosen handmaidens,
the virgin [11] comes from her maternal bower,
and to prepare garlands and necklaces,
she spoils the fields of their most lovely trim.
Now it appears that with her eyes she makes

---

[7] A variety of ruby.   [8] Ceres.   [9] Another name for Mt. Aetna.
[10] Vulcan's smithy was under Mt. Aetna.
[11] Proserpine, daughter of Ceres.

the flowers unfold, then plucks them with her hands.
Not even Apelles [12] better could portray
the Eleusinian goddess's [13] fair child.

26. Lo, while she is composing various flowers,
a sulphurous grotto opening its jaws,
out from the depths of the Tartarean [14] night
the ruler of the Furies [15] bursts in sight.
The nymphs take flight, and captive Proserpine
with broken outcries utters her lament.
The coal-black chargers foam with tepid blood
and snort and pant with foggy, vaporous breath.

27. Lo Ceres, sorrowing, returns to Phlegra,[16]
and lo, twin pines she trims and then uproots,
and having made two brands to seek her child,
she raises them on high to give her light.
Most real the chariot is depicted there,
all rich with beautiful and sparkling gems.
With shining track cleaving the dusky air,
go the huge dragons, beating their green wings.

28. There on another panel is engraved
the youthful god whom Ganges' realm adores,[17]
showing how Jove had drawn him, immature
and yet unborn, from out his mother's breast,
and as his sire is mother too, and how,
being nursed by Nysa's nymphs, he loves the woods.
Strange birth it was and wonderful, to be
but once conceived and yet twice to be born.

[12] Celebrated Greek artist.
[13] Eleusis was famous for the cult of Ceres and Proserpine.
[14] Tartarus, a region of Hades.   [15] Pluto.   [16] In Macedonia.
[17] Bacchus. This stanza presents numerous references to the complicated story of the birth of that god. Through a trick of Juno, Semele, his mother, was burned to death by the splendor of Jupiter, her lover. Jupiter saved the unborn baby by sewing him up in his own thigh, whence he was delivered when matured for birth. In his youth, Bacchus visited India, where he is said to have learned to cultivate the grape.

29. Elsewhere in a chariot of vines
    he sits aloft and proudly circles round.
    Four gallant subjects of Hyrcania [18]
    lightly and swiftly draw the chariot.
    The horrid creatures fondly lick the reins,
    soaked in the liquor which is joy to drink.
    The god, among the plaudits of the throng,
    moves gorgeous and triumphant into Thebes.

30. Silenus,[19] never sober, old and fat,
    comes drowsily upon a lazy ass,
    his face and breast bear stains of russet must,
    his hair is greening, intertwined with leaves.
    Now and then he reels, and lest he fall
    satyrs and fauns prop up his ancient frame.
    His eyelids and his brow are heavy, dull;
    with wine and stupor they are swollen and blear.

31. On this side and on that a merry crowd
    of lads and nymphs are milling in a throng,
    that to the timbrel and the castanet
    brandish thyrsi,[20] ivy branches, fronds;
    green tendrils bearing grapes of red or blond
    are garlanding all Bacchus' ministrants;
    the vines are pictured by fine emeralds,
    of ruby and of jacinth are the grapes.

32. A group of virginal bacchantes here
    stomp and sway about to right and left,
    and there a boisterous throng of Corybantes [21]
    in foolish frenzy wildly run and leap.
    The clashing cymbals, horns, and trumpets hoarse
    now seem to cause the nearby hills to quake.

[18] Tigers.   [19] One of the traditional followers of Bacchus.
[20] A special staff or wand, tipped with a pine cone and wound with
vines and ribbons, carried in Bacchic celebrations.
[21] Worshipers of Cybele, noted for their frenzied celebrations.

This splendid work is of such wondrous art
that in mute metal it expresses sound.

33. The closer to the place Adonis came,
the more astonishment pressed on his mind.
"This is the heaven on earth, and this is where
one turns for the beatitudes of Love."
These words he saw inscribed outside the hall
as he explored and roamed the palace front.
With well-cut inlaid gems it was inscribed,
in symbols of Egyptian hierolgyphs.

THE JUDGMENT OF PARIS

[The remainder of the canto (stanzas 41–177) is almost entirely
devoted to the famous story of "The Judgment of Paris."
The introduction of this classical myth and the leisurely
account of it will strike many readers as odd. A reading of the
summary of the plot of *L'Adone,* however, reveals that such
a practice was part of Marino's scheme for amplification.
There are fourteen classical tales similarly treated, including
such familiar ones as Cupid and Psyche, Narcissus and Echo,
Hyacinth, Hero and Leander, and Polyphemus and Galatea.
That Marino considered the retelling of such familiar classical
myths as one of the richest veins for the ingenious poet is supported by numerous other works by the poet, but notably by
La Sampogna, in which he recounts: Orpheus, Acteon,
Ariadne, Europa, Prosperina, Daphne, Syrinx, and Pyramus and
Thisbe. However, the supreme demonstration of his faith in
the Ovidian strain is *L'Adone* itself.

In the preparation of a work of selected passages from
L'Adone, it has been considered necessary to omit most of
the passages presenting the classical myths; but it would seem
unwise to omit all of them, since they are so evidently part of
Marino's scheme. Hence the inclusion in somewhat condensed
form of the Judgment of Paris, which will allow the reader to

see what the poet may do with a story so familiar in brief
outline.]

41. "If 'twill not burden thee," Adonis said,
    "relate the origin, the way there sprang
    among three goddesses a rivalry,
    and how she of that apple went so proud.
    From the Sabaean nymphs I learned in part,
    but the full history I long to hear.
    By this, less disagreeable may be
    the bitter rigors of the tortuous way."

42. "Since Love had with so many, many snares,"
    the shepherd then commenced, "prepared the strand
    that, after long distress, bound Peleus
    to Thetis in the happy marriage knot,
    there came to grace the brilliant wedding rites
    of such meet lovers, gay and festive all,
    as many gods as dwell in heaven high
    and in the circles of the sea and earth.[22]

43. It was the blessed mount of Thessaly[23]
    where were performed those hymeneal rites.
    Its peak with myrtle and with laurel crowned,
    the trophies of the triumph of true love;
    the stars were all propitious and indeed
    all mortals and almighty gods as well,
    if only bitter hatred had not spread
    cruel dissension 'mid the sweet repast.

44. There is no joy that is from envy free,
    nor can a happy state endure for long.

[22] Clizio's narrative fills out this canto, running for 136 stanzas. Hence
quotation marks will be omitted except for speeches within the narrative.
[23] Mt. Pelion.

Behold, how that great feast, by Discord fierce,
the mother of disputes and strife, is spoiled;
for she, excluded from the company
and from the rich and splendid banqueting,
comes to contaminate the great delights
and the bright merriment around those boards.

45.   She has recourse to all her fiendish arts,
and, counseled by the rage that gnaws at her,
she hies her to the tree the dragon guards
within the garden of Hesperia.
From it she ravishes an apple red
and gold, whose harmless ray delights the gaze.
A lightning flash of minium and gold
it vibrates, and its breast holds gems for seeds.

46.   Upon its shining, brightly colored skin,
whose cheerful gleaming dazzles every eye,
the stern, envenomed goddess of disdain
(no Fury can surpass for felony)
with her own hand, as anger urges her,
inscribes seductive but insidious words.
The motto which she carves upon it reads:
"This is a gift for the most beautiful."

47.   Then she returns to where the memory
of injury recalls her for revenge,
and, hot for malice and with venom steeped,
she hides within the veil of a dark cloud,
and on the table with her guileful hand
she throws the message of the golden bait.
Amid the feast she cast this magic gift
among the host of gods assembled there.

48.   The company all left the food untouched,
left off the lifting of the foaming cups,
and standing fixed in sheer astonishment,
began to view that gold so beautiful.

Whence it has come they cannot tell, but sure
a present from the Fates it seems to them;
so ardent to possess it is the lure,
it seems that Love himself is hid within.

49. But of all those who saw and longed for it
three eager goddesses felt most delight,
and stimulated by their greediness,
which is a native trait of all their sex,
their eager hands they all reached out at once
to make a seizure of the charming prize,
and by their keen, discordant rivalry,
they showed themselves wondrously covetous.

50. Now when that god who ushers in the day [24]
and who once watched o'er King Admetus' herds,
better directing on it his fixed gaze,
perceived the letters which were there inscribed,
his countenance alight with crimson gleams
and brightly flashing with a gentle smile,
he gave Jove notice of the strange new words
which he discovered sculptured on the rind.

51. Having read the scripture on the sphere,
the avid goddesses desist awhile,
and, changing face, upon the sumptuous board
they leave the golden prize untouched perforce.
Worth yields to wish, without diminishing
the ambition which pursues the victory.
Knowing that only one can win the prize,
all wish it but no one possesses it.

52. The trial for the glorious crown disturbs,
embroils in turmoil all the heavenly band.
All reason with opinions various,
one whispers about this, one fears for that.
About this thing they wrangle and contend,

[24] Apollo.

now topsy-turvy is the family,
and now with mighty conflict is engaged
the great solemnity of noble feast.

53. Juno in her greatness is so proud
she calls herself more worthy than those two.
Nor does Athena prize herself so low
that she does not pretend to victory.
Venus, beauty's mother and goddess
who knows that she is destined the most fair,
smiling to herself about the rest,
expects to join laurel to myrtle's crown.

54. All the gods have interests in the case,
and are divided, favoring this or that.
Mars wishes to maintain by force of arms
the apple is to Cytherea due.
Apollo brings Minerva's praise to court,
and calls the others envious, malign.
Jove, after having listened well to each,
applauds great Juno, partial to his spouse.

55. At last, lest evil should occur within
the host disputing in that rivalry,
eager to quell the tumult and the strife
and to compose the quarrels and complaints,
turning to them he said, "Things beautiful
are ever loved, all yearn, all run to them;
but for the beautiful and good, the more
they please the rest, the harder to obtain.

·   ·   ·   ·   ·

59. "I will not make an arbitrary rule;
nor can I be fit arbiter for you,
for should I favor one, I do not wish
to draw the hatred of the other two.
I love each equally, and equal zeal

has ever moved me to support their case;
would I might see all happy equally,
all thus triumphant and victorious.

60. "A shepherd dwells among the Phyrgian woods,[25]
    (in name and office only is he such)
    for were it not that envious fate as yet
    conceals his lofty birth in rude attire,
    to all the world his noble state would be
    acknowledged and his royal lineage;
    a son of Priam, Trojan emperor
    and near related to my Ganymede.[26]

61. "Paris his name, and he is not, methinks,
    unfit to solve the question 'mongst you three,
    since he combines integrity and skill
    sufficient to unbind this conflict's knot.
    Unknown within his native land he dwells
    where Ida mid Gargarus Mountains rears.
    Go thence anon, ye three, and he that bears
    the embassy of heaven [27] will be your guide."

62. Thus he spoke, and with applause the words
    of the supernal rector were received,
    and having been inscribed by Atropos
    were read in fate's eternal diamond rolls;
    the divas at that speech calmed their turmoil,
    feeding their inward pride with vanity;
    now for the journey will they all prepare,
    and each to her advantage decks herself.

63. The haughty goddess, wife of the great king,
    was mantled in her famous regal robes.
    Those garments were devised of double threads

[25] Phrygia, in Asia Minor, territory of Troy.
[26] Jove's cupbearer, a handsome youth of the royal family of Troy who was abducted from Mt. Ida to serve Jove on Olympus.
[27] Mercury.

of gold and have a double golden fringe.
Dotted with suns and flaming, every sun
receives both light and worth from the true sun.
With starry diamonds her head is girt,
a jeweled scepter bears she in her hand.

64. She whom Athens worships [28] has a robe
of finest wool and purest silver thread,
embroidered with tree trunks and foliage
of olive green, and in her hand a branch.
She wears a shining helmet on her head
crowned with a circling bough from that same tree.
Her right hand holds a spear and her left arm
protects her side with adamantine shield.

65. The one whose darts and fire are in her eyes,[29]
cares nothing for the pomp of smithy's art,
but lightly with an azure, silken veil
she drapes the nudity of her white limbs;
the color of the sea and of the sky,
the one that spawned, the one that harbors her;
and light, so light and faintly shadowing
it lets her purest ivory show through.

66. Mercury takes the apple, fixes wings,
agile and swift, on temples and on heels,
and as he beats his wings, he takes in hand
his fatal staff with serpents intertwined.
And following him the rival goddesses
all leave behind their peacocks, owls, and doves;
a little golden cloud their chariot is,
lightly borne along by Zephyrus.

67. The smiling air serenely stains the sky
with crimson flames and lovely golden lamps,
and like the sun, now setting in the west,
with roseate splendor blazes all around;

[28] Athena, also called Pallas or Minerva.   [29] Venus.

and marking all the course of lucent path,
it gilds and purples their cerulean fields;
the while conducted by their prudent guide,
the pride of heaven descends on Ida's mount.

68. On Ida in the cooling summer shade
sat Paris pasturing his gentle flocks,
there where upon a thousand living trunks
was seen the name of fair Oenone [30] carved.
Ah, sad Oenone, if as judge he should
elect the fairest of the goddesses,
what will become of thee, robbed of thy love?
Ah, that thy loss should be another's palm.

. . . . .

72. When lo, he [31] sees the cloud descend, which bears
within its bosom beauty's fairest flowers,
and circling round the spot where he sits fixed,
from gyre to gyre it floats downward toward earth.
And lo, the three fair enemies in turn
rise to their feet, prepared for the new war,
at whose resplendent brightness near at hand,
the wood lights up its gloomy, horrid shades.

73. Upon beholding such a wondrous sight
he bites his lips, he lifts his arching brows,
and on his forehead, which is creased by fright,
the marvel sculptures terror in deep lines.
Against a nearby trunk he leans his head,
and he indeed resembles that same trunk.
His song he breaks off and at once lets fall,
mute at his feet, the rustic flageolet.

74. "O lucky shepherd, O illustrious youth,"
the heavenly messenger then said to him,

[30] A nymph who was loved by Paris but whom he later deserted.
[31] Paris.

"whose splendid light, hid in this marshy veil,
not only earth does honor but heaven too;
thy earnest prudence makes thee worthy seem
for venture never granted mortal man.
Jove sends me with these goddesses to thee
and he commands that thou shalt be their judge.

75. "Seest thou this apple? This the provocation
for the contest now shall be the prize.
She shall obtain it who in this great trial
is with the greatest loveliness endowed.
Bestow it then, with no fear of offense,
on her who merits, not who most desires.
Well wilt thou know how to resolve the strife,
as thou art handsome, expert, and in love."

.   .   .   .   .

[Each of the goddesses in turn addresses Paris, asserting her
claims to glory, and after each speech Paris appears virtually
convinced of the efficacy of the claims advanced by the speaker.]

111. He ponders long but does not know which fair
of that immortal band most moves his heart,
for while he alternately turns his eyes
to this, to that, he finds them equal quite.
There where perchance he first directs his glance,
'tis there he stops, and what he sees approves.
He turns to one, and deems her full of charms,
then eyes another and forgets the first.

112. Fair is Juno, and her whiteness pure
resembles light from oriental pearl.
Graceful in motion, wise in every act,
the warlike daughter [32] of the major god.
But in her face the fair goddess of love

32 Athena.

holds the true portrait of the beautiful;
and every part, wherever one regards,
from tresses to her feet is without flaw.

113. A blush which, from the whiteness indistinct,
blends on her cheek, mingles and fuses there.
The privet bloom is stained with crimson hue,
and where one fades the other shows more clear.
Now by the rose the lily is o'ercome,
now purple, vanquished, flees from ivory.
While there bright flame gives place to driven snow,
here scarlet red stands side by side with milk.

114. Her brow a noble square of diamond gleams,
and as the heavens clear it seems to shine.
Here Love is wont to play, and thence he reigns
as in a palace spacious and sublime.
The dawn its brightness, other spheres their rays
receive from her, in her take their delight,
whose limpid crystal kindles all the sky
with a serene and gently tempered light.

115. Her eyes, desirable and wondrous fair,
unique, and without any parallel,
at once bring shame and splendor to the stars;
the sun is mirrored there and dazzled too.
She sometimes tears the hearts out by the roots,
whenever she but turns her tranquil glance.
In trembling rays which issue forth from them,
her glances sparkle, moist with wantonness.

116. By straight line from those lovely eyes descends
a channeled ridge [33] in right proportion made,
with whose accompanying flower [34] she inhales,
more than she sends forth, pure and fragrant air.[35]
Beneath it, where an opening is cut,

[33] The nose.   [34] The nostrils.
[35] This "flower" draws in more odors than it gives out.

where is unlocked the treasury of love,
a coral gate dividing in two parts
opens a passage for both words and smile.

117. Nor did Aurora in the quiet sky
with such sweet roses deck her streaming hair,
nor stormy Iris offer to the sun
her bosom with such bright enamels heaped,
nor does the dewy conch expose to dawn
a breast adorned with so much living pearl,
as can compare with her sweet, smiling mouth,
which holds the riches of the orient.

118. Scattered in many tassels and loose strands
appear the blond and curling threads of gold,
the tresses, which a wanton negligence
by studied art dishevels skillfully.
Now o'er her shoulders, now before her eyes
scattered and dispersed they flow in waves;
thus simple arts and earnest carelessness
add graces to her glowing loveliness.

119. Having heard the pleas, and having viewed
the eyes and cheeks of those three heavenly nymphs,
and while the contest of divinities
still fluctuating hangs in doubtful scales,
no more of words and tales the shepherd wants,
no more he cares to view their limbs well draped,
but to inspect their beauties more within,
desire and curiosity demand.

120. "Since all joust in these lists on even terms,
further inspection is required," he says;
"nor can your controversy be resolved
unless modesty's veil is drawn aside;
because the outward beauty which appears
although it speaks no words can sometimes lie.

The splendor of the dress oft tricks the crowd
and covers imperfections of the form.

121. "Let each one then ungirt and strip herself
of every ornament of drapes and art,
because the vanity of coverings
may have no part in judging beauty's worth."
Juno objects, and with a haughty air
she stalks away, refusing to comply.
Minerva too, unwilling to conform,
with eyes cast down for modesty reneges.

122. The offspring of the sea,[36] with courteous signs,
shows her complete consent and eagerness;
"I'll be the first to cast aside the gear,
to blossom forth, uncover secret parts,
whence, 'twill be seen and clearly manifest
that I have more than lovely eyes and cheeks,
that that which is concealed also conforms
and matches with the fair exterior."

123. "Well then," Pallas rejoined, "I will undress,
but first, young shepherd, e'er we have removed
our raiment, make her put her girdle by,
lest by her magic she enchant thine eyes."
Then she replied, "I don't object to this,
but thou, who boast to win by loveliness,
why dost thou not leave off thy warlike helm,
why with ferocious aspect frighten him?

124. "Art thou perhaps shamed by the threatening light
which is discovered in those sea-green eyes?"
Paris declared therefore they must compete
sans girdle, helm, or other property.
Their true aspect remained, all cover stripped,
they stood adorned with no more ornament

36 Venus.

except themselves, and with no lordly arms
the warriors three to the arena strode.

125. When those three models of perfection had
at length disposed of all accouterments,
and of their bodies, heavenly beautiful,
were the most secret parts exposed to sight,
the nearby caverns, hidden and retired,
beheld among their shadows these new lights;
nor was there present a created thing
which felt not in itself an amorous force.

126. The sun holds back the course of his sojourn,
made useless to illuminate the earth,
because he sees that all his rays are dimmed
by splendor yet more jocund and serene.
He would descend to earth to pay respects,
happy even to be second best;
then he repented of his hardihood
and to admire them he remained content.

127. The earth, as if 'twere honored, glorified
by such sublimely blessed inhabitants,
with charming gratitude did strive, at least
in part to make response for so much grace.
It is made pregnant with the seeds of love,
and it gives birth before those lovely eyes.
Nature became rejuvenate, and spring
burst forth in blossoms where it is not spring.

128. Against their custom, natural and rude,
the prickly pines bore apples red and sweet,
of pungent briars were born frail violets,
narcissus flourished on the juniper.
Some streams poured honey and some ran with milk,
the sea its richest tribute freely gave.
Silver the fountains strewed, sapphire the shores,
the fields were purple, mountains emerald.

129. The birds of all the forest left their song
     to feed their eyes upon so happy sight.
     Loquacious waters mid the scattered rocks
     then ceased their murmuring from pure delight.
     The breezes, in their presence all confused
     by sweetness, still the whispering of the waves.
     Each wild beast trembles at the spectacle,
     and silent in attention are the woods.

130. Silent, save only that the happy trees,
     who were the pupils of the nearby marsh,
     moved sometimes by the friendly little winds,
     only whispered that they stood all nude.
     And you, spectators of that glorious scene,
     you feel another venom, vipers fierce,
     wherefore, returning to your darling loves,
     you pierce with your sharp tongue their very hearts.

131. The wanton Naiads and lascivious Fauns
     abandon caves or issue from the waves,
     each one conceals himself nearby to make
     a gentle theft with eyes upon white breasts.
     Love flourishes e'en in the roughest twigs,
     and, full of love, the leaves and flowers laugh;
     for stones, deprived of such a glorious pleasure,
     they grieve because they have no soul or sense.

132. Paris himself, amid those joys extreme,
     is reft of life, save only through his eyes.
     Such an excess of light the young lad fears
     will carry off his sight and life at once.
     He has not strength of vision for such rays,
     nor heart sufficient to sustain three suns.
     Triple streaks of lightning seal his eyes,
     he sees one sun in heaven and three on earth.

133. "O deities, what marvels do I see?
     How can I choose the best 'mongst the supreme?

Are these true miracles? Or do I dream?
Which shall I leave and which of them select?
Ah, since in vain to do what I must do
I file my senses, wake my intellect,
mid so grave doubts, O heavenly deities,
may your bright rays reveal the truth to me.

134. "Why am I not he who, with many eyes,[37]
kept guard upon the heifer of great Jove?
He had in front and all about at least
as many eyes as fame has in her plumes.
Ah, would that I were night or serene heaven,
since from the heaven comes so much loveliness,
that I might gaze on things so beautiful
with eyes as numerous as stars above.

135. "What modest light of holy chastity
sparkles in that noble virgin's face?
How much revered that other deity?
What tranquil air of quiet dignity?
Above this one, what lovely infant beats
his wings? What is that sweetness she distills?
She seems to have in her I know not what
of smiling, festive, sweet attractiveness.

136. "However, that does not suffice for me,
still in suspense, my wavering thoughts are stirred.
While now to this and now to that I turn,
I long to find the best, but know not where;
if I'm not to be charged with foolishness,
'tis meet for me to see yet clearer proofs.
I must investigate each one more close,
viewing each one apart, one at a time."

137. Having said this, he sends two dames aside
and keeps queen Juno there alone with him.

[37] Argus, who had a hundred eyes, was ordered to guard Io, a maiden who had been transformed into a heifer by Juno because of Jove's love for the girl.

She boldly promises that if he rates
her beauties over her two enemies,
no prince that is or ever was should have
more powerful scepters or more glorious crowns;
and that she'll give him rule of Asia's realms,
with every nation subject to his yoke.

138. Juno dismissed, he summons Pallas next,
who comes toward him with virile step and bold,
and she also at bargain promises
a glory such as ne'er was known before,
that if she is declared most beautiful,
he will be made invincible in war,
famous in arms, and over every chief
renowned for trophies and for lordly palms.

139. "No, no, till now nought ever had the power
to overcome within me reason's law.
A mercenary tribune I would be
if I today were led to sell my vote.
An honest judge must not be partisan,
nor be corrupted for a price or prize.
Both lose the name of genuine gift and true,
if one gift with another is exchanged."

140. So he responded, then in that same place
he signed to Cytherea to approach.
She stepped forth and a lamp of gentle fire
appeared throughout the leafy theater.
Whatever the defense the cold heart makes
against that object can avail no whit,
the greedy spectator cannot remove
his eyes, his pain mixed with intense delight.

141. What careful, earnest painter could portray
the quality of those most perfect limbs?
They render alabaster dull indeed,
surpass the lily and the privet's bloom.
Feathers of swan and the unsullied snow

are cloudy samples for these paragons.
The white of ivory, the diamond's light
are seen to glisten in her countenance.

142. "Behold me here," she said, "so now commence
to study every part with diligence,
and tell me if the keen eyes of the lynx
could find herein a drop of ugliness.
But while thou dost observe my every part,
in order that thou be instructed well,
I pray direct toward me both eyes and ears,
viewing my features, harkening to my words.

143. "I know thou dost not crave for sovereignty,
nor dost thou feel a need for scepters new,
that thy paternal realm is capable
of satisfying thy utmost desire.
Thou hast no need of warfare, since the realms
of Phrygia and Lydia are at peace,
nor shouldst thou, friend of pleasure and repose,
love other conflicts than the amorous.

144. "Not mortal are the battles fought for love,
nor in them does iron practice homicide.
Sweet are its arms, its pains and sorrows sweet,
and without shrieks or bloodshed are its wounds.
Besides, the country folk on Ida's slopes
should not aspire to royal marriages,
nor should a simple nymph inflame the heart
of him who can oblige the queen of Love.

·   ·   ·   ·

148. "In Greece there lives a damsel, young and fair,
who all the rest excels for loveliness;
not only is this honor granted her
in realms of Argives and Corinthians,
but scarce inferior to goddesses

she's held, and little does she yield to me.
To my devotions is she much inclined,
a friend of love who loves to be much loved.

149. "Jove left the womb of lovely Leda great
with this new glorious sun of whom I tell,
when to her bosom he flew swift and light,
transfigured as a fair and noble swan.
Of purest white, just as she ought to be,
the babe engendered of so white a bird;
and soft and gentle, she is like to one
nurtured in nest within the tender shell.

150. "Such fame has she for beauty in her land,
so much the cry is vanquished by effect,
that Theseus, mighty champion, took up arms
for her, and left the field all stained with blood.
The princes of Argos and Corinth sought
by trial these most favored marriage rites,
but Menelaus, most approved, appeared
the only worthy spouse for Helena.

151. "If thou wouldst win that lovely one, if thou
wouldst with an apple bargain for such joy,
thy recompense for services shall be
the lap and bed of this exquisite dame.
I pledge at first encounter of her eyes
with thine thou shalt her sovereign be. I will
effect it that, forsaking the Greek shores,
where'er thou wishest she will go with thee.

152. "There to Lacedemonia's great realm [38]
thou shalt betake thee by the shortest way.
Only contrive that she lay eyes on thee,
and leave to thy escort all other care.
In all that such affairs as this require,
Cupid, a trusty aid, I slyly lead;

[38] Sparta, home of Menelaus and Helen.

with his companions and my servant crew
we shall dispose her by a thousand ways."

153. She ceased, and flames glanced from her lovely eyes
to melt the harshness of the Caucasus,
whence he—all other beauty now forgot,
before that loveliness incomparable,
supported by the power of that great god
who conquers hearts and batters all defense—
kissing the apple, eyes now fixed on her,
humbly offered it to her, and spoke:

154. "O beauty of all beauties, over all
the beauties heaven holds, Ciprigna fair;
the gentle flame of every happy love,
mother of sweetest pleasure, star benign,
thou worthiest, before whom envy vile,
malign, perfidious, is forced to bow;
if then no other beauty equals thine,
that's reason why its reason should prevail.

                        .   .   .   .   .

157. Overwhelmed with joy and drunk with pride,
Venus receives it and thence turns her eyes,
"Concede the honor of the great contest,"
she said to the two spurned divinities,
"confess now, Juno, that I vanquished thee,
that wrongly thou presumed to rival me.
Bellona,[39] used to victory, grieve not
to own thyself conquered and shamed by me.

158. "One of you thought to overcome me here
perhaps by being sovereign queen of heaven.
The other hoped that with her shining arms
she might frighten away my heavenly charms.

  [39] Athena.

But little good it was. However truth
is checked, 'tis strengthened by comparison.
I am most pleased to have won over such
great ones without a scepter or a sword.

159. "Come now my Graces, come my little Loves,
my eager forces, my unconquered bands.
Crown ye with many verdant laurel wreaths
your happy mother, now victorious.
Go singing verses loud and sonorous,
and all the happy breezes will reply.
Sing hail, all hail to love, that triumphs now
in heaven, on earth, as well in peace and war!"

160. The while the shepherd watched and listened to
the fair to whom fate had decreed the prize,
the two rejected goddesses toward him
with anger turned their wounded, spiteful eyes.
Their aspects shadow pride and fierce disdain,
as if there menacing ruin and death.
Juno indeed cannot dissimulate
her rage, nor keep from venting it in words.

161. "Miserable wretch," she said, "and how
has that blind archer bound thine eyes in bands,
so that, the force of reason being lost,
he robbed thee of the power of faithful sight?
Did the great rector of the skies choose thee?
If he wished to appoint thee for the judge,
the man best suited in the universe,
why then art thou revealed the most perverse?

162. "This choice will prove to be, you may be sure,
far more disastrous than a boon to thee.
And mark this well, the honor and the glory
which by thy verdict thou hast dealt to me
will be the blot on thy life's history

and the undying shame of all thy race.
And that same beauty, evil and accursed,
which was thy prize shall be thy torment yet.

163. "That shameless, wanton woman who with such
sweet arson will enflame thy foolish heart,
will yet be to thy native land the cause
of final conflagration and defeat.
Ilium fallen, Troy destroyed for thee,
(so love inflicts its wounds and so it burns),
will be the sport of warfare and the flames,
a field of blood, a Mongibel [40] of fire . . ."

. . . . .

166. The other then, of Samos goddess chaste,[41]
next turned to him with curt and tortured speech,
nor could her modesty of face conceal
the pride and anger gathered in her breast.
"O lying tongue, foolish and rash as well,"
she says, her bold hand brandishing her staff,
"how well thy villainous decree conforms
to a felonious heart and twisted thought.

167. "Is this how thou distributest the prize,
allured by the vile bait of faulty tricks?
Dost thou repay me thus for glorious seeds,
which I infused in thee from early years,
that thou dost lust exalt, valor oppose,
that thou dost vice embrace, virtue condemn?
And for those soft caresses' foul reward,
dost thou shun honor, despise chastity?

. . . . .

169. "That apple, cursed and abominable,
will be the sower of deceit and war.

40 Mongibello, another name for Mt. Aetna.
41 Athena.

What wilt thou do, what say, thou wretched man,
when carnage thou shalt see so near at hand?
Then penitent at last, with sighs and groans,
thou shalt perceive with tardy sense how much
he errs that, following a faithless guide,
repulsing reason, worships sense alone."

CANTO III

The Kindling of Love

[Cupid returns to Venus to execute the plan suggested by Apollo whereby he may gain revenge for his spanking.

Venus, having been treacherously wounded by Cupid's arrow, sets out to find Adonis, assuming the guise of the huntress goddess, Diana. The first meeting of the lovers and their falling in love is a big moment of the story and is naturally presented with all the rhetorical fanfare Marino has at his command.]

CUPID'S REVENGE

27. In playful fashion he embraces her,
rains kisses on her face and naked breasts.
He laughs, he chatters, then his rosy face
he hides and smothers in her bosom's cleft.
As yet she knows not how that charming act

threatens her with sharp and cruel wounds,
as, watching with amusement and delight,
she presses to her breast the scheming child.

28. The goddess, smiling, close within her breast
sustains the sweet weight resting in her arms.
Upon her knee she lightly dandles him,
then cradles him and lifts him to her face.
Now she bends to kiss his eyes' bright rays,
now the winsome smile about his mouth;
nor does she know that puffed with mortal juice
a cruel serpent nestles in her breast.

29. The brightly colored plumes, the lovely wings,
which had been ruffled in his soaring flight,
likewise his hair, disheveled by the wind,
she gently smoothes with soft, caressing hands.
But still she does not dare to touch the bow,
whence sometimes painful wounds are slyly dealt,
nor yet the faithless darts, for well she knows
what dire contagion lurks in those same points.

30. Now while she holds him thus within her arms,
she wishes to resolve a certain thought.
"My son, tell me," she said, "since it is meet
that there should be between us only peace,
why dost thou take such joy in others' pains?
How art thou so perverse and impudent,
that ever with thine arms thou dost molest
the quietude of heaven and of the gods?"

. . . . .

[There follows a discussion of why Cupid often aims his darts at certain gods—for example, Jupiter and Mars—but does not molest Pallas and Diana.]

41. And she then: "Since thou hold'st in thy control
such power, now for pleasure, now for fear,

I wish to know at least why Cynthia
still lives secure from thy infectious darts."
"It nought avails," replies the lad, "to wound
her virgin breast, concerned with other cares.
She flees o'er mountains, never takes repose,
so idleness ne'er masters her swift feet.

42. "That shining god [1] who with her of Latona
shared one birth, an archer also he,
that one, whose hair is crowned with blazing fire,
often have I inflamed with other fire."
Thus while he coyly played and talked with her,
he gauged the distance and drew close to her;
and while conversing thus he, although blind,
seizing the moment, struck her who had eyes.

43. From out the crimson quiver, which contains
well nigh the full length of the pointed shafts—
appearing accidental but well planned—
the fatal arrow's sharpened point protrudes.
Once he has pierced his mother's side with it,
in timid fear he hastily takes flight.
With one quick stroke the lad inflicts the wound
of heart, and signs Adonis for her love.

44. She turns her face to him Love designates,
for well she can perceive him lying near.
"Alas," she cries, "alas, I am betrayed,
O son ungrateful, cruel, O false boy!
Ah, what sweet wound do I feel in my heart?
Ah, what keen ardor burns yet pleases me?
What strange new beauty shines before my eyes?
Farewell to Mars, to heaven, I'm yours no more.

45. "Cursed be thy bow, so full of cheats,
and cursed, wicked boy, that cruel dart!
Thou a child of mine? No, from this breast
never wert thou born, thou bastard vile!

[1] Apollo and Diana were twins, the offspring of Latona.

I can't recall having conceived such fire,
such venom, cause of all my languishing.
Megera engendered thee of Cerberus,
or Chaos thee begot of blackest Night."

46. This said, with pain and wrath she extricates
the arrow which is buried in her side,
and there between the feathers and the iron
upon the shaft she finds Adonis' name.
Then turning to that wound her eyes and thoughts,
she sees her tender breast is deeply pierced,
and feels throughout her veins how bit by bit
the wanton fire goes creeping serpent-like.

47. Indeed it's true that flame is such, 'tis not
without some pleasure that she languishes;
and even fond of her uncured disease,
there stirs in her a thousand cunning thoughts.
Now first she turns her to the poisoned dart,
now looks upon the tinder for her flame,
and in these words, from her confused desires,
unbinds the knot with dolorous "Ah me!"

48. "Ah, well must I now envy the estate
of every mortal woman, high or low,
since I perceive myself through hostile snare
mocked by him who least should treat me so.
His arrow wounds me and his flint strikes fire,
yet of misfortune this is not my worst;
for certainly Love's flames must all be spent
if Love's own mother does not feel love's fire.

49. "Why am I victim of so vile a fate,
that by a smith [2] my beauties are enjoyed,
a consort who is rough, uncouth, deformed,
a hairy, sooty, gnarled, unmannered one?

[2] Vulcan, husband of Venus.

And what immortal edict, worse than death,
obliges me to kiss those bristly lips,
lips much more apt for blowing on the coals
in horrid oven than to press a kiss?

50. "One who knows nothing else but with a sledge,
raising a tempest on his cursed forge,
to deafen the great caves 'neath Mongibello
while tempering my father's thunderbolts,
bolts which, falling on this side and that,
bring futile terror to men's timid minds;
and, showing features of the master smith,
the bolts are jagged like his twisted foot.

51. "Alas, how oft, bold and importunate,
does he approach his steaming face to mine,
and with that hand, which has but now put by
the pincers and the file, will seek my breast;
and I, against my will, must needs submit
to the abhorrent knot of his bold arms,
and to endure, while he is fondling me,
that soot and smoke forever smudging me.

52. "Pallas, ah wise one, though thou couldst not match
my beauty, still thou didst refuse his suit.
Nor did great Jove wish him in heaven, but down
into the blind abyss he sentenced him;
whence as he plunged into the scorching pit,
he broke a bone and thenceforth he went lame.
And even lame he comes into my bed
and mars another's peace through his defect.

53. "Even now there will not leave my mind
the memory of his offensive acts.
Deeply engraved within my heart remains
the trap he treacherously laid for me,
when in a sturdy, diamond-patterned net
the smutty villain caught me sleeping nude,

and foolishly to the eternal gods
exposed my body's secret parts unveiled.[3]

54. "I still must harbor anger and contempt
for that grave outrage whence I was beguiled,
since with his calumny and my disgrace
he made me subject to derisive smiles.
Let not those who scoffed at me complain
if shame he brought me should revert to him;
and if he wants to cancel horns with scorn,
I will know how to counter scorn with horns.

55. "Aurora oft descends before the day
to earth, the Athenian hunter [4] to embrace.
The Moon at midnight oft deserts the sky
to woo the shepherd of Arcadia.[5]
Then why not I? If my desires should stray,
that radiant beauty shall be my excuse.
I wish this lovely youth that I have spied
to serve as my revenge for injuries!"

56. She ceases, and as huntress at the ford
she pants as from pursuing some great prey.
In flowing silk, diaphanous and white,
she veils those limbs which even whiter are,
which, like a misty vapor o'er the sun,
covers them but still does not conceal.
The hem is tossed about in graceful turns
as Zephyr lifts and crinkles it in sworls.

57. Fashioned by her craftsman husband's hand,
a fine enameled clasp upon her shoulder,

[3] According to this famous tale, Venus was exposed in the embrace of
Mars, a circumstance which she neglects to mention, though the reference to horns in the next stanza brings the matter up obliquely.
[4] Orion.
[5] Endymion. These are references to other goddesses making love to
mortals.

polished bright, its claws of gold attached
to sapphires, holds her habit up in place.
The bow, whence every wounded beast is wont
to covet the assault, thanks to her hand,
is hung neglected, idle at her back,
and so likewise the quiver at her side.

58. Beneath the confines of her brief attire,
save for the foot, which gilded slippers hide,
the living alabaster of the one
and of the other column naked shows.
This world shall never see—unless perhaps
my lady's equal them—forms so divine.
To praise, to portray beauty such as this,
Thrace has no fitting song and Greece no brush.

.   .   .   .   .

FIRST MEETING OF THE LOVERS

61. Venus does not dare to reveal herself
abruptly to Adonis in true guise;
but wishing to invent some sport of it,
she hides her own behind another's form.
A new, deceitful form she has devised,
with what strange sleights I know not how to tell.
So well the gear and gestures of Diane
she feigns, you would believe her to be she.

62. She goes like Cynthia, plain, unadorned,
and wears a gown the color of fresh grass.
All in a mass of gold her aureate locks
negligently o'er her shoulders fall.
No industry, although most shrewdly plied
with artifice, delights us half so much
as does the wild disorder of her hair
which, scorning art, augments her loveliness.

63. Her right hand holds two greyhounds; by her side
     an ivory horn hangs from a golden chain.
     Upon her forehead, spotless white and smooth,
     a radiant moon is sparkling clear and bright.
     At her left side a bow is seen and quiver
     which holds the piercing points of tempered steel;
     and so with dogs, with arrows, horn, and spear
     the wanton goddess seems the one most chaste.

64. Not only for her sport does she employ
     this trick, but to disgrace her rival too;
     and fearing, should the sun discover her,
     he'd bear the news to Vulcan or to Mars,
     she hopes that either he or some young faun
     who flees from him into that shady glen
     will carry the report to Pan and tell
     that e'en Diana is no longer chaste.

65. To ease herself in speeding o'er the path,
     she strips the gilded buskins from her feet,
     then she goes treading steep and rocky ways
     along the length of that dim, winding vale.
     The grass, grown pale and yellow from the sun,
     turns green, each flower opens, stands erect;
     beneath her pilgrim foot each twig and shoot
     throughout the savage woodland springs to life.

66. Now a reckless and audacious thorn,
     but one as fortunate as it is rash,
     pierces the tender alabaster foot
     in passing, calling forth the blood in spurts,
     at which the head of her who caused the wound
     is flecked with gems of heavenly crimson drops;
     but coloring the flowers on their stems
     makes pale the flowers of the heavenly face.

67. Pale and dolorous, she stops to stanch
     those lovely purple drops with soft, white cloth,

the while she sees the rose all sparkling bright,
now with the white of snow, now ruby red.
But for her double wound she tarries not,
nor leaves the pathway of her chosen track.
Pain being conquered by desire, the wound
of foot surrenders to the wound of heart.

68. Now having reached a solitary hill,
a spot where human foot has rarely trod,
she finds there at the margin of a fount
Adonis sleeping in the flowers' embrace;
and now, although sleep casts its shadow o'er
the heavenly features of his countenance,
and covers with a veil those splendors twain,
even in slumber he resembles Love.

69. He looks like Love, when, weary from the hunt,
and having laid aside the faithful bow,
the arrows and the torch, he sometimes rests
in Gnidos' vale or on Idalian slope,
amid the myrtles where in covert shade
canorous birds have found obscure retreat,
and on his quiver resting his fair head,
he takes his sleep beside the murmuring brook.

70. Like some keen, well-trained hound that, on the hunt,
exploring hedges with both eye and nose,
comes suddenly upon the prey concealed
within its den, he stands fixed rigidly;
and in the thicket crouching motionless,
it seems he neither hears nor blinks an eye,
while, frozen there, he stealthily observes
the prey and any possible escape;

71. just so love's goddess, when alone she comes
to view that bright, angelic form and face,
which lend seductive charms to those wild woods,
increasing even the marvels of her heaven,

she stops, immobile, chilled, and on the grass
she sits down, dazed and yet inspired by hope,
and gazes long, and reverently adores
that wondrous beauty which enamors her.

. . . . .

76. Such joy is showered on her from that face,
and such a fire is caught from his closed eyes,
that, bending over him she overflows
with pleasure, with desire, with wonderment.
As she now scans the purple of his cheek,
and now the sweet vermilion of his mouth,
sighing, an "Ah me!" issues from her breast,
but from delight it springs and not from pain.

77. As studious painter, who with fixed intent
to rival nature in fair portraiture,
observing covertly, would steal away
the many flowers of a lovely face,
first images in thought the nude outlines
of that sweet glance and of the gentle smile,
and then with hand, disciple of his Art,
robes it with pleasing colors on the page;

78. so she, as if with furtive brush engaged,
hoping to capture the dear object's air,
now drinks in with her greedy, wanton eyes
the beauties of that sweet, enamored face;
hence of the true and living counterpart,
she drafts an image with a golden dart,
and then with that same dart of Love she strikes,
and fixes it within his very heart.

79. Sitting at his feet she studies him,
his image being printed in her breast;
she sees herself reflected, and the flame
finds fuel, whence it blazes brighter yet;

but she would like to see the lamps revived
of those fair stars which are eclipsed and spent;
and so, 'twixt joy and longing, she devours
the vision of that lovely spectacle.

80. Although the favor of dense, shady boughs
defends the youthful sleeper from the sun,
even so, the air, with fiery vapors charged,
reflects somewhat the summer's fiery torch,
and, spite of that deep sleep, which sweetly binds
the senses and which lulls the drowsy brain,
his visage, nonetheless, is warm and moist,
diffused with drops of sweat and all inflamed.

81. Wherefore the goddess, out of sympathy,
waves above him now her garment's hem
and now a delicate white scarf, to soothe
the snowy brow, the amber of his locks;
and while she stirs the still, oppressive air,
and fans away the heavy, noisome heat,
intent and doting, she, with airy sighs,
ever exhales her inward kindled flame.

82. "O breezes," she implores, "the sweet and graceful
pilgrims of the sky, O fragrant airs,
you who so oft among the murmuring tops
of these same trees are wont to fly in bands,
you for whom my amorous breaths of sighs
lend double force unto your beating wings,
O blessed breezes, now I pray defend
from fretful ardors our beloved Love!

83. "Thus may the hateful wrath and enmity
and chill of winter never injure you;
and when the mountains have their whitest caps,
may sweet ambrosial flakes drop from your wings;
and may both woods and heaven lend to you
defense against the sun of those fair eyes;

and may the tranquil shade and peaceful air
keep you ever soft and blest with health."

84. Whence turning to the greening, flowery fields,
the couch for her beloved one, she says:
"O land, as sacred now and blest as heaven,
O you adventurous flowers and happy grass,
to whom 'tis granted so much grace to hold,
who are permitted to possess such dower,
that for my languid idol you become
the pillow for his head, down for his side.

85. "O flowers born in happy hour, the ray
of Love which strikes you now be still your sun.
But what do I perceive? Now what cannot
the power of lovely eyes perform though shut?
By the fair color of that lovely throat,
and by the fragrance of that heavenly breath,
the rose is vanquished and the lily shamed,
the one turns pale, the other blushes red."

86. She turns now to the eyes and says: "Dear eyes,
let one of your bright lamps console my heart,
eyes so fair and gentle, shining eyes,
eyes of my thoughts, my ports, my very poles,
eyes charming and serene, O smiling eyes,
eyes of my desires, mirrors and suns,
windows for Aurora, gates of day,
possessing power to clear my nights of gloom.

. . . . .

97. "Why," she asks, "do I not touch him now,
softly, face to face and breast to breast?
Time is fleeting; with it soon enough
delight flies off and sorrow follows fast.
Alas, that pleasure which finds not response
in love's exchange is far from perfect bliss,

nor does one take true pleasure in a kiss
when the beloved kisses not again.

98. "What respite from my pains shall I expect
if I allow so fair a chance to slip?
But if he should awake and be annoyed,
where would I turn in my embarrassment?
Complaints and sighs will surely move his heart,
unless indeed he has a soul of stone.
This could not be in one so fair." She bends,
thus dubious, to kiss him, then dares not.

99. Just as the country laborer delays,
if, rushing to a pool to quench his thirst
when Sirius [6] barks madly in the heavens,
he spies a viper resting in the depths;
or as the hunter who, among the boughs
explores the hidden haunt of Philomel,
and as he thrusts his hand into the nest,
instead of birds he finds an asp therein;

100. so she, at once both happy and afraid,
trembles as much as inwardly she yearns.
The beauty which delights also afflicts,
and too great agitation makes her faint.
She longs for that which hurts, and she is forced
ever to fear the thing that she desires.
She now repents that her desire has strayed,
and is repentant for repenting so.

101. Three times with light, sweet breath, approaching near
the mouth, the kiss, three times she stops, she yields,
the spur and rein are both applied at once,
she wishes, wishes not, retreats, draws near.
Love, who never ceases urging her,
at last compels her toward the wished-for goal,

[6] The Dog Star. Reference to dog days, hottest part of summer.

so that she burns to sip the dewy drops
of the celestial rose's purple bloom.

102. She pressed a kiss—she sipped ambrosia sweet—
at which the sleeping youth began to stir;
and then, returned a little to himself,
he shook the slumber from his tipsy eyes.
Stupor did so conquer him with view
of that fair sight, he lay there motionless;
from her who had embraced him unaware,
turning confused and dazed, he tried to flee.

103. But she, importunate, still clung to him;
"Why flee from me," she said, "where wilt thou go?
Thou wouldst bestow on me thy willing gaze
if thou but knew of me what thou know'st not."
And he, completely dazzled then and filled
with infinite delight at such bright rays,
at rays cast by so fair a sun on him,
first closed his eyes, then parted his fair lips.

104. "Oh, what art thou that show'st thyself to me,
all love, all grace, a mortal or divine?
Immortal goddess sure from heavenly realms,
descended now to bless these savage shores,
if," he declares, "our prayers rise up so high,
if reverent affection heaven shuns not,
reveal to me thy station; what art thou,
wert thou of mortals born or of the gods."

105. To Venus then, who wished for nothing more
than that her lamps be fixed to those fair lamps,
it seemed, in opening the double suns
of those two eyes, that paradise appeared;
thereto the warm sweet words of love which he,
all sighing and atremble, spoke to her,
were most agreeable—flames to the heart,
snares to the soul, and arrows to the breast.

106. But still, concealing her identity,
 she fashions a mendacious tongue betimes.
 "Dost thou not recognize, rash archer, her
 who dwells within the first celestial sphere,[7]
 who holds in empire the infernal realms,
 and likewise has these woods in governance?
 Though thou wouldst imitate and follow me,
 thy heart burns less for me than thou hast said.

107. "I took me, just as I am wont to do
 when summer's Dog Star glows and flashes sparks,
 to this dim wood for shelter in the shade
 along the bank of yonder lucid stream,
 where a live current, pouring into it,
 distills itself from pumice cavernous,
 and forms a little fountain, which impearls
 the tresses of the reeds along its fringe.

108. "My foot, then bare of any covering,
 as thou seest now, because of excess heat,
 a thorn both cruel and injurious
 pierced with a rigid, unexpected prick.
 And though I have no need of medicine
 to bring about the healing of the hurt,
 I plucked these herbs, whose virtue is to stanch
 the flow of blood as well as close the wound.

109. "But since my nymphs are roaming far afield,
 and I have no one here to treat my wound,
 pray lend thy gracious hand to me in aid
 (to thee recourse, in thee recovery)."
 Here of her bleeding foot and suffering heart,
 one wound she hides, the other she displays,
 and utters, as a witness of her pangs,
 a sigh divided into two deep sighs.

[7] Cynthia, variously called Diana and Hecate, was goddess of the moon, of hunting, and of the realm of the dead.

110. Adonis was not made of Alpine stone,
      nor born of Lybian serpent to the world;
      but even were a bosom armed with flint,
      or were it with some bitter poison charged,
      the most obdurate heart, the fiercest soul,
      would by so fair a sun be overcome.
      Nor is it strange when one to one is touched,
      dry tinder burns in a voracious flame.

111. Reverence, piety, and love, and fear
      create in dubious heart a dreadful strife;
      and yet, because each desperate chance of fate
      must be forthwith embraced or let escape,
      he falters not, though trembling and gone cold,
      while he prepares for so sweet enterprise
      with gesture both appealing and afraid,
      at which the wanton eye smiles languishing.

112. "Goddess," he said, "to whom the Delians
      present their vows and incense, deck their fanes,
      who does not recognize your triple power
      in the abyss, on earth, and in the sky?
      Excuse the heart that cannot yet express
      with perfect zeal how much it honors you;
      in peace accept the boldness of this hand
      which dares obey you in so worthy cause."

· · · · ·

115. With this discourse he places in his lap
      the animated milk of her fair foot,
      and when with veil most white and delicate,
      he gently wipes away the gelid drops,
      the hand with which he touches her appears
      as gleaming white as the unsullied snow.
      Cupid, who was hovering near, remarks,
      "So fair a foot wants no less lovely hand."

· · · · ·

117. The youth said in his heart: "What prodigies
       and what new marvels do I here behold?
       The heaven of love, from out its crystalline
       abode, rains down a cloud of sanguine dew.
       When have I ever heard that cinnabar [8]
       was born from alabaster in this wise,
       that ivory fountain poured vermilion drops,
       that red from lilies came, coral from snow?"

· · · · ·

122. "Alas, what charming punishment is this,"
       said his companion, "which now binds my wound?
       'Tis not a bandage, rather 'tis a chain,
       which, while it binds my foot confines my heart.
       This crimson juice, which in so large a stream
       of vivid redness stains and streaks my flesh,
       alas, it is my soul expressed in blood,
       intent to sacrifice itself to him.

· · · · ·

125. "But why do I not now remove the cloak
       that holds my splendor wrapped as in a cloud?
       If when this magic veil in part conceals
       my charms, my adversary is o'ercome,
       what will befall when all mist is dispelled,
       will not the feigned surrender to the true?"
       She spoke, and casting off the false disguise,
       in her true image she appeared to him.

· · · · ·

127. Adonis is bewildered when to him
       the goddess shows herself in all her light;
       and so much more his mind is cast in doubt,
       not sure if he is dreaming or awake,
       because he there discovers clearly shown

       [8] Vermilion (poetic).

the true form as he saw it in his dream,
beholding her once more who recently
appeared to him as robber of his heart.

· · · · ·

129. "I will no longer hide me. I am she
for whom love lights the third celestial sphere;
and I am she whose star shines ere the sun
appears in heaven, a rival of the sun.
I mention not that what is beautiful
on earth receives its loveliness from me,
nor that I am the daughter of heaven's king;
I only say Love's mother is in love."

· · · · ·

137. What's heard, what's seen excited him; he burned
with still new flames not yet experienced;
the burning from the fire of his heart
then spread across his delicate, fair cheeks.
In modesty he lowered to the ground
the smiling stars, so frankly reticent,
then with a sigh he raised his gaze to her,
at last he poured his spirit out in words:

138. "O kindly goddess, oh, if there is yet
a better title for great majesty,
what can a lowly servant offer you,
whose pity deigns to grant him so much grace?
A scepter? No, since, disinherited,
he now no longer reigns in his own land.
My life? Not so, since life and death depend
for us poor mortals on the fatal gods.

139. "You are so bright one cannot gaze on you,
but gazing he must surely flame with love;
yet no one, taking fire at seeing you,
can fall in love without offending you.

To serve you and adore you is offense;
vile man who aims so high outrages you,
because compared to what surpasses measure,
proportion has no scale to reach so low.

140. "Human boldness should not reach so high
as to presume to love eternal beauty,
but bend the knee and with humility
devoutly worship one who reigns in heaven.
'Tis true that sometimes a supernal soul
feels for a lesser being strange desire,
and then that bounty, that celestial power,
imprints its merit on the subject loved.

141. "That merit which in mortals is the cause
of love, in you celestials is the effect,
wherefor when any god inclines to love
a frail, terrestrial one, he perfect grows;
so that although the match unequal be,
one purifies the other's weaknesses;
and purging defects from the humble one,
makes noble what is lowly of itself.

142. "Love enamored me of you through fame
before I came to view your loveliness;
I loved you from afar no less than when
the greedy sight perceives a lovely thing.
Now how much more my glad heart sighs and yearns,
since I behold you with my very eyes,
and since more favors have been granted me,
I would, in pleasing you, make myself blessed."

. . . . .

[Venus speaking.]
150. "Not only do I grant thee to enjoy
my eyes and hands, my tender mouth and breast,
but I lay bare my side and offer thee
my amorous heart in fair exchange for thine.

Thou'lt see the love I feel within my heart
has not harmed thee but has transformed itself,
that thou art the sole object of my thoughts,
and that no heart but thine is in my breast."

151. With such seductions the seductive dame
prays and seduces the seductive youth.
Boldly then she moves her trembling hand,
enfolds his neck and gently binds him straight.
Here meanwhile Love, in triumph and in pride,
now raising his victorious standard high,
entwines both bodies in a close embrace,
their tongues are silent and their souls converse.

152. Sweetly the sounds of kisses echo there,
and envious the zephyrs bear them off,
the sonorous trumpet for assaults of love
murmurs its consent throughout the woods;
to which the lovebirds and the turtledoves
respond with scores of kisses and more scores.
Then Cupid, hidden in a nearby cave
and spying on their secrets, smiles content.

153. So close entwining was the knot which bound
together the adventurous pair, so firm
that ne'er more close did vine to elm tree cling,
bindweed to thorn, or ivy to its oak.
A silvery cloud enclosed the twain, and there
ingenious Love observed and guarded them,
whose treachery, avenging his disgrace,
exacts for his one spanking many wounds.

PRAISE OF THE ROSE

154. The goddess fair, ensanguined by the rose,
although a bitter wound had pierced her breast,
did not reveal her anger toward her son,
lest he become more cruel and more proud;
but, keeping in her heart her hidden wound,

she bit her lip and said, "I'll tend to thee
anon; just now I do not wish to spoil
my happiness with someone's suffering."

155. Her eyes then turning to the nearby hill
where stood the bush that pierced her lovely foot,
she briefly paused to gaze on it once more,
for e'er she left she would salute the flower;
and seeing it still shining there, so soft
and crimson-stained, she then addressed it thus:
"May heaven save thee from outrage and harm,
thou fatal agent of my joyful pain.

156. "Rose, smile of love, creation sent from heaven,
ah, rose, now made vermilion with my blood,
nature's ornament, the world's great prize,
the virgin daughter of the earth and sun,
delight and care of every nymph and swain,
the honor of the odoriferous kind,
to thee belongs fair beauty's highest palm,
mistress sublime of all the host of flowers.

157. "Like a proud empress on her gorgeous throne,
thou sit'st in splendor on thy native bank.
A host of charming and seductive airs
wait upon thy grace and pay their court;
a well-armed band of loyal, stinging guards
surrounds thee to defend thee from all harm;
and thou, proud of thy regal state, art decked
with purple mantle and with golden crown.

158. "Thou crimson of the gardens, pomp of fields,
the gem of springtime, eye of April's dawn;
the Graces and the little, winged Loves
weave garlands of thee for their hair, their throats.
Whene'er the zephyrs or the sportive bees
return to thee for wonted sustenance,
thou profferest them liquors, dewy clear
and crystalline, to sip from ruby cup.

159. "Let not the haughty sun puff up with pride
     because he triumphs o'er the lesser stars,
     for here amid the shrubs and violets,
     thou also shinest with proud and lovely pomp.
     Thou with thy beauties bright and rare appear
     the splendor of these meadows, he of those.
     He in his circuit, thou upon thy stem;
     thou the sun on earth, he rose in heaven.

160. "You two shall feel reciprocal desires,
     the sun shall be thy lover and thou his.
     He will put on thy colors, and the dawn
     at rising will bedeck her in thy spoils;
     upon thy crown, amid the banks of leaves,
     thou wilt display his flaming livery;
     and that thou mayst reflect him faithfully,
     thou'lt wear a little sun within thy breast.

161. "Because some mark of grace is due to thee
     for rendering to me so great a boon,
     thou'lt be my favorite, my one delight
     among the many flowers that Flora owns.
     And when the world pays tribute to the fair,
     I would that none be called most beautiful
     who wears not on her cheeks and on her lips
     thy vivid colors." Here she ends her song.

THE PALACE OF LOVE

162. At no great distance from those woods there stood
     the splendid palace of the god of Love,
     but what it held concealed within its walls
     had never been revealed to mortal eyes.
     They had not traveled far when they beheld
     the rooftop flashing with fine, golden scales,
     whence wondrously that splendid edifice
     made luminous all the surrounding shade.

163. That lofty and magnificent abode,
      which rarely yields to view its secret stores,
      at the appearance of this charming guest
      offered him all beauties it possessed.
      And not alone did it reveal to him
      the matchless glory of those splendid halls,
      but also it immersed him in a sea
      of marvels and delights beyond compare.

164. On entering the first tower on the right
      the fair Adonis then advanced his steps
      and found himself within a strange courtyard,
      the fairest and the richest ever seen.
      Square is that courtyard, spacious, smoothly paved,
      the floor inlaid with stones of red and white;
      its pavement patterned like a checkerboard
      in alternating squares of white and rose.

165. A spiral staircase, in the center placed,
      ascends for access to the upper parts.
      Four arches which extend out from the top
      create a cross and link four balconies,
      adjoining which the antechambers lie,
      whence one can pass to various galleries;
      so that one stair embraces and commands
      through four approaches all the royal seat.

166. Within the sectors into which the court
      is quartered off, divided by the cross,
      are four illustrious fountains, one for each,
      carved by the most ingenious implements,
      of labor so stupendous, intricate,
      that one perceives the art to be divine;
      of agate and of alabaster two,
      and one of ophite,[9] one carnellian.

      [9] Marble with green serpentine markings.

167. Neptune in one fountain is portrayed
     striking his trident 'gainst an alpine rock,
     and thereby sending sprays on every side,
     streams of water, gleaming, crystalline.
     He rides upon a conch shell, dolphin drawn,
     and every dolphin spews a crystal stream;
     four Tritons, stationed round, in thousand streams,
     sprinkle quicksilver from their trumpets' mouths.

168. A second fountain holds a basin, carved,
     incised, and resting on a pedestal,
     in which there stand two figures back to back,
     Pyramus and Thisbe, swords at breasts;
     and many a crimson rivulet spurts out
     with purest wine from their sad, mortal wounds,
     from which the ruddy manna trickles down
     through double channels to the bowl beneath.

169. Another fount reveals in rounded conch,
     mouth to mouth and breast to breast conjoined,
     upon a flowery bank Hermaphrodite,
     holding in embrace Salmacis fair;
     beside each one, in aspect like a wave,
     ambrosia streams forth from their limbs and hair;
     and from above their heads a mighty urn
     rains down pure nectar in a gushing vein.

170. The fourth presents young Love, as though asleep,
     reclining peacefully upon a rock;
     the Graces stand close by but lower down,
     having the custody of bow and torch.
     The blind young god, while he lies dozing there,
     from out his quiver spreads a balsam bath,
     and all his lovely, amorous demoiselles
     distill the selfsame liquid from their breasts.

171. For welcoming Adonis to these halls,
     the household stirs in force, solicitous;

and while the goddess occupies herself
with minute pains upon domestic cares,
the youth, who, led by Cupid, views the palace,
cannot but stare in wide-eyed wonderment,
and he inquires who is it owns and rules
this wondrous mansion which he now beholds.

172. "This," Cupid answers, sighing as he speaks,
"containing such a wealth of splendid works,
is my own dwelling, and I prize it so
that I esteem it e'en above the heavens;
here it was my deep, sweet wounds commenced,
here, alas, my burnings first began;
here for her [10] who ever holds me close,
the fatal swelling of my pain began.

173. "Do not believe that any souls divine
escape the power of amorous desire,
for impulse naturally inclines us all
to long for pleasures so agreeable.
Even the king of the Celestial band
by heaven's decree is subject to this law.
And I, yea even I, from whose own hand
rains joy and grief, likewise came under it.

174. "I could not rest from languishing although,
a mighty god, I hold th' eternal torch,
and draw the bow omnipotent, and rule
the elements and planets at my will.
And if thou harken to me I will show
that I was wounded by that very dart,
and that my heart was kindled by that fire,
that Love, himself enamored, burned and wept."

175. Thus the archer, born of fair Cyprina,
addressed himself to Myrrha's handsome son;
and since it pleased Adonis much to hear

[10] Psyche.

the god, he was intent upon his speech.
Love resumed his talk, then paused awhile,
but did not interrupt their strolling tour;
anon he turned to view his charming guest
and then for longer speech he ope'd his lips.

CANTO V

The Tragedy

[The great hall of the Palace of Love presents a scene such as
one may see (on somewhat more modest scale) in many of the
Italian palaces of the period. The decorations, ornate and varied
as they are, are based on a unified allegorical concept.]

THE HALL OF THE FOUR ELEMENTS

112. Now Venus with the fair Adonis mounts
  the spiral staircase with its ivory steps,
  which from the center of the courtyard spreads
  its arches to the four broad balconies.
  Here through a hundred polished crystal panes
  the mammoth hall receives the light of day,
  and in a series of mosaic scenes
  presents the image of the Universe.

113. Four portals fair of pure and polished gold,
     exposed to the four winds, form entrances.
     Rich incrustations covering the walls
     conceal the structure of the hall itself.
     Upon the facings of opposing walls
     the order of the elements is staged,
     and each contains within its proper sphere
     all fish, all birds, and every kind of beast.

114. In every section is portrayed that god
     who empire holds within that element,
     and every element is made and carved
     of substance corresponding to the real.
     The fire vermilion, set with ruby gems;
     cerulean the air, of sapphire pure;
     the smiling, verdant earth of emerald;
     the zone of water is of diamond.

115. The pavement of the hall, which has inlaid
     a foliated border of fine gold
     encompassing the scene, is occupied
     by Tartarus,[1] realm of infernal night;
     and there in horrid attitude appears
     the king [2] of that grim, dismal world of shades;
     and with him crowd the Furies, hags who make
     a pomp of serpents shadowing their brows.

116. In its vast dome a sky serene is feigned,
     a greater work the Cyclops ne'er achieved.
     Compared to its display of gorgeous gems
     India is poor and Ethiopia shamed.
     Enameled background, jacinth in mid-part;
     a sun of porphyry shoots out its rays,
     and for the stars the vaulted firmament
     is bright with ruby and with chrysolite.

[1] Hades.   [2] Pluto.

117. One there beholds the fixed point and the course
circuitous of each celestial light.
There, with its monsters twelve, the Zodiac,
in circuit wide three lesser circles frames.
There too are marked the two bright tropic lines,
where equalize the hours of light and dark.
There are inscribed the two lines of colures [3]
shown intersecting at the polar points.

118. There is the equator, whose great line is placed
precisely midway twixt the other four,[4]
of which the outermost are too exposed,
the one to Austral,[5] one to Boreal [6] climes;
and yonder, formed of small and thickset stars,
behold the regal way of all the gods,[7]
whose whiteness, cutting cross the sky, extends
its track from Centaur to the Gemini.

119. At center of the hall an Atlas huge,
a single towering piece of jasper fine,
supports the vault and fixes both his feet
upon a pedestal of adamant;
there under the high, massive cupola
he stands, his back curved and his chin inclined.
And all the heaven that fills the vaulted arch
presses on him its mighty, grievous load.

A THEATRICAL PERFORMANCE

[This theatrical performance is a faithful representation of entertainments performed throughout the courts of western Europe during the sixteenth and seventeenth centuries. The core of

---

[3] Two great circle lines of the celestial sphere, intersecting over the poles and passing through the equinoxial and solsticial points respectively.

[4] The Tropics of Cancer and Capricorn, the Arctic and Antarctic Circles.

[5] Southern.   [6] Northern.   [7] The Milky Way.

the program is a familiar mythological story, the Ovidian tale of
Actaeon and Diana. But this is interrupted by frequent inter-
ludes, ballets, and colossal spectacles having no observable connection with the main drama.

Budgets for costumes and scenery were astronomical. And
much labor and ingenuity were devoted to the construction of
stage machinery for scenic effects. Nevertheless, the conception
of the revolving stage appears to have been an invention of
Marino, perhaps two or three centuries in advance of the construction of such a stage. (For a more detailed discussion of the
issue, see the appendix.)]

120. Now Night, at hearing the light sound of kisses,
      most envious, made her return to heaven;
      and, borne aloft by light and fleeting Hours,
      with dark'ning shadows armed, she conquered Day.
      The friendly stars accompanied in grief
      the coffin of the Sun with thousand torches;
      and the world, now cloaked with mists and shade,
      seemed turned a sepulchre for buried light.

121. The amorous pair, proceeding arm in arm,
      had scarcely entered that colossal hall,
      when, lo, a gilded theater appeared,
      that, emulating day, illumined dusk.
      Less rich and full of light and gold, methinks,
      would be the fourth sphere,[8] were it to appear.
      Woods, statues, palaces were there revealed,
      when full the splendid curtain was withdrawn.

122. A courtly spectacle has been prepared
      by Mercury to entertain the youth.
      'Tis Mercury who has prepared the cast,
      who tests, trains, and directs each histrion,
      and each of them, in happy role or grim,

      [8] Sphere of the Sun.

according to his aptitude performs.
Not one of them would deign to act before
a vulgar and commercial audience.

123. Invention, Fable, and the Poem here,
with Energy, Decorum, Harmony,
plus Order firm and Wit and rare Conceit
contribute to the theme of tragedy.
The artificer prime is Eloquence,
who towers o'er the rest with Poesy.
And with them Meter, Numbers, Prosody
impose upon the music their control.

124. Golden seats are furnished for the pair,
from which all that is acted may be seen;
and, lo, the first of all to issue forth,
the bearer of th' eternal embassy,[9]
declaims the argument in lofty style
that manifests he's come from realms supern;
the subject he announces for the play
concerns the hapless fall of Actaeon.

125. Then, following the prologue, Actaeon
appears with bow and arrows, dogs and horn,
and he is seen with his attendants joined,
all armed with pikes and gorgeously attired;
and while in hunting for the savage prey
he sends part of his crew to scour the brakes,
assigns the stations and directs the track,
he lauds the hunt with diverse arguments.

126. Lo, at a blast from curving ivory
Adonis spies a sudden rushing out
from every bush and briar, from juniper
and myrtle, hosts of gentle woodland beasts;
doe and chamois scamper, goats and hares,
some from the stage to Venus' lap, while some

[9] Mercury.

conceal themselves behind Adonis' robe,
much to the startled couple's merriment.

127. Now suddenly the hunting scene departs
from sight; the stage presents another set,
since counterpoised upon a turning point
the stage rests on a central pivot strong,
which, mobile yet well fastened to the floor,
turns easily, now lowered and now raised;
and pivoting its mobile weight around,
it comes at last to fasten horn with horn.[10]

128. Just as the world in single globe conjoined
two separate hemispheres together links
by the horizon which from height to depth
cuts midway through the whirling universe,
so this device which rolls around reveals
how several theaters appear in one,
except that earth embraces only two,
while this within its circle harbors more.

129. Therefore, as often as they wish to bring
a different scene before the audience,
the setting can be shifted readily
upon that huge, orbicular machine,
so by a screw device they, bit by bit,
can make it move without a grating noise,
and with such skill can raise or lower it
that spectators may not perceive the change.

130. Various props support the master stage,
both joists and braces, planks and sturdy beams,
and all the boards well reinforced with bronze,
with heavy chains and crossbars tough and thick,
and nails and keys of that same metal made,
with many cranes and intricate machines;

---

[10] A detailed discussion of Marino's "invention" of the revolving stage
is presented in the appendix.

and one piece to another is so matched
that smoothly without flaw they operate.

131. And now that in the hunt the Theban youth
withdraws, departing from the verdant fields,
at once an ironshod lever starts to turn
the platform on its many-cogged vertex;
the scene shifts as the apparatus then
presents a new set to the audience;
so after the first curtain has been drawn
a different spectacle is thus revealed.

132. A pleasant woodland scene appears, dark caves,
fresh hills and somber shades and fountains clear.
There Hyppocrene spreads out her silver stream,
here double-peaked Parnassus lifts twin brows.
Apollo and the Muses, wise and fair,
descending from those verdant mountain slopes,
enact down here the light and graceful dance
which in the heavens is performed by spheres.

133. Each one keeps step according to the time
marked by the lyre, the movement matching notes,
and with the hands and feet and with the voice,
at once strikes strings and pavement and the air.
The dance now finished, in a moment's time
the master sets in motion the machine,
and, turning on the pin on which it rests,
the stage he then revests in a new guise.

134. After that first interlude, once more
the woods are shown, and Cynthia appears,
who weary seeks a shelter dense and green
in vale of Gargaphy her to refresh;
her garments all ungirt and cast aside,
she bathes her weary, sunburnt limbs therein;
and midst the waters pure and crystalline
reclining she converses with her nymphs.

135. Again the scene is changed, and in a flash
    the square is full of Centaurs in a dance,
    one bearing a keen poignard in his hand,
    one a light lance and one a heavy mace;
    save on their arm a shield they have naught else
    to cover them of armor, helm, or plate.
    The trumpet blares out in a martial air:
    "To war, off to the war! to arms, to arms!"

136. Now one with fury seems to strike his foe;
    now, now it seems that blood spills on the ground.
    With art harmonic is the battle staged;
    now they engage, now one makes head, now fails.
    And while this one 'gainst that one hurls himself,
    they clatter, blade on blade and targe and targe,
    and striking so in tempo back or breast,
    thus out of horror strange is born delight.

137. While on their sport Adonis is intent,
    comes Love to offer him refreshment meet,
    and brings one golden and one silver cup,
    filled with ambrosia this and nectar that.
    As much as he requires for nutriment
    he savors only, to restore his veins;
    for other food, wherein is more delight,
    he feeds on with his eyes, drinks with his ears.

138. For the third act, upon the turning pin
    the versatile machine again revolves,
    and Actaeon returns, his face and limbs
    with sweat all streaked and grossly stained with dust;
    wherefore, to give some respite to the hounds
    and band of hunters he at length resolves.
    He gathers up the nets, and in the deep
    and shady wood alone he takes his rest.

139. Now twixt this act and the ensuing one
    there comes a charming novel interlude.

You see a wavy sea; [11] I know not if
of sapphire, silver, or of crystal made;
a strip of shore is visible all strewn
with foam and seaweed, shells and coral bright;
the trembling waves flash with cerulean gleam,
and in it swimming dolphins glide and leap.

140. And scattered wide o'er the unstable field,
with puffing sails outspread and sail yards hauled,
with prows afoam and fiery, clamorous din
two powerful armadas clash in fight. [12]
At length the brilliant-colored lamp of Jove,
streaking with aureate shafts the darkening sky,
makes through the quivering air with glancing rays
a thousand tongues of flame and serpent stripes.

141. The heavens flash, and swords flash from the ships,
the waves rise high, tempestuous and black,
the clouds weep and the struggling legions shed
water and blood o'er all that wavy plain.
One flees the iron and is consumed in fire,
one flees the fire and perishes in waves,
one who is sprayed with water, fire, and blood
is vanquished in a moment, burns and sinks.

142. Such is a war, the tumult and the chill;
reality is matched by what appears.
But now at length the heavens become serene,
the sea from storm turns gradually calm,
and Iris spreads her bright and misty veil,
a banner in the clear and dewy sky.

[11] Water scenes were sometimes represented on early stages by actual flooding of stage tanks, more often faked by an arrangement of revolving corkscrew-shaped rollers covered with blue canvas.

[12] A naval battle was staged in the flooded courtyard of the Pitti Palace in Florence for the marriage festivities of Ferdinando Medici III, 1589. A picture of the scene is reproduced in J. Scholz and A. H. Mayor, *Baroque and Romantic Stage Design* (New York: H. Bittner & Co., 1950), Plate 10.

The galleys scatter and the waves are stilled,
the rainbow vanishes and all is calm.

143. That passed, the wondrous stage again is changed;
there a lovely fount is seen to play,
and there Actaeon stands watching Diane
at bath among her troop of naked nymphs.
Then she with light but fatal wave of hand
deprives him of his erstwhile human form.
With hirsute hide and with broad-branching horns
the luckless hunter is transformed a deer.

144. Close upon this, by slow degrees the sky
from azure pure takes on a paler hue,
with silver light the darkening plain is gilt,
and stars and moon begin to light the sky.
At length, driving Arcturus on his way,
the dawn arises hand in hand with day.
It seems like the true sun and a real dawn
that clears away the mists and lightens gloom.

145. The stage is elevated once again
and half the amphitheater spins round.
A splendid prospect thereupon is shown
with a rich table sumptuously spread,
and there assembled are the almighty gods;
the scene reveals such wealth of viands rare,
such treasures and such splendors are displayed
that heaven seems translated here on earth.

146. Lo, now a concert of musicians next
begins in low, in high, in blended strains,
and concords sound from various instruments,
some played by hand and others played by mouth;
in tempi bright and quick, then grave and slow,
the verses swell for those blest banqueters;
from choruses of nymphs responsive sound
the echoes of a symphony of Love.

147. On the horizon night had just revealed
the sixth step of the stair that leads to dawn,
when lo, pursued by hunters and by hounds,
appears the stag traversing the steep hill.
But now no longer heavy-eyed Adonis
can lift his lids or hold his head upright;
hence in the lap of his companion fair,
o'ercome with sleep, he lays his weary head.

148. In such a guise as the vermilion poppy,
touched by the first rays of the rising sun,
is wont to bow its slumber-laden head
and faint between the lily and the rose;
so sinks his drowsy head within the arms
of her who's nothing loath to such a care;
she could not bear a weight more dear to her,
nor he find lovelier pillow on this earth.

149. This was the cause wherefore he could not hear
the final horror of that tragic death;
nor with what torture dire and dolorous
the youth was slain by being torn to bits,
nor heed Autonoë's grievous lament
or plaints of Aristaeus and Cadmus old;
the tender goddess who so pillows him
wills that he be not wakened until dawn.

150. By now the harbinger of light had called
his winged coursers to their yoke and bit,
roused by the sound of jingling golden reins;
the young and lovely nurse of field and mead,
serene and smiling more than she is wont,
has issued forth with all her purple plumes
to nourish fresh with her celestial dews
the grass and plants and blossoms on the bush.

151. When young Adonis wakened and perceived
the sun was striking on the balconies,

he rubbed his eyes and then began to rise,
invited by his queen and Mercury.
Fair Cytherea took him by the hand
along the way that led them from the court,
she brought him to a garden of such green
that to it e'en Elysium yields the crown.

CANTO VI

The Garden of Pleasure

[Cantos VI, VII, and VIII form a unit and may be regarded as the heart of the poem, the quintessence of its "philosophy" and the triumph of its style. This section of nearly 5000 lines is devoted to a description of the Garden of Pleasure, the garden of the Palace of Love. Actually there are five divisions called: the Garden of the Eye, the Nose, the Ear, the Mouth, and Touch. The fact that critics have referred to Marino as the Poet of the Five Senses must be attributed in considerable measure to the minute and imaginative development of this fantastic passage.

Among the curiosities of this section of the poem are those passages treating the various organs of sensation in a style combining both physiological data and poetic appreciation. In Canto VI we encounter his descriptions of the eye and nose.]

THE PLAN OF THE GARDEN

7. A spacious garden ornaments the bounds
   of that great palace, wonderful to see.
   No misery or hardship enters there;
   there flourish loves, delights, ease, and disport.
   To it fair Venus, without fear of fate,
   has made provision to conduct the youth,
   exchanging heaven for that blest abode
   which seems a heaven, or little yields to heaven.

8. "Think not that without marvelous design,"
   said Mercury, turning to fair Adonis,
   "Ciprigna has established in her realm
   this mansion, so resplendent, so ornate;
   for heavenly intellect, genius divine,
   ne'er forms ought or disposes without cause.
   Her edifice is here constructed so
   it seems mysterious to the mind of man.

9. "The noble structure of the human body
   has in itself such perfect symmetry,
   that 'tis the rule and scale infallible
   of all that heaven enfolds beneath its roof.
   Nature created him that he alone
   of all the animals can sit and stand;
   and as the soul exceeds all other forms,
   so is his body model for all forms.

10. "The marvels which it comprehends and locks,
    mere words have not the power to express.
    No ship on water, palace on the land,
    no theater or temple under sun,
    no tool of peace or instrument of war,
    which does not take its pattern from this frame.
    The compass and the square find every figure
    in its rich architectural designs.

11. "Great miracle, for which most generously
Jove showered the abundance of his gifts;
it shows the semblance of divinity,
the living image and the perfect stamp.
Like some great sphere drawn on a narrow map,
the universe was epilogued in it.
It holds the forehead lofty, brow on high,
to view that heaven to which it is compared.

12. "The major world [1] is portioned in three parts,
the one of the great gods, which stands on high.
The several orders of the rolling spheres,
so fair and well disposed, have second place.
The last and lowest site of all contains
the region of the lowest elements;
to these this other, lesser world [2] conforms,
which is with senses and with spirits blessed.

13. "The power of understanding, in the head,
retains the role of sovereign governor;
midway, holding the sun's place, stands the heart,
which spreads its gentle warmth to all the rest.
The belly, in the lower, corporal seat,
like a sublunar body, fosters change;
in government, in nourishment, in life,
this animated house is tripartite.

14. "The sky and elements are bodies five;
the number of the senses is the same.
The stellar dome of lovely, burning lamps
is like a natural portrait of the sight.
Among them likewise in conformity,
hearing to air, and earth akin to touch.
Nor does it seem that with less sympathy
odor responds to flame and taste to wave.

[1] The macrocosm, or the universe.
[2] The microcosm, or the human body.

15. "Well could omnipotent divinity
    with that benignant zeal with which it placed
    in man such excellence, have given him
    a veil of incorruptibility; [3]
    and of the flower of that fifth essence pure,
    of which the sky has been composed unmixed,
    just as it formed the body like the heavens,
    it could have formed him of celestial stuff.

16. "But since he's born to speculate, 'tis meet
    that every living species shine in him,
    that he conduct the fantasies of sense
    to intellect, with which he is endowed,
    nor should have been of other substance formed,
    than elementary,[4] though it decays,
    to first make senses capable, then mind,
    of grasping what they feel and apprehend.

17. "Of all the wondrous work which with such art
    the supreme Master has bestowed on man,
    the nerves are instruments, by which the mind
    sends movement and sensation to the limbs.
    Some soft, some hard, in every part each one
    is ever on its proper office bent.
    The faculties of motion or sensation
    without them cannot execute an act.

18. "And now go forward, thou shalt see the effects,
    and thou shalt own that Venus is quite right
    to make that spot sacred to her delights
    the example of examples to behold."
    Here ceased Cyllenios,[5] and with such words
    he roused the youth from his astonishment,
    who at that point had come to the approach
    and first great portal of the joyous park.

[3] An immortal body.

[4] The system of elements of which the sublunary regions are composed, in contrast to the composition of the upper heavens.

[5] Mercury, born on Mt. Cyllene in Arcadia.

19. Around the garden, in five vestibules
    five gates give entrance to the visitors,
    and by custodians seated at each port
    the gate of each great vestibule is watched.
    Through every gate one finds a paradise,
    there where the little garden opens out,
    so that with equal space among them all,
    five gardens are in one great garden held.

20. Five gardens does that palace of delights
    embrace within its five enclosing towers,
    so from its balconies a different park
    invites by distant view from each façade.
    Each part is shaded by surrounding walls
    which spread their lines out for a thousand yards.
    These walls compose a square, and in the midst
    of each stand doors which lead from park to park.

21. At each of the four corners of the wall
    there springs a tower angular and high;
    a fifth tower rises in the midst of all,
    so that the cornice soars above the wall;
    and, as I said, one sees the towers set
    all in straight lines and equally apart;
    and pleasing art, with perfect measurement,
    I know not how, frames all the several parks.

22. Before the gate of the first portico
    which is of sapphire and of crystal made,
    a noble and vivacious youth stands guard.
    With diverse colors is his costume bright.
    A vulture in his hand he keeps, a lynx
    beside his feet, one on either side.
    Before, a mirror; on his shield is etched
    the noble one who fixes on the sun.[6]

----

[6] The eagle.

23. The courteous guardian immediately
    made his addresses to the loving pair,
    and with a friendly, smiling countenance,
    received Adonis, took him by the hand.
    "Welcome," he said, "thou living, burning sun
    that kindles flames within our great queen's heart.
    Right it is that of our secret bowers
    none be concealed from him but all revealed."

24. "Tell me," Adonis to Jove's messenger,
    "tell me," he said, "I pray thee, my dear guide,
    this guard, this animal with spotted hide,
    this splendid gate—what signify these things?
    That foul and greedy bird, that shining glass,
    that varicolored robe, what means it all?
    His unfamiliar countenance, strange gear,
    gladly would I know what they denote."

THE EYE

25. The other one replied, "Of all the prime,
    most worthy parts of sensory empire,
    the eye excels in glory, like a prince,
    indeed surpasses in nobility;
    which, placed upon the summit of the mount,
    leaves other vulgar members well behind;
    and 'mongst plebean senses proud it sits,
    from where it watches all and governs all.

26. "Eminent it sits, of senses chief,
    and surely the Creator planned it so,
    that of those it is leader, both for light,
    which is the one most precious quality,
    as well as that it can transmit so much
    and such variety of colored things;
    and also for the swift and ready mode
    of operation that pertains to it.

27. "Since without interval or change of place,
     it joins all distant objects in a flash,
     'tis such that in its acts it deviates
     but little from the action of the brain;
     whence, if that is more rapid and more smooth
     than wind or fire, 'tis called eye of the soul,
     so this, as one of nature's fairest works,
     is often called the body's intellect.

28. "Through eyes descends the sun, through eyes descend
     whatever images the soul receives,
     and of all that she sees and comprehends,
     almost the total credit is the eyes'.
     The eye, much like a bee, is wont to take
     the fairest and the lightest of the flowers,
     choosing the beautiful where'er 'tis spied,
     which to the inner censor it presents.

29. "Native to the fountains of the brain,
     from which the nerves have root and origin,
     with one beginning though by diverse ways
     two separate lines describe two narrow paths.
     Whence eyes, explorers, spies of all about,
     derive the motory ability;
     thence it befalls, as has been shown by proof,
     a single motion moves them both at once.

30. "Of matter soft and damp and slippery
     this splendid member was by nature formed,
     and so it can retain within itself
     impressions it receives perfect and pure.
     That it be mobile, nature gave to it
     a shape orbicular or spherical;
     and furthermore, in this form it can serve
     the better to reflect rays and refract.

31. "The living ray to spirits pupil joins,
     and is projected out from those twin spheres,

which in a pointed pyramid [7] extend
throughout the vision's range, where'er it turns.
And what it sees it draws within itself
as does a shadow, mirror, or a brook.
So while the eager glance escapes the eye
with all its power, the image enters it.

32. "Oh, how much study, how much industry
did the eternal Master gather here,
how many membranes, veins, and arteries,
what various subtile cobwebs, tender sheaths!
Through what a host of transverse ligatures
the pack of threads and films moves variously!
How many nerves, what a variety
of angles and canals pass through the eye!

33. "Out of the membranes and the various kinds
of liquids is a lucid volume formed,
and glassy matter, water, albumen
join in the uvea and cornea,
which are all servants and custodians
of that clear crystal,[8] whence the light proceeds.
All of the others aid and guard this one,
the prime, the central organ of the sight.

34. "In order that it may be less exposed
to outward hurt, immortal Providence
has given it a cavernous recess
sheltered beneath the arching of the brow.
For hedge and rampart he has added there
eyelids of film eternally alert,
and only through their beating rapidly
it is preserved from human accidents.

---

[7] Figure of the triangle formed by the convergence of the two visual
axes on the object viewed.
[8] Lens, retina.

35. "And so that it may open like the sun,
    this microcosm's sun, to copy that,
    much like a crown of rays has added there
    a delicate and silky hedge all 'round.
    This frames the iris in its curving globe,
    which has a border of cerulean blue,
    and in the middle are the heavenly spheres,
    enameled and with limpid sapphires flecked.

36. "These are the open portals of the soul,
    the indicators, faithful oracles,
    the certain guides for dubious reasoning
    and burning torches of the obscure mind.
    They are the tongues of thought, agile and keen,
    loquacious messengers of mute desires;
    the books and hieroglyphs, where all can read
    the letters of the secrets of the heart.

37. "Mirrors living and serene, through which
    are shown whate'er the breast retains within,
    and where in manner clear and manifest
    the soul reveals its every passion plain.
    The smiling pleasures and the bitter griefs
    are there exposed; now ire, now pity shows;
    and, what is more, the flames of love's hot fire
    are visibly revealed within their depths . . ."

. . . . .

THE NOSE

[Mercury speaking.]

116. "A well-drawn profile, sculptured by the hand
     divine, in mid-point of the human face,
     which upward with two curved eyebrows is joined,
     and at the nether end the lip confines.
     And since it has the task of guarding there,
     he armed the ridge with curved and hollow bone,

which as a base supports it, and the rest
is of a softer cartilage composed.

117. "So that, if through some sinister mischance
one of its windows should become shut off,
another might stand open and the nose
have passage for the breath, he fashioned two.
And placed between the one and the other tube
a separating column was installed,
not frail, though pliant, so that through its course
the showers of the head can be distilled.

118. "And though, besides its ornamental worth
and that it offers passage for the breath,
it serves to purge the head of excrement,
yet smelling is the greatest of its gifts.
Sensation here consists of movements slight
of mammillary nodules on its sides,
and at the entrance certain muscles move,
of which the one dilates and one contracts.

119. "Whence is the port of the internal sense
at last exposed down to its deepest roots,
there where in form of perforated sieve
a section overhangs the nostril tubes.
The other part is spongy and with neat
device is formed for needful offices,
which, being like a pumice full of holes,
breaks up the impure air within its pores.

120. "It is the cranium's moist sponge and such
that it absorbs from breath all arid things,
and draws unto itself the quality
of sweet and fragrant objects all about.
Warm vapors enter, pass through it, and rise
up to its ventricles through two canals
which never are compressed, wherefore thereby
both air and fragrance always have ingress . . ."

CANTO VII

The Delights

[Canto VII recounts the adventures of Adonis and his divine companions (Venus, Cupid, and Mercury) in the Garden of the Ear and the Garden of the Mouth. The quality of invention, in which Marino took such pride, is here displayed in full flower.

Among the most celebrated of Marinistic passages are: the contest of the lute player and the nightingale, the description of Flattery, and the celebration of Bacchus—all in the present canto.]

THE GARDEN OF THE EAR

1. Music and Poesy are sisters twain,
   restorers of afflicted human kind,
   with power through happy rhymes to make serene

the turbid tempests of our guilty thoughts.
There are no arts more beautiful than these
or more salubrious for troubled minds;
wild Scythia holds no barbarous heart, except
the tiger's, that sweet singing does not charm.

2. And yet sometimes a wanton kind of verse
can render far less lovely those same charms,
can turn to damage honest pleasantness,
and serve as evil magic for false gods.
A speeding dart, its point with poison stained,
as it strikes home, wounds not so grievously
as melting verses entering the ear
to penetrate the breast and prick desires.

3. The heart that is oppressed with madd'ning cares
they ply with wine of subtle luxury,
as did the daughters of that Hebrew sire [1]
till he became inflamed with profane lust.
By them are instigated men's desires
to foolish and licentious liberty,
and thence their vain, illicit appetites
transgress the decent and the lawful bounds.

4. But if unto the magic power of these
enchantresses, these sirens treacherous,
there comes to join as third dire pestilence
the added warmth of gay debauchery,
what cannot, does not fall? How many grim
and tragic scenes cry out because of this?
Reason is often snatched from out its seat,
the soul reft from the heart, man from himself.

5. Voracious wolf, infamous monster greed,
whose strong desire forever brightly burns,
and who to satiate thy greedy maw

[1] Lot.

yearns for the crane's long neck and Scylla's [2] pouch;
so food enough for such a hungry beast
not earth nor ocean can distill or yield,
and from thy all-devouring gullet's grip,
the unique Phoenix scarcely can escape.

6. Sweet poison, that with juices delicate,
while moist'ning throat inebriates the soul,
from thy gay frenzy he was not secure
who first pressed out thy juice in his rough palms;
among the many who have been cast down
by pressure of thy powerful influence,
Balthasar, Herod, Holofernes too
have left with us a tragic memory.

7. But most of all Adonis is the one
who puts this to the proof, reveals his trust.
Behold where toward the garden's third retreat
with Love's own mother he now turns his steps.
The porter at the gate to guest so fair
yields passage free and open readily;
and on a narrow, hard, and twisting path
he serves as guide from one joy to the next.

8. He stood with sounding plectrum in his hand,
while wooing a harmonious instrument.
A wild boar near, a stag and bull, all stood
transfixed, with ear intent upon the sound.
But at their coming, laying down his lyre,
he made the gate resound upon the hinge;
of silver is the gate, with cavities
conch-shaped, which give a ringing sound when struck.

9. "Of all sweet harmony this is supreme,"
to Myrrha's son [3] the son of Maia [4] said;

---

[2] Six-headed monster in the Straits of Messina, eager to devour sailors passing the entrance to her grotto.
[3] Adonis.   [4] Mercury.

"and, as thy goddess's handmaid and slave,
it lures men through the pleasures of the ear.
Nor is it without provident design
that he resides with Love who fosters Love,
since there is nothing in a suit for love
more readily wins grace than amorous verse.

10. "Whoever harkens as the graceful hand
strikes on the strings of the expressive lyre,
wedding that music's charming melody
with brilliant voices in a sweet accord,
and does not sometimes feel the mighty power
of those same numbers penetrate his heart,
must have a spirit dissonant, that for
the music of the spheres is out of tune.

THE EAR

11. "Nature so formed this sense that it might be
to sweet enticements ready minister,
and yet it is ordained through that same path
each decent influence must enter man,
since all my art and all my discipline
no other passage has unto the soul;
there is one cause but varied the effect,
the one for profit aimed, one for delight.

12. "Because the voice will ever upward mount,
therefore the ear was placed on high also,
and on each side, as if in rivalry,
stands even with the level of the eyes.
Surely, no less than eye 'tis quick and keen,
nor is it less ingeniously composed;
in it are placed and skillfully arranged
many recesses, channels, labyrinths.

13. "Little indeed were they to be compared
with those of other vile and common beasts,

but they could not have been designed more fair,
more excellent, and yet more wondrous strange.
The entrance ever open stands, and twins
they needs must be, their function to fulfill;
they do not move themselves, and they are made
of a dry substance sensitive to sound.

14. "Sound is the object of things moved and heard,
which through the means of air comes to the sense;
by outer impulse struck and shattered, air
retains the quality of that same sound;
whereby the neighboring air, when it is stirred
(just as in mobile water it occurs)
bears the light breath in wavelets circular,
one after one, to the interior gate.

15. "It flows to where for such a use the dry
curtain of sounding membrane is stretched taut;
there, shut in, 'tis broken and dispersed,
and vibrating conceals itself within;
through channels tortuous it roams confused,
till in the sensory system 'tis distilled,
from which, then passing to a central point,
the pattern of the sound is stamped therein.

16. "For the performance minute bones combine,
the anvil, hammer, stirrup they are called;
and all are set within the tympanum,
well jointed and articulated there;
and for this work there serves as aid to them—
I know not what to say—a cord or hair,
so subtile one can scarce determine if
'tis thread or nerve or artery or vein.

17. "Thou see'st how much supernal Love invests
of art and genius in this instrument,
all merely to convey a certain part
of his eternal joys to those below.

Ingrate in human form with soul of hell
is he who scorns the blessing thus bestowed."
And here the messenger of all the gods
brought to a close his sage and pregnant speech.

· · · · ·

[The following stanzas name the many birds that are seen and
heard singing their various tunes in this section of the garden.
Climaxing the passage, the nightingale is introduced.]

THE NIGHTINGALE

32. But over all those lovely, gentle birds
    that here display their graceful flight and song,
    the siren of the woods, the nightingale,
    pours out his spirit subtle, tremulous;
    so fair he tempers his exquisite style
    he seems the master of the winged throng.
    His singing varies in a thousand ways,
    and he transforms one to a thousand tongues.

33. Melodious prodigy! How marvelous,
    that one can hear but scarcely can discern,
    as he breaks off his song, and then resumes,
    now lightly and now full, he holds, he trills,
    now murmurs grave, now subtly thinning out,
    and now he forms a chain of sweet roulades,
    and always, whether hushed or shrill the song,
    he blends, dissolves with equal melody.

34. Oh, what charming, oh what plaintive rhymes
    the wanton bard composes and recites!
    First mournfully he utters his lament,
    and then the canzonet breaks off in sighs.
    In many shifts, now languid, now sublime,
    with pauses checked, then rushing in its flights,
    he imitates in style and compliments
    now flute or lyre, an organ now or lute.

35. Forth from his sweet, seductive throat sometimes
    he utters long, articulated runs,
    whence loudly he exhales a harmony
    such as in gradual waving charms the air;
    and when one note has been somewhat sustained,
    at length precipitously it breaks off.
    And thence an outburst in full-throated tones
    creates a double counterpoint of trills.

36. His throat and every fiber seem to have
    a kind of rapid wheel, a turbine swift.
    His little tongue, which vibrates, twists, and turns,
    is like a fencer's blade, dextrous and fierce.
    Whether the voice in bursts or ripples springs,
    or if in tranquil measures is released,
    'tis sure a heavenly sprite that weaves the song
    so figured and embroiled in all its modes.

37. Who would believe that so minute a soul
    could gather in itself such mighty force,
    and that a singing atom could conceal
    such sweetness in its veins and in its bones,
    that it is other than the vibrant air,
    a feathered voice, a flying sound perhaps,
    indeed a living breath in feathers dressed,
    or a canorous plume, a winged song?

38. Mercury, who saw Adonis stand
    with ear attentive to that lovely song,
    turning to him then said, "What thinkest thou
    of the divinity of yonder bird?
    Wouldst thou believe a spirit of so slight
    a substance held such quantity of breath,
    that such a soul, composed of harmony,
    dwells hidden in a bosom so confined?

39. "Nature displays—it cannot be denied—
    a wondrous art in all of her fair works,

but like a painter who reveals his skill
far more in little figures than in large,
in minute objects she sometimes employs
her greatest care, her greatest diligence.
Yet this excels her customary work,
surpassing all her other miracles.

THE NIGHTINGALE AND THE LUTE PLAYER [5]

40. "I will relate to thee a charming tale
about that song, in truth miraculous,
a case as tearful as 'tis memorable,
to make the rocks dissolve with tenderness.
It chanced a solitary lover once
in piteous sounds gave vent unto his grief
with strings. The woods were silent and the dome
of heaven was covered with the veil of night.

41. "The while love's bitter poison he makes sweet
with sound, that fixes Sleep itself intent,
the sad, enamored youth, who had escaped
the city to conceal him in the woods,
now heard within the dark and leafy nest
the jealous little bird beat his light wings,
and fascinated, charmed, approach with moans,
and murmur to himself the sounds he heard.

42. "The lonely bird, that on a beech tree branch
remained awake to summon the new day,

[5] The following passage of the musical duel is often cited as one of
the most fanciful, most "Marinistic" in the poem. It is interesting to
note that Marino expanded the passage after the first edition was in
the press. Some copies of the first edition contain an abbreviated
version. Others include twenty additional stanzas, just enough to fill
one added leaf to the book. The added stanzas are those here num-
bered: 41, 46, 49–53, 57–63, 66–71.
    The episode, which was based on a much shorter Latin poem by
Famianus Strada in *Prolusiones Academicae,* is of special interest to
students of English poetry because it was from that same poem that
Richard Crashaw derived his "Musicks Duell."

and gently, sweetly, with melodious speech
was supplicating dawn to come again,
heard interrupt the secret silences
of lone and savage wood a loud lament,
which smote the air with accents anguished sore,
of one transfixed by love's unkindly dart.

43. "Then, at once attracted and provoked
by sounds which seem to summon and invite,
down from the treetop slowly he descends,
until he perches on the lowest branch;
and taking up the final cadences
as if he joys to hear and emulate,
he close and closer draws and does not stop
until he rests upon the player's head.

44. "That one, who strikes on the harmonic strings,
feels the light weight but does not leave his song,
rather the tenor of his dolorous notes
he starts to iterate more forcefully.
The doleful nightingale close as he can
follows his style, intent to imitate.
One in his singing languishing complains,
and one echoes the song and the complaint.

45. "The one now on the mournful instrument
redoubling that same dolorous complaint,
the other duplicating the lament,
as he would with the other's grieving grieve;
with alternating of their sweet accord
they held transfixed all the celestial lights,
and well they charmed the idle, taciturn
nocturnal hours to sleep more peacefully.

46. "At first the player scorned the rivalry
and wished to make sport of the little bird.
Lightly he began to pluck with quill
the dainty strings, and then more vigorously.

The other, reinforcing his weak breath,
waits until the passage comes to rest,
and then—oh nature's tireless prodigy—
what one with hand the one performs with beak.

47. "The skilled musician, viewing scornfully
the competition of this challenger,
and angry that a creature so minute
not only matches but surpasses him,
begins to search out on the lute the tones
most difficult played on the highest frets;
the eloquent, loquacious little tongue
persistent follows, always copies him.

48. "The master reddens with disgust and shame
to have been vanquished by a thing so mean.
He turns the keys, sweeps up and down the strings,
sounds chords in series mounting to the rose.[6]
Defiantly the warbler never stops,
but renders each response more vigorously;
and as the youth diminishes or soars,
he deftly weaves the vocal labyrinth.

49. "Astonished now, the lad became like ice
and irate said: 'I've suffered thee awhile.
Now either thou wilt fail what I perform,
or I'll confess defeat and break my lute.'
He grasped the hollow case tight in his arms,
and as to make a final proof of skill,
with tremolo and syncopy and fugue,
he sought all manner of variety.

50. "Without a pause he strikes, releases, strikes
upon the neck from base to topmost fret,
and as his mood directs he murmurs low,
then swells the tone and plays in style sublime.

---

[6] The rose-shaped aperture in the case of the lute.

Sometimes he vibrates on the treble [7] string,
while pressing with his thumb the major chord;
at other times with gravity profound
he plunges to the bordon's [8] lowest depths.

51. "His hand flies o'er the strings, now low, now high,
more nimble than the bird itself the hand;
first up, then down, with unexpected leaps
the speeding fingers move in lively dance.
Inimitably he imitates the stress
of fiery conflict and confused assault,
and equals with the sound of his sweet songs
the bellicose uproar and clash of arms.

52. "Trumpets and kettle drums, such instruments
as Mars employs when marshalling the troops,
with whirlwind roar accelerating fierce,
his art expresses in skilled melody,
and all the while he plays he multiplies
the tempest of roulades in every part;
and while he thus compounds the harmonies,
his small competitor makes no response.

53. "He stops to see if now the little bird
will emulate his tune with matching song.
The other gathers strength within his breast,
nor does he in the struggle wish a truce.
But how can such a tiny, tender frame
faithfully pursue so grand a course?
Such mastery and so great artistry
a simple, natural song can ne'er display.

54. "When for many hours the rival pair
skillfully had vied on equal terms,
lo, the poor bird, exhausted finally,

[7] String tuned to the highest pitch on the lute, called *canto* in
Italian, *treble* in English.
[8] *Bordone:* one of the lower-pitched strings.

languished, fainted, weakened, and then died.
Thus, like a torch that flutters and then fails,
yet brightens just before the light dies out,
from that brave tongue that never sought to yield
the delicate free spirit was released.

55. "The stars on high, that until now had been
enamored of that soft, delightful song,
fled weeping, and from aureate balconies
the dawn appeared, the sun came out at once.
The gentle lutanist, through his great grief,
bathed the lifeless body with his tears,
and in his weeping and his sore complaints
accused himself no less than destiny.

56. "In admiration of that genius rare,
unconquered even in its final breath,
within the bosom of the silent lute
the youth desired to bury him in death.
Nor could the fates assign a sepulchre
more worthy of so honorable a corpse.
Then with the feathers of the bird itself
he wrote the history of the event.

THE ORIGIN OF MUSIC

57. "But who instructed him? The master true
of this great art—if thou know'st not—was Love.
He it was who first taught music here
and was of dulcet numbers author prime,
and so he chose to name after the heart
the cords of the seductive instrument.
What strange, what sweet and bitter harmonies
the wounded heart must learn at Cupid's school!

58. "Let her who knows, who witnessed it, relate
the curious origin of this device;
or have shrewd Love himself, since he is here,

tell whence he learned it, how it came about.
They tell that one day at the fiery forge
which the dark caves of Aetna luminates,
where workers [9] alternate their blows by threes,
the clever infant entered for pastime.

59. "Observing that the rhythmic hammer blows
resounding as the anvils were struck home,
whose pounding thunder, beaten out in time,
made it appear a concert in effect,
he started then to reason on the rules
of measure, until then not understood,
and to the great amazement of his sire [10]
he solved the secret of the intervals.

60. "A somewhat rough and poorly tempered lyre
was the first simple product of the work,
and to compose that sonorous device
he gave his golden quiver for the parts.
To make the keys of gold for it he broke
the arrow, which could even shatter rocks,
his bow itself he fashioned for its bow,
and from his bowstring made the lyre's strings.

61. "The learned god Apollo next improved
the scheme of keys and of its harmonies,
and I, who am intent on all things new,
forthwith revealed these studies to mankind;
and I in shapes delightful and refined
contrived to fashion various instruments,
whence was sprung in perfect form and pure
the faculty that brings so much delight.

62. "It pleases all, but more than all the rest
delights the restless souls of those in love,
nor can tormented heart find other peace

[9] The Cyclops.   [10] Vulcan, who presided over the smithy.

or refuge than in melody and songs.
'Tis true indeed that music has the power
sometimes to call forth doleful sighs and tears,
and thus it mingles two contrary ends;
it cheers the cheerful, saddens still the sad."

POESY AND MUSIC

63. Here ceased the famous courier who bears
in hand the winged scepter, serpent-twined,
because as he conducts the enamored youth
Adonis through the garden for delight,
he has perceived a troop of men and maids
approaching through the nearby grassy mead,
and two fair nymphs,[11] most joyous to behold,
as captains lead the radiant company.

64. One nymph displays her lovely bosom bare,
her snowy breasts all quivering with milk;
she has a verdant garland, azure gown,
and wings whence sometimes to the stars she soars.
A heavenly band of youths and maidens bring
for her gay trumpets, harps, and flageolets.
In her right hand she bears a laurel wand,
and in her left she bears a golden book.

65. Her fair companion has her tresses decked
with blossoms beautiful and amorous,
her parti-colored robe has diverse signs,
figures of keys, of notes, and lines of verse.
Behind her many nymphs and swains with song
and revelry come bearing measures, beats,
with sundry instruments and music books,
and jars with crimson Bacchus brimming full.

66. Then Mercury resumes: "Behold the pair
of sisters from one birth, renowned and worthy,
worthy I say not only of thine ears,

[11] Poesy and Music.

but of that king who rules above the stars.[12]
The first has in her works something divine,
the other ever strives to second her,
and thus with wonder and immense delight
the one attracts the mind, the senses one.

67. "That one who in the lead approaches us,
and to my eyes appears the nobler one,
though she inventor is in her own right,
and from the gods her pregnant art derives;
yet with her twin she is so close entwined
she learns to measure rhythms from that mate,
from her, who yields and follows after her,
she imitates the measures, flights and rests.

68. "That one who to accompany her is wont,
she likewise doth require the other's aid,
nor knows she how, without her sister's moods,
to show if she rejoices or is sad.
From her she learns the accents and the words,
from her in phrase distinct to loose the tongue.
Without her aid a sound would senseless be,
deprived of grace and poor in its effect.

69. "Because of their reciprocal estate,
united as a pair they shall advance,
and with that light by which true genius shines
they will through coming ages shine more bright.
Now Greece is witness to their primal rays,
whom miser heaven promises all grace,
fair Greece, in which for many a lustrum [13] hence
bright spirits will in honor harbor them.

70. "With time they will become the sport and prey
of barbarous races and of cruel years,
the stroke of Mars, to which all noble art

[12] Jupiter.
[13] Period of five years. In ancient Rome a ceremony of purification of all the people was performed every five years.

must yield, or to the blows of tyrant kings.
At last 'twill be for Italy alone
to hold some relics of the ancient loss,
but even there the lovely, pristine light
of the true science will be dim and blurred.

71. "Although now here my charming ones are lodged,
these haunts are not their principal abodes.
There in my sphere of heaven with other youths
forever blessed they dwell as goddesses.
If e'er 'tis granted thee to rise so high,
I will reveal the inn where they were born.
But here with Love, intent on pastimes sweet,
they oft descend from the eternal realms."

72. They came to fair Adonis, took his hand,
of festive semblance they and shining face,
those beauties twain, and with fair human speech
they graciously received him in their band,
and thence proceeded to an open plain
in which there stood a throng of happy folk,
who, him inviting to sojourn with them,
formed in a circlet like a theater.

73. If real or vain I know not, but they had
the semblances of demoiselles and lads.
The groups of dancers alternate their sets,
now tripping the courante, now rigadoon;
wantonly the songs give sweet accord
to festive dances, and the sounds to songs.
Lyres play and psaltries, tymbals, castanets,
to mark the diverse movements of the ball.

74. The concave brass,[14] the boxwood's fretted tubes,[15]
the raucous bagpipes and the trembling fifes
together teach how those shall tread the ground,
controlling with their role the errant steps.

[14] Trumpets.   [15] Flageolets.

O'er ample terrace and on flowery stage
are choruses of happy lovers seen
dancing in galliards and canarios,
in nizzard capers or in staid pavanes.

75. One couple heads the company, and they,
as leaders of the dance and all the feast,
with pacing wondrous masterful and light,
go circling round among the several bands,
so gay to view, and on their feet so quick,
it may be that less rapid and less fair
to music of the wheeling spheres above
the stars go dancing through the plains of heaven.

76. The company all sing, "O goddess blest,
O lovely universal mother, nurse,
sprung at a single birth with nature's self,
and hence of all things born the primal root,
through whom each tribe of mortals is engendered,
and generated lives in happiness;
happy may that beauty here arrive
in these blest realms, through which thou happy liv'st.

77. "At thy command the Fates obedient
weave the threads into a varying web;
and Nature learns to seminate the vines
through thy advice, increasing in thy power.
Through thy laws the tempers of the spheres
and elements are yoked in happy bonds;
without the breathing of thy fecund spirit
the world would certainly unlease its bonds.

78. "Thou dost the heavens and earth preserve, sustain,
flowers, grass, and plants and fruit upon the plants;
thou dost create, command, restore, assuage
both men and beasts and all the universe,
which without thy sweet and joyous gifts
would lone and solitary be, destroyed;

but while it varies in its form and state,
that frail state endures, thanks to thy grace.

79. "O lovely lamp, that with a cheerful light
illuminates the dusk of human gloom,
from which is born a gentle, secret flame,
which burns the heart but yet does not consume.
O planet, benefactor of mankind,
great glory of divinities benign,
that wishes naught for him who it attains
but to enjoy the fair, possess the good.

80. "O binding force of love, a power that links
with firmest knots of mutual embrace
both things celestial and terrestrial
and even subjugates the dark abyss;
through whose control, reciprocal desires
impel both sexes, coupling fertilely,
so that while one gives and the other takes,
exchange of joys is rendered and received."

81. With this devoted hymn, this fervent song,
the throng comes venerating Venus fair,
still in a dance; then coming to a pause
in that sweet concert, there they ended it.
Adonis now, with Venus and with Love
and Mercury, resumed their journeying,
when soon, behold, to his no small delight,
a strange and novel object caught his eye.

FLATTERY

82. A flower, a flower bursts its shell, gives birth,
and as it opes, its blond hair shows unbound;
after the hair two calm eyebrows appear,
and following the brows a lovely face.
But its first show does not resemble well
the middle and the end, which differ much.

To that rare beauty which unfolded first
the body of a curious bird is joined.

83. When the fantastic monster gradually
emerged out in the light surprisingly,
it rose not on its feet but squatted down
among the grass and leaves of its retreat.
With smiling eyes, looks pious and benign,
its face is juvenile and feminine.
Starry feathers cloak its breast and back,
its legs and feet are trimmed with gilded scales.

84. A serpent's tail is to its belly joined,
its claws are like a harpy's, curved and sharp;
it hides a hook beneath the flowers with which
it captures careless, unsuspecting prey.
Its tongue with honey and with nectar pure
is laden, the more sweetly to persuade.
'Tis thus the charming beast beguiles our sense,
a gentle beast, her name is Flattery.

85. That monster Flattery, flee far from her,
O foolish followers of pleasure vain;
not sphinx nor siren has more lying words,
more subtle or deceptive countenance.
Adulatory kisses or embrace
disguise insidious sleights and bitter wounds.
Viper and scorpion, with treacherous arts
she bites while kissing, while embracing slays.

86. Her hair, sometimes rolled into graceful knots,
is held with bands of costly golden chains,
anon, unbound and freed from its confines,
it falls, unfolding over all her limbs;
that lovely hair, so long and thick it hangs,
can cover up her body's ugliness,
so that beneath the fair and golden locks
all of her nether defects are concealed.

87. Lovely and insidious to view,
    either she hides her or dissembles quite;
    thereto her voice, enchanting, magical,
    she pours in streams of pure, angelic notes—
    notes into which Love dips both torch and darts
    to make the amorous wounds and burns more sweet.
    Her numbers, measured and harmonious,
    are heard in sweet, seductive tremolos.

88. Thus Adriana [16] with her lovely voice
    is wont to soften e'en the hardest heart,
    and with her voice and with her face at once
    traverses double paths to wound our breasts.
    And thus thou hearest in thy theaters,
    O Mantua, Florinda [17] dramatize
    Ariadne's bitter pangs, and draw
    from a thousand hearts a thousand sighs.

89. The rivers stopped their course, the winds their flight,
    the little birds their winging at her song.
    The tree of Daphne fled the sweet conceits,
    remembering Apollo's amorous song.
    Indeed Apollo checked his ardent steeds,
    enchanted by the sweetness that was heard.
    And these were the seductive words rehearsed,
    where secret death was hovering in the air.

90. "Ye happy spirits, who go frolicking
    through the laughing season of bright youth,
    gather with prudent hand, ah, gather fast
    the freshest rose in April's opening,
    before the flame that glistens in your eyes
    becomes as cold as ice and dry as ash,

[16] La bella Adriana Basile, the most celebrated of the vocal *virtuose* of the early 17th century.

[17] Virginia Andreini, celebrated actress and singer, who played the role of Ariadne in a melodrama by Ottavio Rinuccini, set to music by Peri and Monteverdi, when it was performed in Mantua in 1608 for the wedding of Francesco Gonzaga and Margherita di Savoia.

before the pearls of your sweet smile are changed,
before your face shows wrinkles like your hair.

91. "Beauty is a lamp, a shadow Age,
and none knows how to check their destined flight.
Too soon an envious pen begins to mar
the pomp of nature with injurious lines.
Time vanishes and quickly disappears,
it turns the hair, dims eyes, and dries the blood;
and Love, no less than he, has fleeting wings;
the flowers of beauty flee with flowers of years.

92. "The spring of happy days is all too brief,
and pleasures past can never be retrieved.
After the green there comes grey Penitence
with slow and heavy foot, alone and sad.
Where flowers once sprang the snow begins to fall,
changing the colors and transforming thoughts,
so he who young was cold in heart to love
soon finds the chill of hoarfrost on his hair.

93. "Wise is he who clasps it to his breast,
enjoys the blessing which is granted him.
And oh how dull, nay cruel, is that heart,
to others cruel, cruel to himself,
who is bereft of joys through his own fault,
joy which is sought so oft, so seldom found.
The soul in which desire for love reigns not
is not alive, does not deserve to live."

94. The swan that sings, the nightingale that mourns,
the siren or the muse that sighs for love,
a breeze or brook that murmurs through the grass,
an angel with a harp, a heaven that gyres,
nothing so intoxicates the heart,
so binds the senses, nourishes desires
with such transcendant harmony as she
here through the ear assails the heart of youth.

95. That unaccustomed beauty now began
to spread live sparks through all Adonis' veins,
just when a ray of sunshine lightly struck,
and soon dissolved it into tender dew.
O mortal pleasure, O terrestrial joy,
how swift to bud, and then how swift to fall!
O pleasures vain, enticing human souls,
begot of vanity, soon vanishing.

THE GARDEN OF TASTE

96. Now is Adonis with his goddess fair
granted entrance through a secret way.
The gate he passes is of ivory
with ruby arch and cornice overhead.
The minister who guards it bears a tray
heaped high with branches and with diverse fruits.
And sampling what he carries in his arms,
an ape and bear stand arbiters of taste.

97. Adonis' guide, conducting him from lodge
to lodge, now leads him out into a wood.
The leaves in weeping there distil a rain
of rare, celestial liquor, fresh and sweet.
Wherefore the birds that lodge among those boughs
find in the selfsame tree their nest and food;
and to that dear and happy progeny
one plant is both a cradle and a nurse.

.   .   .   .   .

109. Among those leafy shrubs Adonis passed,
and journeyed with his heavenly company,
where every tree extends to form an arch,
as though to lock its neighbor in embrace,
and ne'er is bare of flowers or of fruit,
and so bends down, prodigious in its weight.

The olive nectar drips, manna the holm,
the oak tree honey, sugar the tall cane.

110. Here all about grow Bacchus' fecund vines,
where vintage is distilled in dripping rain;
well laden with the sanguine grapes or white,
each vine, in reaching out its arms, dissolves,
so that around the roots a little stream
of purest must [18] collects and irrigates.
The must drains from the bursting grapes and leaves
and flows in a vermilion rivulet.

111. The savory liquid gathers into streams,
accumulates until a river forms,
and nourishes amid its purple foam
strange fish like it in color and in taste.
Foolish is he who dares to taste of these,
because he'll leave his senses for great joy.
He smiles, but lo, so potent is that smile
that his keen pleasure terminates in death.

112. Strange trees, it has been written, here are found
if one may credit such strange prodigies.
The lower trunk spreads out upon the bank
with many twisted, sprawling, knotty feet.
But upward from the forking roots appears
a living woman's quality and form.
The tendrils are her hair, her finger tips
trail out in branching vines and clustered grapes.

113. Such guise did Daphne [19] take on Peneus' banks,
and such did Syrinx [20] on Ladona's shore,
when one to her belov'd Thessalian woods

[18] The pressed out, unfermented juice of grapes.

[19] Daughter of the river god Peneus, pursued by Apollo, was transformed into a laurel tree.

[20] Daughter of the river god Ladona, loved by Pan, was turned into a reed.

and one to Lician stream new verdure brought.
Perhaps in forms as strange the Po beheld
her daughters,[21] following that bitter chance
when Phaëton, who drove his car amiss,
came down to quench his flames within her fount.

114. Beneath the wrinkled, rough, and stony bark
a savage spirit seems to palpitate.
Smiling, they reach their hands to one another
and ever they converse in Grecian tongue.
But if their blossoms or their fruit is plucked
the outrage is not rendered without pain.
Lewd flatterer may sue them with a kiss,
but he who tastes their kisses waxes drunk.

115. With all their tendril stems and leafy vines
perchance they may entwine this Faun or that,
who, being then unable to detach
his generative parts, performs a graft.
They then become like species, arms are dressed
with foliage, the rest is grown with sprigs,
the hair turns green, beard reaches to the earth,
and feet become fixed indivisibly.

CELEBRATION OF BACCHUS

116. All the host of profane deities
fabled in ancient age are gathered here:
Lares, Sileni, Satyrs, and rude Pans,
thyrsi in hand, and vine leaves in their hair,
Sylvani rustic, lecherous Genii,
and twin-horned Satyrs, wildly leaping Fauns,
Priapi and Bacchanti unrestrained,
unclad, their heads with shady fennel [22] crowned.

[21] The Eliades, sisters of Phaëton, wept over his death until they
were changed to poplar trees.
[22] Ferula family of plants, traditionally carried by Bacchus and his
followers.

117. There one discerns Maenads and Bassarides,[23]
    forever drunk and ready still to drink,
    who are intent on draining cups and vats
    of potent Latian and Falernian wine,
    and, fired by inner fury, tossing free
    their limbs in shameless and indecent guise,
    they celebrate their orgies to the sounds
    of mad, licentious songs and bacchanals.

The Hymn to Bacchus [24]

118. "Now with ivy, now with verdant vines,
    let lads and tender virgins deck themselves,
    and let them have imprinted on their minds
    twin images, Venus and Liberus.[25]
    Oh, let them glow and blaze like Semele,
    who burned to ashes from a thunderbolt;
    and let them chant in numbers and in rhyme
    the praise of Cupid and of Bromius.[26]

119. "Along the margins of the fragrant fields
    the zither, organ, and the castanet,
    the tambourin and flageolet let join
    with shepherd's tymbal, whistle, and shrill fife;
    and offer festive jubilee to her
    whose name is Hesperus or Lucifer,[27]

---

[23] Priestesses of Bacchus.

[24] The Bacchic hymn, following the pattern of Poliziano's *Stanze per la Giostra* (I, 111–112), employs *rime sdrucciole:* i.e., rhyming on words ending in two unaccented syllables. However, Marino has further developed the rhythmical *tour de force* by placing the three main stresses of every line of the hymn on words with antepenultimate accent. For example:

    "*Or d'éllera s'adórnino e di pámpino*
    i gióvani e le vérgini più ténere, . . ."

The translation does not reproduce the effect.

[25] Another name for Bacchus.   [26] Another name for Bacchus.

[27] The same planet (Venus) was called Hesperus when it appeared as the evening star and Lucifer when it appeared as the morning star.

so by their music they may fill this isle
with crash and din of their live merriment.

120. "With songs and fables let the satyrs drain
a mighty deluge of the wine of gods.
And let the bowls o'erflow with "tears of Christ," [28]
from Posilipo and Vesuvius.
Let grottos stored with brimming panniers
of grapes gush forth in sweet, abundant streams.
Among the ash, the plane, the willow trees,
let juice be pressed into the chalices.

121. "Who longs to suck the amiable juice,
with spice of balsam and of marjoram,
let him ne'er mix the ruby potable
with Tiber, Adige, or Rodano;
'tis treason damnable, 'tis sacrilege,
and not a drop to drink does he deserve
who ever tempers, mingles, or pollutes
with brooks the purple or the chrysolite.

122. "But let those spirits in their frenzied state
take care and damage not the drinking cups,
nor break nor scar the brimming amphoras,
now burdened with the liquid topaz' weight,
for men are wont to reel in ecstasy,
and stomachs alter in satiety;
and brains exalted by a fervid zeal
become more furious than Hercules."

123. While those thus celebrate with song and dance,
with joyous shouts repeating "Evoè,"
while eagerly at frequent intervals
they drain their goatskin sacks to sate their thirst,
Adonis, passing from those pleasant vales
into the secret bowels of a close,

[28] Lacrima Christi, a famous wine from the slopes of Vesuvius.

discovered there a luscious banquet set,
and ready 'round the board were golden seats.

THE MOUTH

124. "Here, fair Adonis, it is meet," commenced
Cyllenios,[29] "to lay aside all cares.
Now needs must thou consider to repay,
to strengthen nature with restoring food.
And since the several senses have now had
their place within the precincts of these walls,
'tis fitting that we honor taste, which dwells
within that feature of delight, the mouth.

125. "The mouth, 'tis true, is the first messenger
of speech, the unique office of mankind.
Reason cannot expound a single thought
not first discovered and expressed through it.
Divine interpreter, through whom is shown
whate'er the intellect of him who speaks
would print within the breasts of other men,
the voice subserving as the go-between.

126. "But mouth serves further to bring us increase
of vital humor, nor is quelled by heat;
to which, when food sometimes refreshes it,
the tongue becomes the judge and guarantor; [30]
nor through the throat e'er passes any food
whose savor is not first distinguished there.
Then testing through its knowledge of all foods,
it sends it to the stomach for its store.

127. "And since neglect to feed the appetite
can cause a man to waste away and die,
and since a man not readily fatigued
will seldom falter in his laboring;

[29] Mercury.
[30] *Credenziera,* one who tastes food before it is served to nobles.

he who created all, decrees that food
which nourishes should also bring delight,
hence always this effect with that combined
gives sustenance and pleasure at one point.

128. "Dost thou observe how many sturdy guards
are stationed to protect and shield the tongue?
That it may not be wounded by the chill
and wintry breath of snowy Aquilon,[31]
it is encased and stoutly fortified,
as if with towers and with rampart walls.
And that no other storms may injure it,
it is concealed beneath a concave roof.

129. "From throat to palate it ascends forthwith,
as thick and pulpy as the need demands.
From a wide base it sharpens at its tip,
its substance spongy and its color red.
The root from which it springs is doubly strong,
that it may more adroitly lift and turn.
It curves and dips and vibrates volubly,
has nerves and muscles but no cartilage.

130. "Hence I declare the sovereign Maker thus
constructed it for the intent alone,
because it was to be the instrument
of nourishment, which is derived from taste;
without that taste, useless and vain would be
all things delicious he bestows on earth.
And this immortal flame within thy heart,
without Ceres and Bacchus would be cold."

131. Thus speaks the lord of eloquence; then he
conducts the fair Adonis by the hand
to where the splendor of a royal board
brightly illumines all the woodland gloom.
Arranged with special art and diligence,

[31] The north wind.

the gold and amber vessels gleam in rows.
Of bright and precious substance there are ranged
the many handsome settings for a feast.

132. Among the vessels there Adonis sees
two greater than the rest, all emerald,
the gem of Love, which smiles a lovely green
and is receptive to engraver's tools.
I know not whether any sculpture made
today by Giambologna [32] can compare
with that intaglio and superb relief
which was incised thereon by Daedalus.

VASE DEPICTING THE BIRTH OF VENUS

133. On one great vase in noble portraiture
appears the lovely goddess of the place; [33]
so semblant is the image to the real
that being is near vanquished by the feigned.
The gory, rude conception [34] there appears,
and her most fortunate nativity;
oh wonderful to see how first was born
the genatrice of Love, child of the waves.

134. Saturn is there, who cut from his own sire
the obscene members,[35] gave them as a prize
to Doris, mystic nurse of nascent love,
who gathered them within a crystal conch.
Zephyr is there, who, issued from his cave,
begins to beat his many-colored wings,
that region's gentle, faithful minister,
and lightly drives the wavelets toward the shore.

[32] Also known as Giovanni da Bologna, 1524–1608, celebrated sculptor.

[33] Venus.   [34] See next stanza.

[35] Saturn drove his father, Uranus, from his throne and mutilated him.

135. There through the liquid element you see
     at first the pregnant, fertile foam afloat,
     and thence the silver, changing into gold
     and forming into tresses of blond hair.
     Those lovely tresses captivate the wind,
     and toss and curl, thus emulating waves.
     Then, lo, the forehead rises gradually;
     and now the waters burn with two fair eyes.

136. Oh, marvel! One beholds the candid foam
     transform to lovely limbs of gleaming white.
     A new sun rises from the Aegean Sea,
     which brightens sea and the surrounding air;
     a sun of beauty which will comfort men
     and likewise sweetly will consume our souls;
     thus is fair Venus born into the world,
     a conch for cradle, seaweed for her drapes.

137. Now while with roseate and dewy feet
     sublime she treads the vertex of the wave,
     and with her ivory hand she brushes off
     the briny damp that sparkles on her hair,
     the denizens of foamy palaces
     depart their deep and marshy dwelling place,
     and following their great, cerulean lord,
     they render homage to the amorous light.

138. Palemon [36] a frolic coachman came,
     astride a graceful dolphin's curving back,
     and darting like a fugitive sea bird,
     he cleaves the furrows on his twisting course.
     A host of tritons, dwelling 'neath the waves,
     all ranged in pairs to form a gentle team,
     slowly draw the conch where she was born,
     while some on other duties churn the foam.

[36] A sea god.

139. Here one with curving horn, his cheeks puffed out,
trumpets its raucous voice to heaven's vault;
here one, to shield the goddess from the sun,
streams out a silken veil above her head;
and one, careening far on wanton wheels,
drives there as over adamantine ice;
and since the sun so revels in her charm,
he makes a mirror for her lovely eyes.

140. The daughters of great father Nereus
cease not to sport and dance among the rest,
who gathered in a gray and charming choir,
sing to the sound of plectrum and the lyre;
they offer gifts of amber and bright gold,
of whitest pearls and deep vermilion cloth.
Thus o'er the fields of ocean such a band
receives her, guides her, and accompanies her.

VASE DEPICTING THE BIRTH OF CUPID

141. The other vase sets forth in effigy
scenes of the birth of Cupid, her great son.
Now see her languishing while she awaits
the slow, approaching hour of sweet birth,
in that fair season when the newborn earth
comes into flower, wearing fresh attire.
The dawn, more jocund than is wont, brings in
the first day of the world's fairest month.

142. The lovely goddess on a verdant couch
reposes gently for her accouchement.
The meadow seems to smile, the Indian rose
for pleasure reddens near the flowering musk.
It seems the waves on Cyprus scarcely stir,
and fish are dancing near the grassy shore.
With sands so peaceful and with waves so clear,
the sea seems without tide and motionless.

143. The little Zephyrs, not to make themselves
     annoying in her sweetly bitter pains,
     remain almost asleep in crimson beds
     among the banks of leaves and rosy buds.
     The wanton breezes gather choicest scents
     to sprinkle gently o'er the dewy robes,
     garments bathed in her celestial blood,
     where so much beauty sighs and languishes.

144. Before his eyes are open to the sun,
     or lips to milk, within his narrow room
     the babe anticipates his hour and beats
     against his mother's breast with lively kicks;
     and the closed portals of the womb divine
     the impetuous infant opens and springs forth.
     Without a midwife's aid he issues thence,
     his cradle flowers and leaves his swaddling clothes.

145. Scarcely delivered from her ivory lap,
     he slips into her arms and fondles her.
     He chirps a little cry, and quickly moves
     to fix on her left urn his little mouth.
     The Graces bless the milk, which is infused
     with honey, sweet as Hybla ever gave.
     And alternating oft from nurse to nurse,
     he's suckled part by tigers, part by lambs.

146. Singing, the spinners of all mortal fate
     weave everlasting thread lines for the child.
     The most ferocious beasts go peacefully,
     disporting gayly in those sunny fields.
     The lion courts, and with a friendly roar,
     licks the handsome bullock playfully.
     With happy neighing and with noisy hoofs,
     the warlike steed applauds the baby's cry.

147. The wolf is kindled with an amorous flame,
     kisses the lambkin with a harmless bite.

The dogs embrace the hares, the hirsute bear
gives suck to gentle heifers at its breast.
The cruel panther joys in carrying
upon its spotted back the harmless deer;
the dragon longs to touch the teeth, though sharp,
of his old enemy the elephant.

148. Cytherea sees, and is much pleased to see,
the strangely amorous sporting of the beasts,
and smiles to see that such proud animals
should from a little child feel such a smart.
It seems the frolics of the boar alone
she dares not watch, presaging something dire;
she senses that a life cut off by him
will mean the deprivation of her joy.

CANTO VIII

The Transports

[Canto VIII relates the adventures of the lovers in the Garden of Touch, the grand climax of the exploration of the gardens of the five senses. Here the poet details the long-expected initiation of Adonis into the *sommo piacere,* the "pleasure of pleasures." The importance of the passage is signaled by the formal prologue-invocation, one more mark of Marino's classical discipleship.]

THE GARDEN OF TOUCH

1. Young gentlemen and ladies amorous,
   in whom there burns the sweet desire of love,
   for you I write, to you I speak; now lend
   your favoring ears to my enchanting song.
   There's naught in what I write that will avail

to animate the man of hoary age.
Let grey hair, wrinkled brow, and solemn looks
eschew the tempting bait of vain delights.

2. We often note that bent and feeble age,
which nurses frozen veins and hollow bones,
incapable of ultimate delight,
abhors those pleasures it cannot pursue.
A man not apt for love comes to despise
the very tone of amorous reports;
and blessings which he is forbid to taste,
through envy he condemns in other men.

3. Far, far off, you stern and modest souls,
get you far from my soft and flattering muse.
From verses of such tender wantonness,
O virtue uncorrupted, stand aloof.
Ah, pray do not unleash at what she writes
the sharp reproofs of rigid censoring,
whose calumny with most malign aspersions
blames what is scarcely reprehensible.

4. Do not expect to hear the grave conceits,
dissimulations sly, of moral tome,
which, noting in the good only defects,
would pluck the thorn and throw away the rose.
I know well that among the sweet delights
of merry, harmless pranks the amorous soul,
as in a game, can handle cleverly
both iron and fire without a burn or wound.

5. Both harmless bees and cruel vipers suck
the selfsame flowers of Sicilian fields;
according to their instincts ill or good,
the one turns juice to poison, one to honey.
Now should it chance that from my verses sweet
some will draw venom or distill vile gall,

others perhaps will be less harsh and stern,
who'll glean from them a profitable guide.

6. If innocent, the author need not care
   that on his page immodest strains appear.
   The use of charms and fantasies of art
   is not a fault, or else the fault is slight.
   Who in my rhymes, so rich in tales of love,
   finds shameful matter or discovers scandal,
   let him excuse or blame the youthful fault;
   for though the pen be stained the heart is chaste.

7. The sergeants and handmaidens have removed
   from the white cloth the vessels of bright gold
   in which those two, the captives of sweet love,
   partook of viands choice and delicate;
   then came the golden basin to their hands
   to pour out scented streams, and after that,
   across the table gay with flowers there passed
   a fine white linen cloth to dry their hands.

8. Then Venus, having risen from her seat,
   conducts Adonis toward the final tower.
   The porter of that most delightful realm
   comes quickly to unlock the golden door.
   Upon his bare left arm a falcon rests
   and clamps its talons on his naked wrist.
   Moles, tortoises, and spiders ever go
   along with him, a faithful company.

9. Closed in this charming and capacious zone
   there lies the garden of that master tower,
   more spacious than the others and as full
   of such delights as Love could conjure up.
   An ample circle with its pleasing shade
   composes here a rounded theater,
   that, in the circuit of its lofty walls,
   shelters the verdure of a charming lawn.

10. Adonis enters and it seems a new
    effect of amorous sweetness stirs his heart.
    There's no lascivious object, tender act,
    that here before his eyes is not displayed.
    Semblances of lust and of delight,
    portrayals of soft charms and flatteries,
    love and frivolities, are crowded there
    no matter where the viewer's gaze is turned.

11. That cheery and enticing place appears
    a paradise full of angelic joys.
    Here Sigh breathes forth his breath of hidden fire,
    Glance ranges free and Smile luxuriates,
    Sport runs amain to give a kiss to Jest,
    Delight lies in the lap of soft Caress,
    Pleasure with a whiplash drives away
    grave Cares, and turns to sport with Transport sweet.

12. Amorous Thought inclines his head, his eyes
    bent on the ground, and sadly bites his lip.
    Entreaty sues for ease from Grief and peace
    from War in suppliant and humble guise.
    Signal, the silent courier of Desire,
    reveals through eyes what presses on the heart.
    With eager lips, sucking another's lips,
    pressing fiercely Kiss consumes himself.

13. Upon the threshold Adulation stands
    to guide the pilgrim to that sweet resort.
    Promise invites him in, takes him in charge,
    while, always laughing, Joy accompanies him.
    Vanity greets all who enter there,
    Credence is deceived by every snare.
    And Riches, all in scarlet robes attired,
    to him her lavish treasures proud displays.

14. There Idleness, that languishing reposes,
    stirs lazily and rests at every step.

Sleep follows him, with dazed and wrinkled brow
and barely manages to stand upright.
Adorned with lilies callow Youth appears,
with wreaths of roses woven in his hair.
With him linked hand in hand in company
go Beauty, Grace, Delight, Frivolity.

15. With ravenous Desire comes eager Hope,
a faithless wanton and a strumpet false.
With faces masked and strolling side by side
go sly Deceit and Falsehood, thick as thieves.
With tresses hanging down to hide her face
Occasion rushes by in swiftest flight.
Among all those skips foolish Happiness,
and License uncontrolled leaps all about.

16. The gaudy strumpet, Luxury, in hand
bears bait and gun, and Infamy applauds.
Completely nude stands brazen Infamy
and prizes neither honor nor good name.
Ingenious Fraud conceals with lovely flowers
the serpents in her hair, disgusting, vile,
and hides the venom of her bitter tongue
behind a smile and gentle, soothing voice.

17. Audacity at his first venture trembles,
and Pallor, dear to lovers, stands aside.
There fly with light wings in the gusty air
the Perjuries of Love, errant and vain.
To placate Anger, gently, easily
go fretful Vigils and disturbed Complaints,
and Fears that show a jocund, placid guise
though insecure, and interrupted Joys.

18. Here the earth laughs, birds sing, and flowers dance,
and even the branches make a melody.
The breezes sigh, the rivulets complain.
To sighs, plaints, melodies Echo responds.

Even the beasts make love among the shades.
The fish love deep within the gelid streams.
The very rocks and shadows of that place
exhale caressing sparks of amorous fire.

19. "Farewell, Adonis, I will leave thee now,"
Jove's messenger announced, arriving there.
"Through pathways novel and unknown to thee
it was my pleasure to conduct thy way.
Here we are in the region where all war
with Love must terminate in peace. And this
the region of that gentle sense to which
each other sense must yield fidelity.

20. "Each other sense can be quite easily
deluded by false objects; this alone
cannot; the ever faithful minister
of truth it is and parent of delights.
The others, not possessing our whole frame
but one part only, sometimes are at fault.
But this with universal action spreads
its force through all and comprehends the whole.

21. "More I would tell thee, and would gladly help
resolve some subtle doubts through my discourse;
but 'tis no time for talk, for I am sure
it is not words thy mistress now desires.
Here will I stay and dainty garlands weave
of violets and myrtle for sweet Erse.[1]
Go then, enjoy thyself. More company
for these diversions could not but annoy."

22. This said, he turned him to the Cyprian,
a flicker of a smile upon his lips;
and then he left them, nor was seen until
the day of their departure from the close.

[1] Daughter of Cecrope, loved by Mercury.

But yet before he gave his last salute
as he was parting from the amorous pair,
he joined their hands together as a pledge
of mutual love, in token of their bond.

23. In leafy shade the pair remained alone
when Mercury had taken his farewell.
A fountain marked a nearby grassy bank
where nature seemed to take immense delight.
The waters fed the woods, the shady woods
were then reflected in the limpid pool,
so that one garden shows itself as two
distinct, the one the real, the other feigned.

24. From this quiet fount a little pipe
conveys a streamlet on its tortured course.
'Twould seem like crystal and like silver pure,
did one not hear the sound of murmuring.
Its sands are golden, whence the blind bow boy
is ever intent to take them in his hands,
from which he fabricates his golden darts,
immortal pestilence for mortal men.

25. In two twin branches then divides itself
the amorous stream: the one of honey is,
as full of sweetness as the taste could crave;
the other spoils the sweet with bitter gall,
that gall, that poison whence of old Fame used
to arm the cruel archer's bitter shafts.
The cruel archer who with venom vile
infected even his own mother's breast.

26. Free from its venomous and turbid mate,
the honeyed streamlet takes its single course,
whence through a channeled rivulet of gold
it traces with fair lines the meadow's green;
at last it empties in a secret bath
which is erected midway in the woods.

And of this delicate and soothing bath
do Wantonness and Pleasure hold the key.

PLEASURE AND WANTONNESS

27. Before that harbor's entrance Pleasure sits,
    intent on dalliance with Wantonness;
    a youth with varicolored feathers winged,
    his smiling face is kindled with bright sparks.
    His gilded shield, his hauberk brightly decked,
    rest carelessly discarded at his feet.
    The peaceful warrior's helm, which for its crest
    a siren shows, lies useless mid the flowers.

28. A curving lyre hangs on a nearby branch,
    and oft the breezes stir it into life.
    With amber clear and subtle, through blond threads
    he combs and parts his tangled, shaggy hair,
    entwined throughout with many snares and barbs
    of freshest rose and myrtle newly blown.
    A diadem about his head, adorned
    with lovely rainbow lights, makes him a crown.

29. And no less beautiful of face appears
    the alluring damsel resting in his lap.
    With ivy she entwines her golden locks,
    and watches o'er white ermine flocked nearby.
    A goat is at her side, and with one arm
    she holds a Lybian panther round the neck.
    With her left hand she leans against a tree
    a polished mirror, bright and crystalline.

30. As Venus and Adonis came in view,
    before the glass she combed her errant locks,
    and meanwhile dried the brilliant glittering
    of eyes that were all moist and sparkling bright.
    Oft toward a nest of chattering little birds
    that warbled in the arbor she would turn,

and turning thus, she raised her short, loose gown
more than was meet for proper dame to do.

31. The charming, wanton figures toying there
struck young Adonis with great wonderment,
and with his soul suspended o'er his brows,
he stood immobile contemplating them.
The damsel with a charming, rosy blush,
a blending of enticement and of mirth,
taking her gallant's hand, rose from the grass,
and hastened toward the youth approaching them.

32. A garment gleaming white and striped with gold,
a cloth of softest silk with silver spun,
enveiled her beauteous limbs, and as a sail
is swollen out and tossed before the wind,
so fluttering it opens and reveals
its lining in a hundred pleats and folds.
The hem flaps free and does not well conceal
the naked charms of her extremities.

33. Suspended from the wings of dainty ears
she bears the weight of two exquisite pearls.
A well-wrought setting of resplendent gold
sustains their weight within a circling sphere.
A twining necklace of bright em'ralds falls
upon her bosom with shrewd negligence;
on her white hand, which coyly she extends,
the living milk is lit with orient flame.[2]

34. Defense from summer's heat, which, while it boils,
inflames the face with fiercely burning hue,
is offered by a great, soft instrument
of many feathers whiter than the snow;
and for the fanning of her vanity
and all her foolish show with double breath,

[2] A ruby.

        she has two crystal mirrors stationed there
        wherein she views her counterpart with pride.

35. This damsel spreads her nets for fair Adonis;
        each act was amorous, each word a dart.
        At times she'd break her sentence off so sweet
        and languidly that she could even crack
        the diamond of reason with her guile,
        much more the fragile glass of common sense.
        The while she talked, she colored broken speech,
        now with soft sighs and now with charming smiles.

36. "If as much beauty as thy face reveals,
        so much of courtesy lies in thy breast,
        for certainly," she said, "thy countenance
        presents such expectation to our eyes,
        thou'lt not disdain to come and solace thee
        in the enclosure of yon happy bower;
        within that bower my finger points for thee,
        as thou art worthy, so shalt thou be served.

37. "This is the spirit,[3] if thou know'st him not,
        who yields the boon that brings men happiness.
        All search for him, all long for, beg for him,
        all strive to master him by diverse means.
        One thinks in riches to discover him,
        another looks to honors, some to friends.
        But rarely does he stir from this abode,
        nor dwells he elsewhere than in my soft lap.

38. "Scarce was he loosed from that vile urn [4] where all
        man's ills were pent when he was called to heaven;
        but he had first to cast aside his robes,
        that naked he went there, without a veil.
        He oft descends from heaven to these haunts
        where I conceal him from unworthy eyes.

       [3] Her companion, Pleasure.   [4] Pandora's box.

From others I conceal him with great care,
and only with a few I share my dear.

39. "When first he soared in that immortal flight,
a rash deceit sprang up throughout the world.
With that same mantle which he left below
his adversary Grief adorned himself.
That fellow goes about decked in his clothes,
and thus resembles him in outward form;
wherefore each mortal, tricked by the deceit,
instead of Pleasure follows after Grief.

40. "I then am his companion, I am she
who turns to joy all sorrow and travail.
From us alone thou'lt have, if thou art wise,
that pleasure of all pleasures in the world.
Of those who follow after him and those
who follow me, countless is the throng;
nor shouldst thou be less happy than all these,
since thou today mayst join so great a band.

41. "Here it is meet thou bathe. To that intent
the gracious spot and season's heat invite.
Our law requires it, and indeed thy age
and flowering beauty do consent to it;
but more, that beauty who accomp'nies thee—
O fortunate—is burning equally.
None is admitted to these woods, this bower,
who knows not frolic mirth and dalliance."

42. To these gay words Adonis, all confused,
made no reply but stood there taciturn,
who, still unused to tender amorous ways,
held his head down, his eyes fixed on the ground.
He is surrounded by a host of nymphs
who will not suffer him to pass beyond.
While this one strips the quiver from his side,
another steals his belt and one his clothes.

43. To that insistent troop that captured him
the youth submits but not without great shame;
and save for one light cloth, a meager garb,
he finds himself quite nude from head to foot.
Now he directs his glance, a joyous glance,
toward his fair mate and sees her also nude,
who all of her most secret parts unveils
before his eyes, exposes to the woods.

44. Into the green and shady cloister there
with show of modesty she now withdraws,
now covers, now reveals her guarded charms;
she, as her own abductor, steals away.
She now turns pale, then shows her pallid limbs;
each gesture seems by chance, yet all is art.
Aloofness coy and studied carelessness
give added charm to her fair, naked limbs.

45. The savage bushes tried to cover her
within entwining arms of leafy shade,
and yet the wanton Sun with curious rays
was fain to spy upon her nakedness.
Even the beech tree shows its sympathy—
that beech on which the bow and garments hang—
although not comprehending in itself
how it put forth more buds and grew more dense.

46. With her white hand the Cyprean untied
the silken knot that bound her lovely brow
restraining the bright treasure of her hair,
and scattered free a deluge of spun gold;
whence in the guise of a thick, golden veil,
concealing her white breast among the waves,
her aureate tresses tumbled from her head,
cascading in a thousand rivulets.

47. She tried to hide her breast behind that veil,
but as the bird that bears the name of Pheasant

deems herself concealed from spying eyes
when in a leafy bush she hides her head;
just so, if with her scattered hair she sought
to make a shadowy mantle for some parts,
yet in that golden shade is seen all beauty
only in the sun of her fair eyes;

48. besides, that gentle cloud shone no less bright
than did the sun itself, serene and clear.
Yet she would try to veil her lovely breast
and next her back and then her graceful limbs.
But still the golden threads could not remain
in place against the ivory, smooth and white;
and what the hand would try to cover up,
a playful breeze uncovered willfully.

THE BATH

49. Now they approach the bath. And here the boast
of Baia's ancient baths is put to shame.
'Tis artfully designed a perfect square,
and each side is a hundred ells in length;
commodious retreats stand all around,
on every side are three great sheltering halls.
The chambers and the loggias are arranged
in triple rows, a basin for each one.

50. At mid-point of the lofty edifice
there stands a jasper pillar of huge girth,
through whose interior veins the fountain pours,
so fashioned by a master's craftsmanship
that water through twelve channels streams to fill
twelve alabaster basins in those halls.
Of brightest silver are the channels, whence
like silver are the streams that issue there.

51. To ample basins formed of polished stone
the waters flow, but lazily and slow,

so that the falling liquid can collect
in the first row of loggias lowest down.
I say the lucent wave flows lazily,
moving along with tardy, crystal steps,
for while it travels through so rich a channel,
it eagerly admires its splendid home.

52. And whence thereafter through a hidden tube
to its own chamber each is funneled through,
plunging with a mighty roaring sound,
some bright and clear and others darker shades.
Each hall resembles some great cave or tomb;
the sunlight coming in like moonlight seems.
Pallid it enters by a narrow path,
and thus within 'tis neither night nor day.

53. A set of arcs sustains the portico
into whose lap the streaming water rains.
And where the liquid gorge ends finally
the walls of the interior are adorned
with marble streaked in strange new forms and shapes
of lovely markings and of lucent veins.
The dim recesses and soft, shady seats
placed all about invite for sweet repose.

54. But of no mortal workmanship appears
the splendid art of that fair arching dome,
which shines, encrusted with the richest gems,
for no plebeian stones are there perceived.
One which the sky, one which the grass inspires,
and one which emulates the fire are there.
No stucco forms are there, but subtle work
of richly toned enamel on gold plate.

55. Within the confines of the jeweled fount
so limpid and serene the water flows,
that it usurps adornments not its own,
describing all the glories of the vault.

Great Cynthia would not disdain to be
discovered in so beautiful a pool.
Perhaps Narcissus, in a stream so fair,
more eagerly would woo his lovely face.

56. Wherefore, methinks, the once loquacious nymph,[5]
who for her love [6] fell silent and became
a haunting voice, would eagerly frequent the spot
where he delighted to admire himself.
Pursuing shadows of the final words
here fly across the stream from arch to arch;
as in the temple of Olympia
responses to the words are multiplied.

57. Here came the couple, and at once observed
another couple in a near recess,
nor had they far advanced before they heard
low murmurings of voices and of kissing.
Adonis turned his steps in that direction,
the better to observe the cause of it.
He looked but soon cast down his eyes to earth,
and deep embarrassment showed on his brow.

58. There on a bed, but seated on the side,
he has discovered a lascivious satyr,
who from a nymph enfolded in his arms
is gathering the flower of all delight.
He fondles with one hand the ivory
of her fair, tender flank in soft caress;
with his left hand, which is elsewhere engaged,
he tries for parts more tender and concealed.

59. Caught in the knotty, muscular embrace
of her impulsive swain, the youthful nymph
makes sounds of protest, and with modest eyes,
pretends to be defensive and aloof.

[5] Echo, the nymph who died for love of Narcissus.
[6] Narcissus.

She turns her face to rob his greedy kisses,
denies his pleasure and thereby allures;
but while she struggles and rebuffs his zeal,
by cunning movement she returns his kiss.

60. With mock retreat and clever blundering
she feigns attempts to extricate herself,
yet in those rude rebuffs she all the more
becomes imprisoned, tangled, and entwined,
in such a guise that never more secure
were blocks of wood e'er jointed, wedged, and nailed.
I doubt if Flora, Phyrne, or Thaïs
could e'er invent more gross indecencies.

61. A strange enjoyment from that shameless sight
crept serpent-like into the youthful breast,
for 'gainst the magic, tyrant force of Love,
a feeble heart has no power to resist;
thus from the bait of a seductive sight,
desires already roused acquire new strength;
and goaded to pursue its natural course,
it is no marvel if it breaks the leash.

62. His goddess, who with many amorous knots
has bound his heart, eager to follow him,
now urges him along the path ahead
with subtle manner and with clever speech.
"Enjoy now," to herself she says, "enjoy
the fruits of your sweet sighs, O happy pair!
Breathe your sighs and pour out your complaints,
your happy loves, O you most blessed ones.

63. "Good luck to you. I know not yet if he
who has me prisoner will be so kind."
The goddess thus addresses her fair sun
beside her, and she smiles the while she speaks,
proffering at once with her right arm
a lovely ivory zone for his left side.

And now the damsel [7] who had led them there
fired from her gun a thousand tempting lures.

64. As flame to flame combined increases fire,
as torch to torch adds ever brighter light,
or as in mating stream to stream there grows
by gradual steps a mighty river's force;
just so the youth at this indecent sport
redoubles flames and seems to be consumed,
and, wholly prey to eager Wantonness,
he now forgets his former modesty.

65. Now of its own accord increased in size,
he feels the sharp dart rigid at the heart,
so that the urging of that burning heat
he is no longer able to sustain,
whence breathless with desire, which ruthlessly
assailing, pricks his heart with its sharp spurs,
and longing to attain full happiness,
turns to his lovely, kisses her and says:

66. "I die, I die, alas, if timely pity
brings me not immediate relief.
If you will not have mercy, now, at once,
my life, suspended, will at last expire.
The flame so hotly burns, my fleeting soul,
my vital spirit, now must burst its bonds.
That loveliness, for which 'tis meet I die,
arouses all my members with its sparks.

67. "No sooner did that haughty Cupid come
to challenge me with all these subtle charms,
I drew my bow, and now I fear the cord
will break from the extremity of strain.
I can endure no more. No longer scorn
the too great ardor of your humble slave,

[7] Wantonness.

for I indeed would, as you well can see,
attain the glory of the final goal."

68. So saying, he the hem of his light robe
with languid gesture put somewhat aside,
and thus revealed to her without a veil
the fierce impatience of his hot desire.
"Wait," she says, "till preparations meet
have been provided, for thy hope is sure.
Anon Convenience, ready serving maid,
will show us to a chamber yet more fair.

69. "Pleasure postponed brings its reward in peace,
increasing not a little through delays.
Suffice it that thou knowest a mutual fire
consumes me with reciprocal amour.
The hour of lighting the first torch, I swear,
thou'lt have me in a more secluded place.
Be of good cheer, and take my pledge for it,
thou soon shalt bring thy ship into the port."

70. As sometimes with a savage Irish hound
a skillful hunter, seeing him on fire,
although, perchance, the hunted prey has passed
within close range of all the restless pack,
and though the hound is straining to be free,
he will not yet release him for pursuit;
at every tug he holds tenaciously,
he grips the leash and keeps the collar fast;

71. just so did Venus manage, clever dame,
to add heat to his passion by her art;
while he was fain to open wide the door
of that supreme delight with amorous key,
she checks the force of that first appetite
of youth with kisses and with blandishments.
She takes him by the hand and leads him thence,
inviting him to turn his steps elsewhere.

72. Free passage from those shady bowers lies
    through several exits to the ample court;
    and there is seen inscribed above each door
    the special virtue of the bath within.
    Each fount possesses powers of different sorts
    as other people's trial testifies.
    The vigor and the savor is declared
    expressly both for feeling and for taste.

73. Oh miracle, to find a vein that pours
    from one stone fountain into various urns,
    and yet that can contain within itself
    diversity of gifts and qualities.
    Who can declare the virtues of each one?
    Some more, some less, are chill or steaming hot,
    one turbid and another crystal clear,
    one sweet, one salty, one with bitter tang.

74. The temper of that pool to which the dame
    retired with her most charming paramour
    had drawn its source from that insidious fount
    which joined Salmacis to Hermaphrodite,[8]
    and held within it hidden properties
    for kindling the tepid appetite;
    besides the blended herbs which it contained,
    it was endowed with virtues of its own.

75. There various mushrooms were and ragwort too,
    whose flower and root present an obscene form.
    Mint, which by nature is libidinous,
    and fern, a well-known stimulant for love.
    And there such compound of the simples which
    were gathered once on slopes of Lampsacus.[9]
    Love, tell me now, how in that lovely pool
    the goddess' form was naked to behold.

    [8] Reference to the legend of the lovers who, locked in close embrace,
    became one body, both male and female.
    [9] Principal seat of the cult of Priapus.

76. Not so fair the Nereids appeared,
    their tresses flowing, gliding midst the waves,
    the day the sea received for the first time
    the wound inflicted by the Argonauts.
    I know not if her star [10] when brightly born
    of ocean ever showed so fair a sight.
    The bath appeared to be the sea, her breast
    the dawn, her lovely face the rising sun.

77. There she stands, the image of a nymph
    incised of precious ivory and clear,
    a statue in a sparkling fount perhaps,
    a portrait by some noble artist carved,
    in whiteness she is like one and in pose,
    'tis only movement shows the difference;
    and different from the sculptured stone as well,
    her hair of gold, the scarlet of her face.

78. Before the flashing of her sparkling stars
    the cool and crystal waters seem to burn,
    the humid stones along the neighboring banks
    are flaming from the unaccustomed light.
    Upon her lovely cheeks the softest flames
    of roses and of rubies show themselves,
    as for her fair breast, in a milky sea
    two perfect apples quiveringly float.

79. Now like dame Fortune o'er her brow she coils
    the ample volume of her golden locks.
    Now part she loosens, streaming out behind
    like comet's tail, her shoulders to adorn.
    A breeze which tosses and dishevels them
    conforms their undulations to the waves,
    whence her damp tresses, scattered by the wind,
    appear like gold which silver floods distill.

80. Stirred by the touch of beauty so sublime,
    the amorous wave seemed to dissolve with joy,

[10] Venus.

and greedily enfold her in its breast
as if in jealousy to freeze her there.
It wrapped her, but to what avail? It scarce
concealed her from the fair Adonis' view.
Indeed, she glimmers through the gelid wave
as shows a gem through glass, a lamp through gauze.

81. Oh, how her gentle movements as she bathes
    make amorous assault upon his heart!
    Now she submerges, now she rises up,
    now she immerses her vermilion lips
    and now upon her love with ivory hand
    she splashes pure enamel crystalline,
    now she sprays his breast and now his brow,
    and makes the fountain weep for sheer delight.

82. Adonis too, stripped of his handsome gear,
    at once delighted and amazed, he has
    neath a cool effigy a soul aflame;
    so freezing outwardly, he burns within;
    and while his eyes were fixed on that fair fire,
    he pulls up by the roots a little sigh,
    so profound, so fraught with fervid love,
    he seemed to send his heart forth on that sigh.

83. "Ah, what wild thunder," sighing he exclaims,
    "or what white lightning now bewitches me?
    What flames do I see flash in lovely eyes,
    what snows lie trembling on the fair, white breast?
    Perhaps this soul from heaven has been transformed
    a water sprite, or this an earthly sky.
    Heaven is brought to earth. Come who would see,
    down here the sun is in Aquarius.

84. "Paris, methinks, saw not such loveliness
    in that same goddess in fair Xanthus' vale,[11]
    nor burned with such an amorous fire when he

[11] Place where Paris judged the beauty contest between Juno, Minerva, and Venus. Cf. Canto II.

beheld the Greek,[12] admired at such great cost;
as I now see her with her tempting charms,
and feel my soul dissolve in living flame;
a flame I deem as great as that which burned
to ashes his own native Ilium.

85.   "Father Neptune, say if you recall
the time she issued from your briny spray,
say if you saw then in the lovely limbs
such magic splendor and such radiance.
Tell me, O Sun, does not her beauty seem
more bright today than it is wont to be,
greater than when in heaven, envious,
you charged her shamelessly before the gods?

86.   "Endymion, unworthy of this sight
which I behold, thou wast less fortunate
when to thee from her heavenly balcony
the goddess of the silver orb came down.
Admit, unhappy Actaeon, admit
that for a finer form I burn and sigh;
and very different is thy fate and mine,
for I gain life from mine, and thou hast death.

87.   "O immortal one, why wash yourself
in waves if they are far less pure than you?
The waters are made cleaner with your stains,
and made more lovely by your blemishes.
Since I am destined for delights so rare,
for such a sweet, propitious paradise,
permit that I may wash thee, dry thee now,
with living tears and then with ardent sighs.

88.   "And if 'tis true that such an amorous flame
can burn even in fountains and in streams,
let me like Acis be consumed in waves

[12] Helen.

or like Alpheus let me liquefy.
Perhaps my lovely flame, in gazing down
into these clear and tranquil depths, will join
the ranks of the cerulean deities
in summer's heat, and glide into my arms."

89. Thus he discourses, while the frigid waters
take vigor from the amorous torches' heat.
Love binds them, binds their bodies and their hearts
with rugged and inextricable snares.
Of traps which will appease their fierce desires
he makes their arms the cords, their kisses knots;
and his own blindfold he employs to rub
the cold and dripping members of the pair.

THALAMUS

90. The sun had reached the end of his long course
at which the flowers were left disconsolate.
The flying shadows and the drowsy gloom
were escort to the silences and chills.
Night, beggared of her customary splendor,
covered up her hair in a brown veil;
because Love's star appeared not in the sky,
aflame, but bent on other offices.

91. A little secret chamber where the air
is sweetly stirred with gentle, perfumed breath
Love opens for the zealous, amorous hearts—
Love the porter, Love who turns the key.
Inlaid with finest crystals are its walls
and beams, as bright as if with diamonds,
and everywhere in wild extravagance
clear mirrors stand, the bellows of desires.

92. The marriage bed, sweet with Arabian scents,
is hung with curtains of a Tyrian dye.
Those spoils of India which bacchantes hung,

concealing Ariadne and their lord,
those corals and sapphires the nymphs devised
to curtain Thetis' love for Peleus,
would seem but poor beside the wondrous bed
made by the Graces for these happy loves.

93. Regally it shines, adorned with gems,
    its columns are of cedar, sides of gold.
    Its coverlet might shame the Orient,
    its pillows every treasure would outmatch.
    The crimson hangings spread around reveal
    a heaven of fantastic workmanship.
    Soft sheets of scented linen, gleaming white,
    stand out against the trimmings and the gems.

94. Four curious columns at the corners stand
    whose capitals support the canopy;
    in form of tree trunks subtly carved, with gold
    and emeralds are their twisted shapes adorned.
    Here as in a green and dome-shaped cage
    among the branches lodge a flock of birds,
    from which, if one should agitate the boughs,
    the song of an angelic choir would rise.

95. This was the tranquil port which now received
    the noble couple from the dubious surge.
    'Twas here he plucked the vintage of his sighs,
    and reaped the harvest from the seeds of Love;
    here, as the sun was setting, Venus took
    the fair possession of Adonis oft;
    and here, as ever, when one sun had set
    the other rose, more lovely in her eyes.

96. Whereat the dam of silence and sweet sleep,[13]
    calm, dewy, and obscure, enfolds the hills,
    until her fillets, shadowy and dark,
    are torn away by morning's early rays;

[13] Night.

meanwhile the goddess in that dark enjoys
the embraces of those white and graceful limbs,
without a light to shine, except the one
dear light which casts its brightness in their shade.

97.   And still from dawn to even in her lap
she holds him close and binds him with her arms.
Both night and day are one to her, and if
at times her duties force her to depart,
though she is absent but an hour or two,
she utters sighs for such anxiety,
she seems to have within her heart those flames
that burst from Aetna or destroyed great Troy.

98.   When the swift sun, mounting the dome of heaven,
with his straight, fiery shafts strikes on the hills,
there where the rolling mountains' leafy backs
a verdant prison weave of sylvan shade,
to sojourn where her darling lover dwells
she oft withdraws her solitary steps,
and by a stream or in a grot delights
to share the hours with him, and thoughts and speech.

99.   And, ever constant in her warm desires,
she sits, she lies, and whiles the day with him.
In concert with the rippling of the streams,
the gentle murmur of their kissing sounds.
No ray from other sun here touches her
save from fair eyes in which she mirrors oft;
no scorching breeze from summer's noontide blows,
save from his sighs, which evermore she feels.

100.   She sometimes roams abroad through fields and woods,
in following the track of his loved feet,
a bold and lovely huntress of the wild,
errant companion of her hunter mate;
and sometimes in her hand she bears the bow
or at her side the arrows of her love,

so that each faun and sylvan deity
deems one to be Apollo, one Diane.

101. Thus sometimes when a youthful heifer calf
strays off through lonely and deserted fields,
so tender it cannot yet tread the grass
with sure and steady footing all alone,
nor are the new buds of the arching brow
yet curved in full and perfect crescent form,
the careful mother follows everywhere,
and hovers over her to guard her close.

102. So jealous is the goddess for that face,
she fears lest Love might burn with love for him.
She fears lest in a whirlwind Boreas
might swoop down from the clouds and bear him off;
she fears lest Jove, concealed in golden shower,
might spread his snares for such a handsome prize.
She wishes to conceal those lovely lights
from spyings of the sun and all the stars.

103. Whether the world is growing bright or dim,
whether night spreads or folds its darkened veil,
Venus mistrusts Aurora or the Moon,
afraid that one may bear him off to heaven.
She hates, as rival, the presumptuous air;
the birds, the trees, the flowers fill her with fright,
she's almost jealous of her own sweet kiss,
and even of her too voracious glance.

104. Under the curving, massive battlements
of shady hill, unknown to sun's fierce rays,
girt by a deep and solitary vale,
there lies in hollow rock a mossy cave.
Rarely do any try the secret path
to its recesses save Repose and Sleep.
Both savage beasts and shepherds reverence
its sacred shades, its gloomy, hidden depths.

105. This spot bold Nature, imitating art,
     has marvelously adorned with rude designs.
     She has with rustic painting covered it,
     of leaves and flowers both inside and out.
     She's made a shade of ferns and anice plants,
     a screen against day's warming injuries.
     Ivy defends the entrance 'gainst the sun,
     armed with the branching of a hundred wings.

106. Here for a shelter from the sunny fields
     the charming couple often would retire,
     in happy leisure passing blessed hours,
     safe from the ardor of the major orb.
     The airs were gentle nurses for their sleep,
     bed curtains were the branches and plumed grass,
     their confidants the valleys, and the hills
     and solitudes their only company.

107. Against the great blond archer god [14] who aimed
     his fiery rays straight from his golden bow,
     the green Briariuses [15] formed a shield
     for the two lovers with their twining arms.
     Stirred by the delicate and playful airs,
     in alternating whispers pine and beech
     seemed to converse, with every leaf a tongue;
     Love nurtures them more than the sun and rain.

108. One certain day, behold she views him there,
     having returned all breathless from the hunt.
     The blond and curly gold three times or four
     returns to dry the clear white ivory.
     She chains his flanks with her fair arms, and takes
     him in her lap, sits in the lap of grass;
     and gazing lovingly at him she loves,
     she feasts her eyes, as eagle at the sun.

[14] Apollo, the sun god.
[15] Briarius, a giant with a hundred hands; here figurative for trees.

109. She holds eyes joined to eyes, faithful and dear,
     and likewise face to face and breast to breast.
     Whene'er he kisses, smiles, with mouth and eyes
     she eats, she drinks the kisses and the smiles.
     "Oh, who shall e'er divide thee from my eyes,
     O thou who ne'er art parted from my thoughts?
     What other care can come that would avail
     to make thee callous to my suffering?

110. "Now well I see with fire equal to mine
     (who would believe it true?) thou dost not burn,
     and that sometimes, unused to loving well,
     thou dost bestow caresses that are feigned;
     since sport is oft neglected for fatigue
     when thou return'st so tardy from the hunt;
     as with some children, above everything
     thou dost prefer a puerile pastime."

111. So saying, gently with a precious veil
     she dries the delicate perspiring drops,
     a living dew, which streaks the freshest flowers
     of morn upon that charming human face.
     She gathers in her hands the golden threads
     of his fair locks, repairs their wanderings,
     and with her tender tears she washes him,
     with pearls of sweat she mingles pearls of grief.

112. Then he replied to her: "Oh, dry these tears,
     and cease to sound these melancholy notes!
     Sooner wilt thou see these locks with snow
     all covered o'er, these cheeks with furrows streaked,
     than ever put to flight for other love
     the love which from my heart can never fly;
     and if thou art immortal, my loved flame,
     immortal too shall be my hot desires.

113. "By that torch inflaming me, I swear,
     and by the piercing dart that wounds my heart;
     by the eyes I swear and by the locks

in which Love gilds the dart, inflames the torch,
Adonis ever shall be thine alone,
so splendidly that sun shines in his sight.
If I swear other than the truth, my love,
may I become the prey of the wild boar."

114. And she to him: "If thou, my love, but knew
how sweet it is loving to be beloved,
and hadst thou learned how hard a thing it is
to have to wander far off from thy love,
thou wouldst sometimes, when resting at my side,
give me more certain signs of mutual love,
and we should then be equal in our love,
contented thou, I happy, and both blessed.

115. " 'Tis true that nothing mars the happy thought
when the loved object always is in sight.
And in souls bound with sturdy, loyal chains,
no separation causes love to fail.
Let Lybian desert part them if it can,
the deepest ocean or the unscaled peak.
Indeed to leave one's love is even worse
than to desire and never to enjoy.

116. "Let us enjoy each other, let us love!
Love is the sole, the one reward for love;
two souls are made one soul, two hearts one heart,
through the high virtue of an amorous faith.
The heart, the soul changes its hostelry,
lives in another, in itself it dies.
Love then inhabits the abandoned shell
and there fulfills the part of heart and soul.

117. "O sweetness infinite, ineffable,
O pleasant wound, burning delectable,
where, like the Phoenix,[16] burned to ash, the heart
has both its cradle and its sepulchre,

[16] Mythical bird which died in flames only to rise from the ashes
to a new life.

whence the soul, wounded by two bright eyes,
not dying dies, and cares not for its death,
and, pierced by Love, it sighs and languishes,
all without hurt and without iron or blood.

118. "Thus sweetly can the spirit learn to die,
tinder to flame, a target for the dart,
can feel within the sweetly bitter flame
and from a mortal wound immortal death.
A death that pleases both the heart and sense
no death is, rather it is life, is birth;
and Love that burns and pierces her,[17] the more
he makes her die, the more he renders life.

119. "Now if indeed thy wish responds to mine,
and my desire truly responds to thine,
and if thou long'st as greatly as I yearn,
and if it pleases me as thou dost wish;
if one desire is shared within two breasts,
and if one spirit nurtures both of us;
if thou dost seize my heart and giv'st me thine,
why not then of our bodies make but one?

120. "O thou sweet spark of my illumined soul,
O sweetest martyrdom of my pierced heart,
O light and pupil of my glowing lamps,
O my caresses, O my kiss, my sigh,
turn to me those founts of sparkling gems,
pure sapphires whence all graces are distilled.
Yield me that source where fate has granted me
that from a ruby cup I drink my death!

121. "Turn to me those lovely eyes. O vital eyes,
eyes, the shining mirrors of my eyes;

[17] The reference is to "the spirit" (*l'anima*) above. The Italian
pronoun can, in the present context, be translated "her" or "it." I
have chosen "her" in order to preserve the sense of the obvious *double-
entendre*.

eyes, those bows and quivers, heated forge
of arrows tempered in a bath of pleasure;
eyes of the heaven of Love, two fateful stars,
of beauty's sun the living orient;
stars serene, whose lovely light can cause
perpetual eclipse for my own star.

122. "Grant me that mouth. O dear, beloved mouth,
the jeweled exit of the realm of Smiles,
a hedge of roses, whence a little viper
amorously exhales a scented breath,
coffer of pearls, whence blessings overflow,
a crimson chamber, cavern odorous,
a refuge where Love steals away and hides
when he has robbed a soul or stabbed a heart."

123. She ceases, but what style could hope to match
the lovely tenor of each smallest word?
Unworthy, true, is every other tongue
save that which forms the words thus charmingly.
So speaking, gazing, greedy to enjoy,
she sates her thirst without destroying it;
and thus since more she burns and is consumed,
she kisses the sweet lips and the sweet lights.

SONG OF KISSES

[The following stanzas (124–149) represent a new and elaborated treatment of the *"Canzone dei Baci,"* a youthful composition of Marino for which he gained an early celebrity.

Perhaps the passage might better be entitled "Hymn to Love."
One does not read far before realizing that the lines are concerned with more than kisses. Much of the imagery in the passage
is traditional and repetitious, with endless references to the life-
death-rebirth convention. Conceits are abundant, are tumbling
over each other in fact; and not a few of them are ingenious,
according to the Marino canon.

Almost the entire scene is talk. This matter of the narrator's

technique is reminiscent of Shakespeare's method throughout a
very large part of his *Venus and Adonis,* though there are perhaps different explanations for the adoption of the method.
Marino seems to have been guided by a certain sense of delicacy.
As long as the actors are talking, more realistic details of action
are not given, though there are many erotic *double-entendres.*
With Shakespeare's characters, the action never went much beyond talk—pleas and arguments.

One other significant aspect of this section—a passage to which
Marino must have attached considerable importance and devoted much of his well-known ingenuity—is the studied development of verbal patterns, which results in creating the effect of an
ode of celebration.

The poem has a radically different brand of eroticism from
that to which many twentieth-century readers are inured. It is,
nevertheless, one of the most characteristic of all Marino passages; consequently, we may be certain of its exceptional contemporary popularity. In any case it is not hard to understand
why Marino felt the absolute need for some such treatment of
the theme of sexual love. It is central to the story of Venus and
Adonis.]

124. She kisses; after kissing looks and looks
     upon those beauties kissed, now these, now that.
     He kisses back, then sighs and sighs again
     over the tasted sweets; now he, now she.
     Two lives live in a single life infused,
     and one speech in two speeches utters breath;
     the hearts conjoin upon their outer lips,
     the souls rush to entwine in one another.

125. From time to time to intermittent sounds
     echoes the grotto rough and cavernous.
     "Tell me, goddess," says the one, "your kisses,
     spring they from the heart as from the lips?"

Replies the one: "The heart in biting lips
is kissed. Love is creator of the kiss.
The heart distills it, lips deliver it;
the more soul joys in it, the less the mouth.

126. "Not kisses these, loquacious messengers
they are of mutual amorous desire;
the tongues, though silent, speak to one another
and have expressed much in their silent way.
The sighs and kisses are the accents mute
come from my heart, which thy sweet kissing bites;
the kindled spirits answer each to each
in voices understood by them alone.

127. "The kiss can speak, and over sighs and looks
bears off the palm, though they are tongues of Love,
because plunging the arrow in the heart
the souls are then entwined at the lips' edge.
What sweet restorer for the fire I feel,
to pacify our mouths and ease our pains!
Our mouths, which long for nectar have both thirst
and juice, are both the roses and the bees.

128. "That lovely crimson hue which stains the lips,
it leaves no doubt that there is red blood there.
Now if 'tis true the soul maintains its seat
within the blood, as certain sages claim,
then as we, kissing, tourney in the lists,
by blood thy soul is really kissing mine;
and while thou dost return the kiss, and I
rekiss thy lips, my soul couples with thine.

129. "It hangs upon the tip of the loved lips
there where the blossom of the soul is plucked,
like body animated in itself,
the kiss, which is extracted from the soul.
I know not what sweet rage of love it is
that murders it, nor where 'tis laid when dead,

but even there where it has been entombed,
divinest kiss, thou'lt bring it back to life.

130. "While in encounter one goes mouth to mouth,
while in the wounding one goes kiss to kiss,
such pleasure takes possession of the souls
that then they spread their wings to soar in flight;
the hearts, being but narrow urns, cannot
contain the sweetness that is showered down;
they pour their very souls out through their lips
and on their lips they seem to pant for death.

131. "The spirits tremble, gripped with burning zeal,
and then the kiss excites the soul to die.
Tongues change from mouth to mouth and hearts change breasts,
spirit with spirit, heart with heart are joined.
Eyes flutter, and an amorous pallor stains
and curtains the bright flowers in the cheeks;
and sometimes prudent lovers in their dying
delay their death to gain a double death.

132. "Thy soul in dying flies away from thee,
but I receive it dying in that kiss,
and in that vital death, which shatters it,
the while thou giv'st me thine, I give thee mine;
and him who sees me sigh, who sucks my lips,
I suck also, and dying gaze upon;
and when I gaze and kiss thee, to win death,
I wish the soul were every uttered sigh."

133. "Then make me, O my soul," he answered her,
"exchange my death with an immortal life.
Let my soul to heaven fly, that it
may be companion of eternal gods.
Make me now live and die, and, if't may be,
make me then revive to better fate.

At one time, let me, sweetly languishing,
live in thy mouth and die within thy breast.

134. "A single harbor mid these rosy sweets
unites both my desire and thy desire.
Our souls, our hearts, our spirits all in one
are joined together now to live and die.
The wounder in his turn reveals his wound,
and she who wounds is slain causing a wound;
whence while I perish and thou perishest,
our dying pleasantly revives our zeal.

135. "Ordain, O my delight, for my delight
that ceaselessly I hang upon thy lips.
But do not with a niggard kind of love
refuse thy white breast to my crimson lips.
Nor let the scornful rigor of fair eyes
oppose, I pray, my amorous appetite.
Dying I shall live in thee and thou
in me, so I shall render what thou giv'st.

136. "If there is nothing in us of our own,
nothing to be called just thine or mine;
if much or little of my heart's not mine,
as I believe thine is no longer thine;
since thou art my bright flame and I thy fire,
and what the one desires the other seeks;
since with his own divine hand Love has made
and signed and sealed this contract binding us;

137. "consent that I return thy kiss, and grant
that I embrace thee e'en as thou dost me.
Strike me, wound me, kill; oh make me swoon
until the soul sweats and the heart grows chill.
Inflame my flame for thee, thy flame for me,
and spring the trap for each of us at once;

let arms and lips be twined in double knots,
and let our tongues perpetual motion find.

138. "Amid the lovely flowers of thy soft lips,
Love, like a graceful, charming little bird,
with hundreds of his playmtes, wanton, gay,
flies playfully, and there conceals his bow.
Nor is he willing that I satisfy
my hunger there, being jealous of his sweets,
for lo, no sooner do I seize a kiss
and ease my pain than he attacks my heart.

139. "But when I can escape from him and take
my refuge where thy face shows deepest red,
O happy me, I sweet ambrosia sip,
such as the gods enjoy in paradise.
O gentle Zephyr, thou for whom I long,
I feel the breath of roses at that smile,
whose fire, which consumes my heart and soul,
while cooling ardor yet illumines more.

140. "Ah no, these are not kisses that I take,
they are the perfumed airs of Araby,
richer than the embalsamed cinnamon,
of sweetness which I cannot comprehend.
They are perfumes of Love, which he distills
by means of burning the enamored souls.
These red recesses as much honey hold
as does Hymettus, Hybla, or Parnassus.[18]

141. "Happy me, to merit that sweet ill
which has occasioned me so much of good.
But I am foolish in my sweet delights,
for I attempt to kiss and speak at once.
Such is the pleasure that I would not wish
my mouth to be engaged save in this act.

[18] Places famous for the honey they produced.

And my heart grieves together with my mouth,
when kisses must surrender place to words."

142. "And I," she says, "who might well boast to reap
infinite glory in supernal realms,
ne'er have experienced delights above
that can compare to this my present joy;
take what thou wilt, and ask as much of me
as pleases thee, command me at thy pleasure;
lo, at the slightest touch of thee, my love,
my heart, all sighing, trembling, leaves my breast.

143. "O my heart, into my heart now darts,
now penetrates that tongue, arrow of Love,
and in my ruby whetstone would make sharp
its point, which sweetly urges me to death;
and while I feel myself about to die,
it brings a sweet vendetta for thy death.
Thou seem'st a serpent set to strike, for oft
are serpents mid fair roses wont to hide.

144. "And if because it's sly and venomous,
comparison with viper suits thee ill,
let's say, at least, much like the swallow's tail,
as fluttering in rapid flight it sports.
Or rather does ingenious Love teach thee
to toss it like an olive's wavy branch.
It flutters so that well thy archer mouth
emulates the eyes and wounds my heart."

145. "Are not," he answered her, "oh, are not these
the eyes whence those sweet arrows pierced my heart?
The eyes whence my heart sweetly burns within?
Fair eyes—" and at this speech he kissed her eyes.
"O lovely eyes," she adds, "celestial eyes,
the source from whence my heart is showered with sweets.
Heart because of which I heartless live,
treasure whence I'm poor, life whence I die!"

146. Then he resumed: "So thou and thou alone
      art the sole heart whence my heart gets its life;
      my heart—" And more he wished to say, when she
      drank with a kiss the word and heart as well.
      She melts for him as he for her, as melts
      the snowflake in the bright rays of the sun.
      Kisses resound, and ne'er from hollow cave
      has Echo answered to a sweeter sound.

147. Then forms a close-tied knot out of two hearts
      that peak of pleasure, end of all desire.
      In ecstasies of love their breasts compose
      a murmuring of the profoundest sighs.
      Their souls become distilled in a warm dew,
      a sweet oblivion presses every sense.
      Their tongues turn cold, their faces pale and wan,
      eyes waver and are turned up toward the heavens.

148. Souls weary, drunk with joy, and languishing,
      now swoon, transported to a heaven of love.
      The broken accents, oft-repeated sighs,
      sweet wars and wounds, I know not how to tell.
      O ye fresh breezes and ye rippling waves,
      who witness it and hear it all, you tell,
      and ye, the confidants of happy loves,
      green myrtles, shady laurels, lofty pines.

149. Meanwhile the light departs, the shades return,
      beyond Morocco is the sun concealed.
      The orient sky is turned a dusky hue,
      earth changes a green mantle for a brown.
      Now the cicada to the cricket yields;
      the nightingale surrenders to the owl,
      who chatters to the stars and utters plaints
      unto the lovely planet's fleeting rays.

CANTO X

The Marvels

[For the entertainment and enlightenment of Adonis, Mercury conducts the lovers on a flight into the heavens, a venture calling up frequent reminiscences of Dante and Ariosto. Mercury, in the role of the irrepressible pedagogue with a captive audience, discourses in fulsome fashion on numerous matters which might be puzzling to a mortal on his first trip to the moon. In Mercury's lectures we cannot fail to detect Marino's satisfaction in parading his own learning in matters astronomical. To Marino the announcement of the telescope and the findings of Galileo through his observations of the moon and of the moons of Jupiter represent a subject of thrilling novelty and of vicarious pride. To the reader, noting the time of Galileo's first publication of his observations *(Sidereus Nuncius,* 1610), this enthusiasm on the part of Marino hints at a reaction on the part of the public—at least one segment of the public—which is in striking contrast to that of the church authorities, who censured and persecuted Galileo for his teachings. One wonders if the reading public in any generation between the early seventeenth century and the mid-twentieth century has been more concerned about the surface of the moon than was Marino's, if we may judge from the present passage.

It is amusing to observe that in the same breath that Marino lauds Galileo he is presenting a scheme of the heavens which is purely Ptolemaic, apparently ignoring the fact that Galileo's efforts were directed toward the establishment of the Copernican cosmography. This same pattern, of course, was adopted by Milton in *Paradise Lost* half a century later.]

INVOCATION

1. O Muse, O thou who through the curving paths
   of heaven tirelessly dost turn thy course,
   and while thou guid'st in concert all the gyres
   of crystal stars, some swift and others slow,
   with thy harmonious feet in happy dance
   thou tapp'st the pavement of the starry heaven,
   whence of that harmony the sound is formed
   which is the primal measure of our song.

2. Thou, power divine, immortal intellect,
   Urania, guide thou the genius bold,
   that mounts and soars beyond its proper bounds
   to wander far through the celestial realms.
   Oh, let thy breath of favor lift my wings,
   that on so steep a course I may not fail.
   Guide thou my pen, O thou who movest heavens,
   and to a new style dictate new conceits.

3. Typhis [1] first raised sails above the waves,
   Orpheus with his lyre went down to hell,

---

[1] Pilot of the Argonauts, the first pilot, according to a legend of the ancients.

Daedalus plied wings through upper air,
Prometheus to the sphere of fire took **flight**.
'Tis meet that pain should follow recklessness,
through rash and stupid ventures such as those;
but greater far the terror and the risk
of the uncharted course I now attempt.

4. I venture upon unaccustomed ways,
remote from senses and from intellect,
whence, when I think to raise the mad desires
of either faculty to that high realm,
as a weak optic power, bewildered, dazed,
when in the presence of a brilliant light,
the one is blinded, while the other one,
lame and infirm, grows weary at the height.[2]

5. And if indeed it may sometimes befall
that awful splendor overwhelm it not,
and that my thought, supported by thy aid,
may visit that serene, untraveled road,
it cannot well conceive those lofty spheres
unless it find terrestrial forms up there.
I know without thee one so slow of pace
could ne'er succeed to gain so high a goal.

6. Thou, who once bore up from sphere to sphere
the wise, devoted lover of Beatrice,[3]
and that gay author [4] who immortalized
the misery and fall of Agramant [5]
guided so he knew how to conduct
the British knight [6] upon the flying horse,[7]

[2] In this involved conceit the intellect is identified with sight and the senses with motion, hence with bodily travel.

[3] Dante.   [4] Ariosto.

[5] In *Orlando Furioso,* leader of the Saracen forces against Charlemagne.

[6] Astolfo, knight in Charlemagne's army.

[7] Hippogryph, which aided Astolfo and other knights in flights through the heavens.

now grant that I also by grace attain
the secret precincts of thy glorious fane.

FLIGHT TO THE MOON

7. Now through serene and spacious fields of heaven
   Luciferus took flight before the sun,
   and he, while shaking free the jeweled reins,
   opened the crimson gate to a new day.
   His steeds were breathing forth a living flame,
   and cleaving clouds like lightning with their hoofs,
   whence at their coming the nocturnal shades
   slowly yielded to the golden breeze.

8. From cages on the Cyprian isle, where feed
   a family of gentle, simple birds,
   Love gathered six of them, and with gold bands
   he bound them to the chariot in pairs.
   You see them turning toward the newborn day
   their tiny heads and lovely, graceful necks,
   their colorful and iridescent breasts
   varied and beautified before the light.

9. Cooing they advance, with jocund tread
   they set their feet in motion for the flight,
   the flight on which the goddess wished to soar
   with the fair youth who gave his heart to her.
   Mercury was stationed at the reins
   to act as driver for the glorious course.
   And high upon the chariot's crescent poop
   the loving couple happily reposed.

10. The doves at one great bound launched into flight,
    their wings with silver bright, their yokes of gold.
    The heavens opened and the winds grew calm,
    the poles became serene, the clouds dispelled.
    A multitude of gayly singing birds
    followed with musical accompaniment.

A thousand wanton sparrows flashed about,
their festive voices twittering of love.

11. Those innocent, cherubic choristers,
from whose bright beaks we learn of love and peace,
Love's ministers elect, now have no fear
of greedy merlin and rapacious hawk.
The eagle, sporting with them, hides his claws,
more pleased to have the arrows pierce his heart.
And thereabouts the fiercest birds of prey
are made companions of their enemies.

12. Attendant archers flank the chariot
in squads, before, behind, and round about,
some to console the weeping dawn speed off
with notice of the goddess's approach.
Others greet the sun with messages
to rise from Ganges and to clear the path.
But each first upward to the fleeing stars
bears the announcement of the wondrous news.

THE SPOTS ON THE MOON

24. Now having passed the perfect zone of fire,[8]
which dries the goddess's [9] cool countenance,
surmounted thence and drawing near the place
where circles the first heaven [10] in its course,
and having broached its body gradually,
which like a mirror shows without a crease,
the master of the arts and languages [11]
began to give a discourse on the place.

25. "Adonis, I perceive thou long'st to know
the secrets of the sphere where we are come;
I see thee with attention gaze upon

[8] Region of fire, between the earth and moon.
[9] Cynthia, goddess of the moon.   [10] Sphere of the moon.
[11] Mercury.

the goddess' face, the mother of the months;
thus though thou sayest nought of thy desire,
and dost not utter thy demand to me,
I read each thought depicted on thy brow
more clearly than if 'twere expressed in words.

26. "This orb we are approaching is the moon,
that with its splendor whitens all the sky;
the shining guide of sober, dusky night,
the eye of horrors blind and shadowy.
It generates the dews, convokes the clouds,
and is the minister of fertile damps.
Illumined by another's light it shines,
the sun's light takes, and to the sun gives back.

27. "This body's real magnitude is less
than is the sun's, nor does it darken it,
for in its measurement it scarce contains
one thirtieth of earth's full area.
But if it broaches the terrestrial sphere,
it equal seems, and makes a shade for it.
For one sole moment it is seen to conquer
Sol, all other times it yields to him.

28. "Various forms it has and many aspects,
now 'tis round, now horned, now full, now shrunk,
and ever holds its eyes turned to the sun,
which shines upon it from a distant zone,
whence always one of its two faces serves
to hold a part in its great loveliness.
Each month it rounds its period entire,
and sails the heavens, changing hemispheres.

29. "Because she is closer than the other orbs,
she wields upon you greater influence.
Mistress of senses, goddess of disease;
she alone creates and cancels these.
How much, O Ocean, hides within thy womb,

in thee how many scaly creatures dwell,
and yet thy movements at her movements shift
their state, their semblance, and their changing modes.

30. "The flower and the fruit, the root, the plant,
the sea, the stream and fountain, wave and fish,
all these derive from her their moving power,
and move according to her wax and wane.
She is sole governess of intellect,
of what the womb holds and what issues thence;
and everything which in itself retains
some humid quality conforms to her.

31. "There is no thing, propitious or benign,
which Saturn, Jove, or any other orb,
fixed or moving, staid or vagabond,
sends down upon the fair terrestrial globe,
which passes not through her; what influences
rain down on earth pass through her blessed sphere,
through that clear, shining lamp of silver, which
is ornament of the nocturnal shades.

32. "Whence it occurs that that revolving face,
e'en though 'tis changing, ever variable,
yet cherishes a happy countenance
remaining ever fixed in fair aspect.
Let any who is born her subject know
he may expect nought but inconstancy,
a fate that drives him to much wandering,
to lead his life far from his native land."

33. The heavenly physicist meant to proceed
with fuller, more explicit lecturing,
when in the middle of his talk the youth
cut short his teacher's words, addressing him:
"To search the cause of something curious
a warm and keen desire possesses me,

a thing which since my eyes encountered it
has ever held my mind in wonderment.

34. "With certain cloudy spots impressed, I see
the triform goddess's [12] pure, radiant cheek.
Tell me the cause; mid thousand doubts I hang,
nor any sure opinion can I find.
Pray now explain what strange, unclean contagion
mars with ugly stains that lovely face?"
So did he reason; then the other one
once more resumed his talk and thus declared:

35. "Hear then, since thou so deeply wouldst inquire,
I'll strive to satisfy thy questioning.
But reason ought to tell thee that for this
the eye serves better than the intellect.
There's been no dearth of scientists on earth
who have observed these blemishes in her.
Each one has striven to investigate,
but rare is he who comes nigh to the truth.

36. "Some claim between the Sun and Cynthia
dense matter of some sort is interposed,
which acts to blur reflection here and there
of that great splendor which he sheds on her.
If this were true, as these would have us think,
her face would not always remain the same;
nor would the one who studies her observe
those spots in one same place and shape are fixed.

37. "Then there are those who think that Cynthia,
being so close to your own elements,
must necessarily partake somewhat
the elemental nature of the earth.
Thereby would they contaminate the boast
and purity of our ethereal realms,

[12] Cynthia: in her triple role as goddess of the moon, the hunt, and
the underworld.

as though a thing of heaven clear and pure
could be infected with a mixture vile.

38. "Others there were who said that orb to be
like opaque crystal that is backed with lead,
and therefore that the shadow of earth's peaks
is there reflected causing darkened spots.
But what is bright enough to strike upon
steel or glass across so vast a space?
What lynx-eyed vision could avail to view
an image in a mirror from so far?

39. "It must be said then that another cause
more secret is concealed, explored in vain,
which human zeal and ingenuity
are not permitted yet to penetrate.
Now I will show thee that this planet's face
is not, as others think, polished and smooth,
but in its deep, obscure recesses has,
no less than earth, both vales and rugged hills.

40. "Its surface, though 'tis little understood,
I tell thee true, is like the earth itself,
uneven, rough and swollen, creased and humped,
in parts concave, in other parts convex.
There thou shalt see (but without near approach
to them sight cannot recognize such things)
more rivers, other fountains, other seas,
and realms, towns, provinces, mountains, and plains.

41. "And this it is that causes dusky signs
to show down there on Trivia's [13] fair face.
Although thou canst not see them now, I would
that thou shouldst notice other spots therein,
which are more crowded, more minute and dark,
for they are rocks and hills, meadows and woods.

[13] Trivia: another name for Diana, "goddess of three ways."

These too are on the purest of white cheeks,
but from the earth the eye perceives them not.

GALILEO AND THE TELESCOPE

42. "A time will come when these her marks will be
clearly observed without impediment,
thanks to a marvelous new instrument
through which things distant can appear close by;
and one surveying the bright lunar orb,
with one eye closed and with the other fixed,
will shorten the tremendous interval
by a small cannon with two crystals set.

43. "Through thee, O Galileo, the telescope,
to present age unknown, shall be composed,
the work which brings remotest object close
and makes it show much larger to one's sense.
Thou only, the observer of her motion
and of what in her parts she has concealed,
thou shalt, without a veil to shroud her form,
behold her nude, O new Endymion.[14]

44. "In this same glass thou'lt spy not only each
of her minute details from near at hand,
but also, by my aid, thou shalt observe
Jupiter girt round with other lights,[15]
whence in the sky the Arno's demigods [16]
will leave their names inscribed forevermore.
Then Julius [17] shall yield to Cosimo,[18]
Augustus vanquished by thy Medici.

[14] A handsome youth, loved by Cynthia.

[15] A reference to Galileo's discovery of the moons of Jupiter.

[16] Galileo named those moons the Medici Planets, for the Medici family, rulers of Florence, on the Arno.

[17] Julius Caesar, whose fame is surpassed by that of the Medici which shines in the heavens.

[18] Cosimo II de' Medici, Grand Duke of Tuscany, who was Galileo's protector.

45. "Cleaving the breast of ocean, vast and deep,
    but not without grave peril and bitter strife,
    Liguria's Argonaut [19] down on the earth
    will yet discover a new land and sky.
    Thou, second Typhis,[20] not of sea but heaven,
    searching how wide it circles, what it holds,
    thyself wilt e'en discover without risk
    new stars and lights once hidden to all men.

46. "Much dost thou owe to heaven that grants to thee
    the invention of the wondrous instrument,
    but far more heaven owes to thy superb
    device, which makes its beauties manifest.
    Full worthy is thy image to be placed
    among those stars for fitting ornament,
    and those thy frail glass lenses to repose
    immortal mid eternal sapphire lights.

47. "Never until the heaven extinguishes
    the gleaming radiance of the stars themselves
    should that celestial splendor which shall wear
    for thee a crown of honor e'er be dimmed.
    Brightly will thy glory live with stars,
    and thou in flame endure, forever bright,
    and with their lovely, burning tongues of light
    the stars will tell thy story evermore."

48. Scarce had the secretary of the gods
    concluded his enlightening discourse,
    when he saw the sacred chariot mount
    upon the lesser of the two great lamps.
    Adonis, now alighted, finds himself
    in a strange world, mid other fields and woods.
    Whence he arrived by unmarked pathways near
    a grotto nestling in a narrow vale.

[19] Christopher Columbus, native of Genoa, in the state of Liguria.
Argonaut: explorer.
[20] The pilot of the ship Argo on the voyage in quest of the
Golden Fleece. This is addressed to Galileo.

CANTO XV

The Return

[After a long separation of the lovers, involving the captivity of Adonis by the sorceress Falsirena, they are happily reunited. The episode which follows, the chess game, comes under the category of amusing diversions and consequently can hardly be said to contribute to the plot. It does, of course, add to Marino's general purpose of presenting in fullest variety the world of pleasure.

The chess game is described in language appropriate for an Homeric battle scene, a device for mock-epic style familiar to English readers through Pope's game of cards in *The Rape of the Lock*.

Students of chess will discover that certain pieces go by designations different from those with which we are familiar: for example, pawns are infantry, foot soldiers; for bishops they had archers; and for modern rooks or castles they had elephants with a kind of fortress-carriage on their backs. They are referred to either as towers or as elephants.

The passage is modeled after a Latin poem by Vida, *Scacchia ludus,* which describes a game played by Apollo and Mercury in the presence of the other gods.]

THE GAME OF CHESS

119. The pact confirmed by all with this accord,
lo, comes a spirit graced with sparkling wit
and nimble hands, who jests and skips about;
Sport he is called and is akin to Love.
He, in a trice, upon the table fair
sets out a chessboard wondrously designed,
chased with a border of fine gold; the rest
of ivory and ebony is wrought.

120. Of sixty-four compartments square in form,
all quartered by straight lines and by traverse,
neatly disposed in eight enchanting files
containing eight compartments to the row.
Each chamber is exactly square in shape,
in space all equal but diverse in hue,
which alternately contrast white and black,
to make a pattern like a dragon's back.

121. Reciprocally to white square black succeeds,
and variegates the field in every part.
"Now here," the goddess said, "thou may'st perceive,
as on the battlefield, the strength of art;
it seems a charming likeness of fierce Mars
and faithful imitation of real war,
to lead assaults and order strategems,
and for two rivals to combat or flee.

122. "My royal father does not scorn, at times,
to witness such a pleasant spectacle,
when from the burden of his government
he wishes to refresh his weary mind.

Wherefore the wielder of the trident plays
a game of chess against his Nereids
for Jove's amusement when he comes to grace
the table of his friend Oceanus."

123. That said, she empties from a golden urn
onto the board two troops of figurines
which, carved from polished precious stones, display
in various shapes and costumes human forms.
In two divisions are the squadrons ranged,
these under the white ensign, those the black.
Equal they are in number and in power,
but different in semblance and in name.

124. Sixteen against sixteen they stand, and as
their color separates them, light and dark,
just so they have their varied shapes and names,
just so their different offices and trusts.
Here there are kings and queens, each one erect
with head encircled by a royal crown.
Here too are archers,[1] soldiers, armored knights
and elephants [2] with turrets on their backs.

125. Lo, now the troops are in formations drawn,
some in the sovereign sites, some in the mean,
the sections are divided, posts assigned.
The kings supreme, the last line occupy,
one here, one there, directly opposite,
each takes the fourth post in his row to start;
on the dark square the white king takes his stand;
the Moorish king stands on the ivory.

126. A royal spouse each king has by his side,
one has her on his right, one on his left;
each queen maintains a square of her own hue,

[1] *Sagittari:* now called *alfieri,* standard-bearers, correspond to our bishops.
[2] Correspond to *torri*—castles.

the dark the dark holds and the white the white.
In the same row twin archers stand confined,
the one on this flank stationed, one on that.
These to provoke the quarrel sally forth,
or for the royal couple stand as guards.

127. Not far off are two champions on horse,
both speedy to engage in open fight;
at the extremities of either squad
the Indian beasts [3] make strong the corner posts.
Then double cohorts of foot troops assist,
with eight confronting eight in ordered lines,
who in the first attack most fierce advance
their firm, intrepid breasts against the foe.

128. Thus if to battle 'gainst the Ethiop
the fair young knights of Gallia were arrayed,
or if a flock of crows assailed the swans,
the pitch black and the milk white would contrast.
The one compares in whiteness to the gleam
of untouched snows upon their native Alps;
the other wears upon his countenance
the dark of night before the breaking dawn.

129. The lovely Cyprian directs her prayers
to Mercury, and with those winsome charms
to whose appeal there's none that would not yield,
just as there is no marble will not chip,
asks that to fair Adonis he explain
the game's rules and the moves of every piece.
And he, mid thousand Loves who hover round,
proceeds to the instruction with these words:

130. "Each warrior proceeds out of the ranks
into the lists, encounters man to man;
if one in white advances, lo, in turn
we see another issue from the black.

[3] Elephants.

However, by their rule no more than one
at one time is allowed to take a step.
And all goes to one end, the game concludes
with prisoning the king in narrow place.

131. "And that he may the sooner fall to earth,
with steel in hand all charge into the breach;
one here, one there attempts to clear the way,
and bit by bit the field becomes less thronged.
If one defeats a rival in the fray,
he takes the station of the fallen foe;
but when by peril threatened, each one may
retreat a pace, except the infantry.

132. "Each is not equally endowed with skill
for marching and for fighting in the field.
Infantrymen [4] can move a single yard
straight forward only 'gainst the enemy,
except that when a rival is attacked,
they change their course and strike him from the side;
moreover for the first assault they may
advance in double steps, two squares at once.

133. "The elephants can forward go or back,
or bear to right or left their heavy load,
but always they move perpendicular,
nor ever turn to angle on their course.
To him who bears the arrows and the bow,
free pass is given along paths oblique.
He goes by flanking moves, and when he shoots,
he touches both the boundaries of the field.[5]

134. "The agile knight will never make his charge
in one straight course as other warriors do,
but, proud in show, he will traverse the lists,

[4] Pawns.
[5] The "archer" (bishop) is free to strike diagonally to the extremities
of the board.

veer in his charge with spin and whirling curve,
and always in his leap he gains two squares;
he leaves one color, takes the other one.
But for the royal lady, far more proud,
no law controls her free maneuverings.

135. "She wanders everywhere, both far and near,
and can perform the moves of all the rest
save that in curving line she may not go,
also she is forbid to leap or vault;
the horse alone has such a privilege,
the others may not curvet in their course.
But otherwise, if nothing blocks the path,
her movements have no limits or restraints.

136. "The sovereign king maneuvers cautiously,
on whom the hopes of all the camp are placed,
for if he's captured venturing on the plain,
the host of all his force will be destroyed.
Therefore for him each warrior arms himself,
for him all risk their lives in bloody strife;
and he, spectator of the fierce debate,
surrounded by such guard, fears no offense.

137. "Little does he intend to strike or wound,
through open combat rarely joins the fray.
To fight is not his aim, it is enough
that cautiously he guard against deceit.
But if some unskilled duke dare to attack,
he knows well how to wield the sword and lance;
he wounds or slays, but when he leaves his throne,
he may not pass the limits of one stride.

138. "These are the laws which I recount to thee
of this contest, and may not be transgressed;
but that the practice may be clear to thee,
thou first should watch to comprehend the game."
Thus he declares, and now the board is brought

and pieces set, at which he makes a sign
for Venus to assume a seat to play;
he likewise sits, prepared to risk his fate.

139. The dawn of battle breaks; and first to move
is the white troop, which Cytherea leads.
She, pausing somewhat in her thought, commands
the trooper of the queen to take the field.
He steps two paces out, and, no less proud,
the black commander sets one opposite.
The two encounter in mid-field, and each
attempts to gain advantage o'er his foe.

140. Here and there to aid this cause or that,
a number of the men advance a pace.
Mars lightly sports about the field, and still
no band has yet engaged another force;
but in a duel of two forward scouts,
the black now in the white one stains his blade.
He steals that place, ah miserable, nor sees
the nearby enemy, who strikes him down.

141. He falls upon the fallen. The black king
shifts from the mid-point to a corner post,
where with his faithful guard, at point removed
he feels himself less open to attack.
Lo, now, with sharp encounter, fierce and bold,
a knight from the left wing of either troop,
as, issuing in devastating charge,
fills the surrounding plain with heaps of slain.

142. But while the gentle daughter of great Jove
was all intent upon the infantry,
sly Mercury, in a sagacious move,
insidiously tries a furtive ruse.
The ruthless courser moves among the foot,
and dashes swiftly through them all unchecked,

he curves and pivots and with subtle tricks
brings sudden threat to the unwary king.

143. Lo, he has come to where he menaces
the final ruin of the royal throne
and the extremity of the right wing
where one of the great Indian ramparts towers.
Adonis's fair goddess sighs and groans,
not knowing which one first to render aid.
She cannot save at once both this and that.
Indeed the king's life must be guarded first.

144. She draws the king apart, and helplessly
the wretched elephant is shot to earth;
but the proud rider who has scoured the plain
does not escape unpunished from the fight.
He tries the risk of flight, but is opposed
by men on foot who press him from all sides.
Borne down at last by the virago queen,
he terminates his life in glorious death.

145. Just as a bull, who having lost a horn
in fighting, grows ferocious, bellows loud,
and staining the fine sand with blood, confronts
the weapons with his breast, and will not flee,
just so the irate Cytherea, who,
with little counsel but with greater rage,
longs to retrieve so notable a loss,
incites the avenging army 'gainst the foe.

146. She risks her men to slaughter willingly,
nor cares that more than one is sent to death,
even though she cannot fail to see
the fall of those is linked to her own fall.
The clever envoy of the immortal race,
with better judgment guides his strategy,
foresees the blows and with his art mature,
directs the whole, proud of the spoils attained.

147. In silence he oft cogitates and plots
the mortal ruin of the fair white queen.
At one point he had cleverly concealed
his right flank archer on the other wing,
and moves a helpless pawn in the queen's path;
then uttering a sigh he slaps his thigh,
as if repentant, thus in clever mode,
pretending error, he conceals his fraud.

148. No sooner did the occasion show itself
than Venus thinks to seize fate by the locks,
she pounces on her prey, not noticing
the queen was left unguarded on her flank.
For the opposing trooper who steps forth
she starts to deal his death with her own pawn,
when Cupid, grieved to see so fell a blow,
gives her a warning sign with lifted brow.

149. The goddess checks her hand, arrests the blow,
for she perceives the peril threatening,
and now the trooper who had been so keen
to rush in front of his cohorts retires.
The herald of the gods, irate at this,
utters a cry and trembles in his rage.
He claims the queen is forfeit and declares
a foul; and Venus makes apologies.

150. "Who," she says, "denies to one the right,
once having moved into a danger zone
in haste, to shift it to a safer spot,
since we have made no pact forbidding it?
Now that from so great risk I've rescued her,
let this be our confirmed decree henceforth:
whichever of two moves is first must count,
that stands perforce, be it by black or white."

151. This just decree was pleasing to them all,
and they made ready to observe the end.

The messenger divine restrained his ire,
his breast transfixed with many piercing thorns;
a secret thought was born within his heart
to fight with treachery and sly deceit.
He now is wary of deceits; henceforth
must Venus gauge her actions cleverly.

152. Sometimes by sleight of hand he manages,
I know not how, to deal two deadly blows
and carry off two bodies at one play,
much to the damage of the hostile troops.
Now, now, with fingers so adroit and swift
that eye their moves can follow with fatigue,
he sends a quiver-bearer to attack
but makes him jump in fashion of a knight.

153. He leaps into the throng in manner false,
in imitation of a horse he stamps,
he shakes himself and schemes to bring to earth
the white virago at whose side he camps.
The goddess then smiles bitterly in scorn
and blazing out with living fire, she says,
"You are indeed the author of deceits,
but please be more adroit in hiding it."

154. In chorus loud the host of witnesses
began to laugh to see his cheat exposed.
The hall reverberated with the sound
of dainty clapping hands and beating wings.
Ashamed at their amusement and confused,
the irate god rose from his gilded bench,
and asked Adonis to assume his place
and to play out the half-completed game.

155. At this predicament Jove's messenger
and infant Cupid form a mutual pact
together, each one keen in rivalry,
to join in with the others in the match.

The quiver-bearer joins his mother's side,
while Mercury supports Adonis' cause;
and now these clever rivals fix their terms,
as for the wager they declare the stakes.

156. As forfeit Mercury, if victor, claims
a golden net, the knots with diamonds twined,
for this he hopes would serve his purpose well,
ever to make secure his secret prey.
If Cupid wins, he wants the magic wand
that plunges into Lethe one who wakes,
thus to be able in nocturnal frauds
to put to sleep a watchful guardian.

157. The young Adonis moves with sage advice,
and, prudent for his troops, commits no fault.
When to the king on his majestic throne
a fierce white horseman threatens to give chase,
an archer slays him with his bow, but soon
the archer falls, struck by a trooper's blow,
and that one by another; lo, each knight,
each elephant and archer joins the fray.

158. The battle rises, mingled and confused,
with alternating roles and accidents,
as when the Ionian Sea begins to swell
and toss, tormented by conflicting winds.
The bold white Amazon darts back and forth
among the ranks of hostile blackamoors,
and in her sallies and retreats she brings
to earth one bowman and one elephant.

159. She passes midst the foe, and thundering
she cleaves the press like dart or lightning flash;
their squadrons all hold back and everyone
yields ground, surrendering a path to her.
She, trusting her facility to range,
whence she can always make a quick escape,

in her maneuvers spies out hidden lairs,
opens a breach, and levels rows of troops.

160. Envious then the leader of the blacks
calls to the skirmish his own warlike queen,
and, lo, infuriated by the fight,
precipitously she too cuts a path.
She scatters in disorder right and left
foot troops and bowmen, knights and elephants.
Who can recount the slaughter and the din
created by those two high-minded queens?

161. At last these two come face to face, well matched,
of equal strength and equally arrayed.
Now, now the white lifts high her pointed shaft,
assails her adversary on the flank.
But if this one is slain, that one repents;
with fate unkind, she by an arrow dies,
thus it befalls that victory is won
by mortal blow but short-lived is the joy.

162. Anon the husbands of the vanguished queens
both seek to draw back to a safe retreat,
bewildered, harassed in the bloody fray,
which has so many warriors sacrificed.
However, not completely robbed of strength,
they still can battle to defend themselves.
Three troopers has the fair Cyprina still,
one archer and a towering elephant.

163. And thou, Adonis, hast an equal force,
save for the towering beast that bears the fort,
who in the fatal combat not long since
was by the hand of sagittary slain.
The rest the struggle now has carried off,
a horrid tempest swallowed up the folk.
A sad and tearful scene it is to see
the grim arena almost void of men.

164. The captains with no consorts at their side
     stand lonely mid the carnage and the strife;
     though weary and afflicted by their lot,
     they bend their wills toward second marriages.
     With this in mind the white commander views
     the faithful servants of his former wife
     as choice for royal consort, but at first
     he thinks to test the courage of each heart.

165. He urges one to leap the hostile trench,
     another to attack the citadel,
     to see which has the most intrepid mind,
     which is the boldest and best versed in arms.
     The game forbids by law that subject maid
     may e'er aspire to marriage with the king
     except for one alone, who shall succeed
     in scaling the opponents' last defense.

166. The chosen handmaidens cut short delays,
     the bright reward makes all the path seem smooth.
     But one who holds the third post on the right
     outstrips the rest, while they are held in check.
     Ambition now puts wings on her swift feet,
     in spite of all restraints she forward flies,
     and little can the ruler of the blacks
     impede her on her glorious path of war.

167. Whence as she lures the enemies, she spurs
     her friends by her example to bold deeds,
     and though a black advances toward the breach,
     too late he comes and misses by a step.
     And, lo, unscathed, the maid in white at once
     attains her goal, the vacant marriage bed,
     and to the plaudits of her comrades gains
     the scepter and the crown which she has earned.

168. With pride and joy over the diadem,
     she looses rein on her new course with zeal,

and once possessing freedom of the field,
repays their devastation to the full.
There falls, transfixed, a dusky Amazon
who lacked but one pace of her final goal;
the other troops dispersed, the king, confused,
is finally hemmed in by the assault.

169. The son of Maia, at Adonis' side,
     wishing to assuage his hopless grief,
     and looking for new arts to please, observes
     that Venus has her mind on something else;
     since she, intent on touching foot with foot
     of the beloved youth beneath the board,
     heeds nothing else, and would be sad indeed
     if she should win the game and lose his heart.

170. The god now sees his chance, and furtively
     into the golden casket which is tomb
     for corpses of those soldiers slain in war
     he reaches with his silent, nimble claws.
     A dusky archer and a jet-black knight
     he snatches, and returns them, now revived,
     to fight again; but since his moves are watched,
     he gets an aid to carry out his scheme.

171. Sly, he incites to execute the fraud
     Galania, a nymph of Venus' train,
     no less adroit of hand and sharp of wit
     than youthful and demure of countenance.
     When all Adonis' squadron is laid waste,
     she slips out two fresh warriors on the field,
     of which one wields the bow, the other one
     in battle neighs and prances, snorts and stamps.

172. The goddess of the myrtle and the rose,
     when noticing the new and startling aid
     supplied the enemy, deems it most strange
     how she at once could win and also lose.

Raising her glance, amazed and dubious,
she catches a sly smile from Mercury,
at which, the trick perceived, "That's quite enough,"
she says, and scatters pieces far and wide.

173. Then springing from her seat excitedly,
consumed by wrath which seethes within her breast,
she rushes at Galania and strikes
a blow that robs her of her loveliness.
Ah, what a fool is he, how ill advised,
who ventures to oppose a will divine!
The wretched maid was beaten on the head
with chessboard, which now hangs around her neck.

174. With furious force the sad, afflicted nymph
was so belabored by the wrathful queen
that, bent and changed into a hollow shell,
the pattern of the chessboard marks her back.
The light of her fair eyes now fades away,
the gold of her blond head now vanishes,
her neck, in semblance of a snake or fish,
contracts and stretches out, jerks back and forth.

175. Her body shrunk becomes at length concealed
within a spotted shell up to her neck.
Henceforth she needs must travel on four feet,
and make her progress with great tardiness.
Into a turtle is the nymph transformed,
wherefore she hides herself in caverns deep;
and evermore she carries everywhere
the burden of her dwelling on her back.

CANTO XVI

The Crown

[A king is to be chosen to rule jointly with Venus over the Island of Cyprus. The whole affair is conducted less like an election than a male beauty contest; the features and costumes of the handsome young contestants are reported in detail, their assets and their blemishes are closely examined by a group of elderly male judges. The final verdict rests, however, not on the decision of the judges but on the determination of the gods as revealed through the power of the chosen one to lift the golden crown from the statue of Venus and claim it for his own. Like the sword in the stone, the crown cannot be budged by any but the appointed one.

The candidates in the contest are, almost without exception, beardless youths whose charms are catalogued in language reminiscent of the conventional descriptions of the heroines of romance. The pleasure of viewing their delicate features and

exquisite costumes is heightened by contrasting descriptions of
the dried-up old men who are serving as judges at the court.]

THE CONTEST FOR THE CROWN OF CYPRUS

78. Prince of Epirus, Cupidorus fair,
    was first of claimants to present himself.
    His eyes were of a gentle sapphire blue,
    over which projected smiling brows.
    His lips were of the purest Tyrian hue,
    within which were encased bright, lucent pearls.
    His glance was calm, benign, his step was proud,
    a child matured or, say, a youth unripe.

79. Upon his brow the whiteness of pure milk
    is seen, without the slightest blush of red,
    but in his cheeks, where white is ruddied o'er,
    pomegranate tints contend with snow in one;
    the blend is such that they are equalized,
    as they were fused of rose and ivory,
    but now and then with two small dimpled spots
    a smile is wont to bring a deeper red.

80. On his blond head the Tagus [1] rolls in waves,
    his hair rains down diffuse in a rich mass,
    and down his back it is allowed to fall
    in tumbling billows streaming carelessly.
    Sky blue his mantle; and his tunic fair,
    whose border does not reach below the thigh,
    is of a shiny satin which reflects
    the azure color of his lovely eyes.

81. A silken bonnet, creased upon the crown,
    in color dyed a pure ultramarine,
    shadows his brow, and it displays a plume
    whose hue is like to the cerulean sky,

[1] River in Spain, golden colored from its sand.

and at the bonnet's crease a buckle fair
fastens and binds it with a brilliant pin
of sparkling ice, composed of that same gem [2]
which for incising only yields to blood.[3]

82. The living alabaster of the feet,
which shames the whiteness of the Milky Way,
is clad with buskins of an azure hue,
laced along the calf with crimson strands,
in which gems were inlaid by clever hands
of craftsmen in an intricate design,
and golden figurines in bold relief
were fashioned for the buckles' ornaments.

83. Not so many eyes the pompous bird [4]
has in his roseate feathers spread about,
when as an April or an evening sky,
with hundred flowers or hundred stars adorned
he opes the wheel of that rich theater,[5]
proud and beautiful, to a new day,
and showing off its treasures to the full,
is for himself the spectator and scene;

84. as, filled with pleasure and with pride, the youth
attracted all the glances of the crowd
when, moving toward the altar which contains
the semblance of fair Venus, he advanced;
usurping stares, he stole away the hearts
of all that vast and noble company,
and stupefied them with the marvels rare
of his arched brows and of his gemlike lamps.

[2] Diamond.
[3] Culcasi's note suggests that this refers to ruby ornaments, but the context does not appear to allow that reading. Probably it refers to the use of blood for cutting diamonds.
[4] The peacock.
[5] Peacock's tail, resembling the shape of a classic theater.

85. But yet the eye of Envy, which is keen
    as Argus [6] to spy out another's faults,
    examining the measure of that space
    which is the margin of the fount of smiles,
    at length made observations that the path
    where part the lips appears somewhat too broad,
    and that, in fact, the mouth, the shrine wherein
    the treasure of Love is put, sins by excess.

86. Uccubus, whose decrepitude, alas—
    his beak'd nose almost joined his pointed chin,
    his gullet cracked, and sunk his hollow cheeks,
    with only three teeth left in his loose mouth,
    his temples and his eyebrows peeled of hair,
    and bald his head, wrinkled his face and shorn,
    of wavering pulse and feeble intellect—
    pronounced this calumny against the youth.

87. The lad now hastened up the ample stair
    until he stood at fair Cyprigna's feet.[7]
    He offered prayers, used all his strength, and pressed
    for the desired award, but got it not;
    because when he prepared to take from her
    the crown within his hands, she held it close,
    and so at last backward with downcast eyes
    he turned his steps, confused and taciturn.

88. Just so a stag, whose tree of branching horns
    sometime is shed and fallen in the brake,
    in shame conceals himself in lonely vale
    and sojourns in a solitary den;
    and so a peacock who by chance has lost
    the jeweled fan with which it is adorned,
    wishing to flee the sun and hating light,
    weeps in sorrow for his missing plumes.

[6] Giant with a hundred eyes.
[7] At the foot of the statue of Venus.

89. Lucindus next came striding on the field,
who rules the race of far Bithynia.[8]
Let Pindus'[9] swan now sing such loveliness,
or Phoebus shower me with supernal streams.
Never from Ind to Mauritania
beheld the sun a white so delicate.
His body vaunts a richness of the flesh,
developed to a stage tender and soft.

90. Across the field where that fair face holds reign
the purest rays burst from a brow serene.
Injurious to the greatest planet's beams
the moving splendors of the two fair suns,
in whose gay, amorous lights an emerald green
nurtures moist glints of passion's ardent flame.
Tresses he has more red than blood or fire,
his brows are of a gold or saffron hue.

91. What rises in the middle of his face
is curved, 'tis true, but modest in its curve,
and of the extremities that mark its ends
one forms a point, the other ends an arc.
A little passage of the deepest red
locks and unlocks the lips in a sweet smile,
and where Love seldom bars them from the view,
between two shores of rose a sea of pearls.

92. His robe white damask flecked with diamonds
down to the heel, with cincture tightly bound,
which is completely lined with ermine fur
and hides the breast, but with the collar free
reveals to view the snow of fair, white neck
all bare, whence even ice would be consumed;
the cuisses of the same material,
with hammered silver shaped in lacelike trim.

[8] Province of Asia Minor adjacent to the Bosphorus.
[9] One of the haunts of the Muses.

93. A cap he has of velvet, also white,
     encircled with a band of finest gold,
     and on the left side is a heron's crest
     which a rosette attaches to the brim.
     A necklace which of rubies is composed
     adorns his throat, another girds his flank.
     The shoes he wears have silver ornaments,
     and golden buckles serve for clasps thereto.

94. Now he perceives himself observed, admired,
     displays himself to censure of the throng,
     nor does the star of Love, at its first rise
     at the beginning of a darksome night
     spread through the hemisphere so bright a light
     as he now sheds afar within those walls;
     he seems in his appearance like the dawn
     that with the sun's bright rays springs in the east.

95. All this is true, and there is only this
     where anyone could charge him with a flaw,
     that some few freckles on his cheeks are found
     which trifling blemishes cause injury.
     Perhaps 'twas Cupid's work, as he prepared
     to whet his arrows on the grinding stone,
     and while he was refining the gold tips
     he let some sparks fly in the young lad's face.

96. Mauriffus then, shrewd member of the court,
     intent on scanning every feature close,
     approached, weak and nearsighted as he was,
     with silver-rimmed eyeglasses for his aid,
     and has perceived his beauty languish there,
     for lack of grace, almost without a soul.
     "Of what avail," he said, "are cheeks of white
     and red, if there be want of grace and charm?

97. "This is that *je-ne-sais-quoi* pleasing note,
     which charms the eye and makes the heart content.

A living spirit, a pure ray from God,
the salt with which Love seasons his repast.
In him I see it not, and lacking that,
in vain he hopes for the triumphal goal.
We will now see whether our goddess shows
the outcome as it has appeared to me."

98. During this time the handsome youth proceeds,
till he has reached the altar for the test;
but all his effort proves of no avail
to carry off the prize that he desires,
because as though it were with nails affixed,
he finds the guarded crown unmovable;
whence, overwhelmed with grief and red with scorn,
as he had mounted, so he now descends.

99. Clorillus entered the arena third,
Clorillus fair, who in his early years,
a ward, deprived of both his parents' aid
through death, endured untimely suffering.
Whence, since the fates assigned him the domain
which the great tyrants over Cyrene [10] hold,
his mighty scepter reaches out as far
as the wide tract of Lybian plain extends.

100. The ever shifting and tempestuous sands
resolve cadavers into mummies there.
Fierce Africo [11] with its dark tempest brings
grim floods of sand, whirlwinds of yellow dust;
and he who dares to cross becomes engulfed
at times mid grains of the inconstant flood.
Strange shipwreck where a man submerged appears
pilot on land and pilgrim in the sea.

101. But what can greed for empire not provoke?
In Cyprus he another fortune tries.

[10] Capital of Cyrenaïca, district of North Africa.
[11] A wind off the desert.

Not white his handsome face, yet 'tis not black,
black are his eyebrows and his pupils brown.
His brow shows two diminished little stars,
indeed two clear, full moons, without eclipse,
than which 'tis certain, by your leave, O stars,
the eighth sphere has no lights more wondrous fair.

102. Brown tresses inundate this third young prince,
a lion's skull he for a helmet wears.
Pleasing is his mouth and rubicund,
which is not too compressed nor too spread out.
He shows a friendly smile and jocund air,
of stature medium and delicate,
so that each member of the audience
stands stupefied and covetous at once.

103. Gleaming garments mantle his fair limbs,
of silvery and particolored cloth,
with many sunflowers in gold relief
embroidered on the border of the cloak;
and they are covered with a host of gems
from which so bright a splendor flashes out
that they would dazzle the beholder's sight,
were it not for the brightness of his eyes.

104. No one more fair and nobly formed could e'er
be born upon this earth, subject to death;
and surely one who viewed him from far off
would judge him an immortal at first glance.
But coming closer he was recognized
for mortal on account of one defect.
A single blemish was discovered there
which made obscure his many other charms.

105. "I do not wish, indeed," Sonorre said,
a subtle critic and a friend of truth,
whose venerable beard with double strands
poured o'er his breast in flowing silver streams,

"indeed I would not shame those other parts,
but of his hand, only his hand I say,
it lacks the purity of milk or snow,
and is too short and thick to suit good taste.

106. "Among the gifts that Nature in herself
unites, the hand claims not the highest praise,
since its own beauty does not ravish us
but it makes other features far more fair.
This skillful artisan can beautify
the face and breast with color and with flowers,
and adding red to lips and gold to hair,
what beauty beauty boasts is thanks to it.

107. "Fair eyes and flaxen tresses, pardon me;
sweet lips, excuse my zeal, I beg of you;
though you be freshest roses, rubies bright,
though you be glowing flames and threads of gold,
I still would yield the palm of loveliness
to alabaster whiteness of the hand.
As purple yields to pearls, just so must gold
give place to ivory and fire to snow.

108. "Though beautiful, the brow, the hair, the mouth
are not, as is the hand, a pledge of faith.
Those are for gazing on, this touches you,
and renders happy who possesses it.
From those Love shoots his dread and fiery darts,
while this can heal the wounds that he inflicts;
those light the tinder which inflames the soul,
this soothes the burning and relieves the hurt."

109. He ceased with these remarks, nor were his words
fallacious, as was manifest in fact,
wherefore if fair Clorillus had indeed
ascended to the summit of the steps,
yet when he had arrived thereon, alas,
it was not vouched him to remove the crown;

so, turning to the post he lately left,
a new contestant ventured to the fore.

. . . . .

150. After him proud Lucifernus comes,
a Saracen of Scythia so called.
Subject to him are Saca, Bactrian;
Margian he won, his home Sarmatia; [12]
he hopes to carry off the envied crown
because of his full beard and flowing hair.
Rugged limbs he shows and robust frame,
head long and thin, full nostrils, narrow brow.

151. His piercing eye, 'twixt black and greenish hue,
strikes terror in the hearts of all around.
And with grim lightning flashes he displays
the fierce and savage gleam of those dark lights;
his bearing haughty, offers signs and threats
of havoc and of dire atrocities,
which seems like Aquilon when, raging fierce,
he battles with the wild Aegean Sea.

152. Over a coat that is blackberry dyed
is stretched a net of gold, subtle and rich,
whereon the angles of the mesh are linked
and intertwined with knots of inlaid gold;
he wears a cape suspended from one shoulder,
which is draped under the other arm;
the border of it dangles to the earth,
and trailing wipes the pavement in long streaks.

153. A curving scimitar hangs at his hip,
short and broad and fancily inlaid;
a quiver at his back and curving bow
at his left shoulder on a transverse strap.
About his head a globe of snow-white cloth

[12] Ancient names for provinces of Russia.

arises, as the barbarous custom is,
a towering heap of convoluted bands,
in form much like a pyramid bizarre.

154. With head held high and nostrils showing red,
with furious and formidable face,
puffing a dense cloud of smoke he moved,
much like a lion menacing his foe.
He bared his back, which showed well set and stout,
he swung his sinewy and sturdy arms,
arms threatening great force and violence,
with veins and muscles standing in relief.

155. All stand and gaze at him, quiet and fixed,
except for Scommus, old and ill-disposed,
a satirist more than a jester he,
his slow feet burdened with a humor vile,
which nourishes a hidden piercing chill
within his secret ligaments and joints,
whence bent and stooping o'er a crooked staff,
he leans the burden of his weary frame.

156. He shook his head, he creased his brow and showed
expressions of contempt and mockery.
"Be off," he said, "and there beneath the Bear
hold sway among wild beasts, monster from Hell.
What, has the governor of love's sweet realm
a need for prowess in great feats of strength?
No, no, thou art more worthy to command
on Arimapo's peaks or Riphaeus.

157. "Who, in that iron-grey hue and in that face
'twixt ash and olive cast of that great hulk
of muscled cavalier does not perceive
the image of the Furies or of Death?
See you not what sanguine lightnings dart
and flash oblique and jagged from those eyes,

with which he boldly would commence to sow
vile hate among the beauties and the loves?

158. "A prince, a king—I will not say—of realms
which often are the gifts of insane fate,
but yet unworthy of the name of man,
a bestial spirit clothed in human form;
vile thoughts, crude heart, brute ingenuity,
a villain soul intent on vicious schemes,
I see in thy felonious countenance,
which shows thee to be base born and ill bred.

159. "And entering thus the honorable trial,
this goes beyond the worst audacity,
as if he were the god that lightens day,
or that fair lad who bears the bow and torch.
Ne'er villainy was dear because of valor,
but gentleness is more than beauty prized;
Love strikes him soonest who is least ferocious,
and gentle beauty wounds more readily."

160. His speech concluded, turning now his eyes
to the barbaric, insolent young prince,
he watches him descending from the altar,
impatient, trembling at the strange rebuff.
Accusing with his gloomy countenance
the goddess of injustice, cruelty,
hating the flame and arrows of the son,
he rolls his eyes about, gnashes his teeth.

161. Just so an untamed bull upon whose back
the hard and weighty yoke has never pressed,
when he has left within the pleasant vale
the victor rival who has vanquished him,
bellowing he roams the desert path,
a frustrate lover and disconsolate,
who filled with anguish and a heavy heart,
abhors the fountain and cares not for grass.

162. The dying, half-light of the sun, almost
immersed within the sea, was growing pale,
and that great shadow which was wont to stretch
across the sky discolored heaven's face.
With steaming sides and coats all flecked with foam,
the flaming coursers folded in their wings,
inclining toward Hesperia's distant shore
to pasture in the golden, western fields.

163. Dismayed at the dark shades and little pleased,
the youthful throng began their slow return,
and, the assembly being now dissolved,
the elders toward their lodgings made their way.
But till the greatest planet should arise
from Indus to arouse the coming day,
for fear of theft and treachery they left
a host of guardians to watch the crown.

164. The light of dawn was harsh and feeble still,
the sun was moving upward on his course,
nor yet had morning's early rays dried up
nocturnal dews upon the humid grass,
when all the handsome, proud, aspiring youth,
together with the noble parliament
came with the same solemnity and pomp
to gather in the customary place.

165. At once began the trials to select
the best of all that were assembled there,
but not a one was found who could surpass
what others had performed the day before.
The ministers and judges of the realm
stood horribly abashed, their heads hung low,
confusion in their breasts and in their hearts,
as though of every hope they were bereft.

166. But in the west Apollo, tired at last,
had brought to rest his gilded chariot,

and his fair sister with her shining horns
was scattering from heaven the darksome clouds;
wherefore, since everyone desired to go
and rest his limbs within his harborage,
the senate had departed thence, when lo,
the model of all beauty entered there.

167. The fair Adonis, who with secret aid
of Mercury and Venus and her son,
thus late, although by easy paths and short,
had reached the city, where his sire had ruled,[13]
by night made entry through the lofty gate,
after the congregation had all left,
and by the lamplight he began to view
the many wonders of the noble fane.

168. At length within a corner of the shrine
he stretched his weary limbs on the hard floor,
and scarcely had the night dipped in the west,
when shortly from his sleep he was aroused.
Awakened, by the light of kindled torches
he started to observe the altar well;
meanwhile the guards, heads resting on their cloaks,
after long watching had succumbed to sleep.

169. There he meets Barrino, a clever Greek,
of rude extraction, vile and fraudulent,
for whose uncouth, diminutive physique
sour malice and betrayals compensate;
with pointed head covered with frizzled hair,
but with no more than four hairs on his chin,
which are of reddish cast but somewhat dark;
he has a felon's look and squinting eye.

170. He cloaks with brow intrepid and secure
his evil thoughts and animus malign,
the color never changes in his face

[13] Adonis was the son of Cinyras, former king of Cyprus.

which is bespecked with red and yellow spots.
He joins to ready speech a perjured tongue,
has smiling lips but poison in his heart.
He for a little gold would blaspheme thus:
"I do not know, I do not worship Jove."

171. He, while he moves about and walks in stealth
among the precious sacred ornaments
and seeks some means how, if no guard looks on,
he may some treasure ravage secretly,
spying the youth who as the sun shines bright,
at first him he surveyed from head to foot,
then he draws near, salutes and flatters him,
and warmly praises all his handsome parts.

172. He jests, and playfully and by degrees
he sets the field for his deceptive scheme,
and he persuades Adonis, for a joke,
to pluck the golden crown with his fair hand,
as if only to try if from its place
it can be moved, and if it fits his brow.
The youth, not pausing to consider well,
lightly took it up and put it on.

173. That other, stunned, can scarce believe his eyes,
is filled with envy for him and with hate,
and when the youth has worn it for a while,
the sly one begs him for it with feigned smile.
Trustfully Adonis grants it him,
wherefore Barrino hides it 'neath his cloak,
and with the trusty favor of dim light
the clever theft was made before his eyes.

174. At once he hastens to Astreus' [14] inn,
who long aspired to both the crown and realm.
Astreus was astir (he scorned repose)
even before Aurora had come forth.

[14] An official mentioned above, in stanzas 45 ff.

Now he begins his fable to compose
and lends such skillful color to his lies
that all those present when he tells his tale
lend trust to the incredible deceit.

175. He tells how on the summit of the stair,
there where one terminates the long ascent,
before the sacred throne where stands in gold
the image of the great divinity,
before the goddess, bowed and suppliant,
at night he was beseeching aid from her,
when lo, he felt, he found, he knew not how,
his brow encircled with that royal crown.

176. Happy the good old man gives thanks to heaven,
and through great joy sheds pious, heartfelt tears.
He takes Barrino by the hand and sets
his steps along the well-trod avenues,
and without formal order he proceeds
to where the third day's trial is to be held;
he waits not till the sun has left the realms
of Eos,[15] and the others follow him.

177. Meanwhile the conqueror of shadows drives
the lazy stars toward the antipodes,
and that black veil which horribly conceals
fair Juno's lovely, serene countenance,
parts with its eastern rays, slashes to bits,
and draws aside the hateful, darkling shades.
Now the fiery steeds in swift return
with their loud neighing summon the new day.

178. The herald of the gods, who had observed
the treachery of that deceitful thief,
now quickly changed his habit and his form
and brought Adonis to the company.

[15] Aurora.

He had assumed the guise of one unknown,
a grey old pilgrim from a foreign land;
and now he turns his glances toward the court
and those forthwith addresses with these words:

179. "Now shall a wicked fellow make so bold,
against decrees of fate and heaven's law,
that from the goddess who in Cyprus rules
he'd rob her treasure with rapacious hand?
Is he indeed unpunished, yea, e'en hailed
the island's ruler true, legitimate?
And is there no one here who will denounce
his crime to the deluded populace?

180. "This morn, when drunk with slumber lay the band
that held the temple in their custody,
I saw this noble youth take up the crown
and then entrust it to this evil one.
So let the goddess, whom I call to witness,
expose the fool as partner in the crime,
how falsely he usurped the stolen prize,
and show how in that tale he tells he lies.

181. "Therefore it seems to me strange and unjust,
contrary to celestial ordinance,
that he should go about so proud, bedecked
in gold, and cloaked in honors not his own,
and unto him who merits Caesar's name,
is judged by heaven worthy of the throne,
such honor is denied by this wise court,
and he defrauded of due praise and meed.

182. "But that this villainy be seen by all,
and that all doubt shall surely be dispelled,
then if the test is true as has been claimed
let him replace the crown where it belongs;
and once again from that same holy hand,
as he first took it let him take it now;

and should he fail to pluck it off, then let
the rich and famous vie for it once more.

183. "But riches, valor, and whatever gifts
the fates may pour with prodigal increase
can be of little profit to the man
who strives against a star's great influence.
Now should it come to pass that that bright crown
for which this noble court is in such strife
may not be plucked by any other hand,
let it be seen if this one can succeed."

184. The dignity of that imposing tongue
and countenance divine moved all the throng.
Then at Barrino each one gazed, who stood
in silence, trembling, pallid, and confused.
At once a gentle fragrance filled the air,
and turning 'round, the winged messenger
all in a moment vanished, disappeared
like foam upon the wave, smoke in the wind.

185. At so strange, unexpected prodigy
Astreus cried out, filled with solemn zeal:
"Praise to the gods, 'tis warning from the sky.
Who can avert what heaven has ordained?"
Barrino is now seized; with looks dismayed,
his heart o'erflowing with a frightening chill,
impelled by force he comes before the shrine,
and, impotent, confesses the whole truth.

186. Now 'mong the senators the lesser ones
concur in favoring Adonis' cause,
but then the richest and most powerful group
disdain him, murmur, criticize, and rage.
Astreus wants all to return at once
to make a last attempt to take the crown,
but quite in vain they try, not one can lift
or shake it from its firm, tenacious hold.

187. Now of those many youths who on that day
    would prove competitors for beauty's prize
    no more remained, when young Adonis came
    to overcloud the honors of the rest.
    The air became serene when he appeared,
    the light so shone day's splendors were increased,
    and as he walked, mid glorious applause,
    he won a thousand spoils of hearts and souls.

188. An early blooming rose sometimes appears
    upon a bush mid brambles and dry twigs,
    born in the snowy season of the year
    when all the fields are lying nude and brown.
    The elders, viewing this adventurer
    were captured by his wondrous loveliness,
    now deeming him, compared to other youths,
    a shining Phoenix mid the common birds.

189. He was within the bounds of that estate
    which makes the step from boyhood into youth.
    And from the calm, enamored lights shone forth
    a trembling ray of sweet serenity.
    Upon his delicate and tender cheeks
    the crimson of young May was freshly flowered.
    On lips the color of the living rose
    a sunny smile of angels seemed to spread.

190. Of rich vermilion is his vestment dyed,
    and gleams with ornaments of purest gold.
    An oriental band confines the waist,
    the border of the robe reaching the knee.
    Upon his shoulder rests a jeweled strap,
    from which sonorous ivory is hung.
    He bears a quiver at his back; and, lo,
    his feet are clad in boots of silk and gold.

191. His bare head has no other ornament—
    nor can one match the glory of his hair—

save for a strand of myrtle, thin and loose,
which strives to blend the emerald with gold.
It seems he turns a sphere at every word,
it seems at every glance a sun rolls round,
it seems at every smile he bears a flower,
at every step he tramples on a heart.

192. No more will I attempt to speak; nor yet
could I portray such beauty with my brush,
nor, blinded by the splendor of such rays,
could I reflect a portion of such light.
Hence, lacking art to carry out my aims,
since style is by the subject overcome,
as imitator of Timanthes [16] old
I'll place a veil of silence over it.

193. Among those gathered for the great event,
who waver in opinion dubiously,
how well might covert truth have lain concealed
beneath a cloak of false, deceptive veils,
were not that truth now clearly manifest
beyond further contention or dispute,
not only to the sage ones but to fools—
the brightest sun of those two lovely eyes.

194. The splendor of those eyes dazzles all eyes,
and that fair mouth locks every other mouth,
whence everyone concludes that verily
no beauty on the earth can equal this.
"Whoever seeks for mortal thing," they said,
"that soars to such a price is mad indeed,
not just for what the outward eye beholds,
but too for what the inward mind believes."

195. Just then a dove that, fugitive, alone,
had been that day miraculously spared,

[16] Ancient Greek painter.

from bloody, sacrificial knife escaped,
upon Adonis' shoulder came to rest.
Whence old Astreus, who rejoiced at this,
together with a host of soothsayers,
interpreted the act a fair presage,
foreseeing an auspicious state of things.

196. Here rose a universal, swelling shout,
of mingled praise and happiness combined:
"For him alone is gained, to him is due
the trophy, worthy boon for his fair eyes."
And with applause such as none had received,
(so that from many envy was perceived)
was heard a murmuring, clear and distinct,
which kept acclaiming thus: "He's won, he's won."

197. Just when the great event is to take place,
behold, outside the people raise a shout,
and lo, a troop of squires invades the shrine,
each bearing in his hand a gilded staff.
Whence, with the multitude in dire suspense,
they clear a widened passage in the hall
before a youth who, at first sight, appears
to have fair lineaments and graceful limbs.

198. Falsirena had him summoned forth
from out the far-off regions where he dwelt,
and where he ruled in lordly sovereignty
over Catizis, Pygmies, Arcamons,[17]
whence she brought him by her secret arts
and made him join the contest of fair youths,
that thus Adonis' rule might be denied
by the most horrid, most deformed of men.

199. Through a marvel unaccustomed, strange,
by two deformed seeds, shapeless he was born.

[17] Skeletons.

He was engendered by a dog and dwarf,
who was by force subjected to the beast.
She was the sister of Feronia,
who had been so displeasing to the youth,[18]
and who had so increased disgust in him
while the enchantress held him in her cave.

                    .   .   .   .   .

205.   . . .

He is called Tricane for his teeth, and he
reveals a form part human and part dog.
His body from the waist bears human form,
but what advances him is like his sire.

206.   Therefore was he named for the great teeth
which stuck forth from his snout at least a span,
the gleaming tusks that, like a savage boar,
caused him to spray his chin with bloody scum;
and often with these weapons in a fight
he ripped and slashed his foe more than with iron.
He speaks, but with a deep and horrid voice,
and with a raucous uproar howls and barks.

207.   His face was truly neither black and seared,
nor was it really white or bright of hue.
His hair was frizzled and his temples pinched,
in color the strange blend of Ethiope.
His head was huge, his bust was infantile,
defective part was with excess conjoined.
Here Erichthonius, Atlante [19] here,
a grafting of the dwarf and giant showed.

208.   Breast swollen, arms too long but haunches short,
a bristling beard, his pelt shaggy and stiff,

18 Adonis. The reference is to an episode connected with Adonis' captivity by Falsirena.

19 Atlante, a giant. The reference to Erichthonius is puzzling. He was
a mythical figure, the first inhabitant of Athens.

his eyes vermilion, lachrymose, and crossed,
his glances burning with ill-omened fire,
brows furrowed, cheek somewhat 'twixt dark and wan,
and under pallid lips are yellow teeth.
His hands are armed with vicious claws, and well
he shows he is the son of such a beast.

. . . . .

211. With magic liquors and with secret chants
the Witch had turned him to a youth so fair
that scarcely under sun could there be seen
more lordly or more gracious countenance;
and with him for attendants other men
converted likewise by her magic arts
from minute creatures of a race she ruled,
emaciated, horrible, deformed.

212. She bade him confidently turn his steps
toward Amatunta's halls without delay,
because to gain the throne of Cyprus isle
he would encounter no impediment;
she said that he would carry off the palm,
and triumph o'er all others' rivalry,
that all the beauty in the world combined
would seem an ugly sight compared to his.

213. Now here he came urged on by her and drawn
by his own light and frivolous desires.
Three times around and round the counterfeit
turned his false snout and eye in canine style.
He neither bowed his head nor bent his knee
in reverence or sign of a salute,
but midst the mighty throng assembled there,
he bore him haughtily of port and mien.

214. The cuckoo, now he's decked in other plumes,
advances toward the altar, proud to view.

He wears a scarlet vest of wild goat fur,
a collar with a double strand of pearls,
his vestments scented with a fragrant juice,
a blend of precious musk and ambergris.
A scimitar all damascened he wears
at his left side, a poignard at his right.

215. A scarlet cloak across his shoulders draped,
which is gold-streaked in herringbone design
and trimmed with gilded lace, and from a cloth
of similar design his hose were made.
A little bonnet of fine beaver fur
is topped by sweeping plume of purple dye;
his hands adorned with gloves of Araby,
and with a mincing, tripping tread he moves.

216. The magic lasted only till the time
that he approached close to the holy fane;
but when he stood before the form divine,
the meretricious phantom was dispelled,
the cloud was burst, the incantation spoiled,
and that false beauty quickly disappeared;
and e'en for the attendants suddenly
the marvel was transformed into a jest.

217. Like a man who, hidden by a mask,
deceives the crowd with lying outward show,
but greatly changed appears when he has doffed
the once deceptive veil of his disguise;
so did that grotesque specimen appear
when once he was returned to his true form;
and even Saliceus, who was esteemed
most vigilant of censors laughed at him.

·   ·   ·   ·   ·

229. Before the throne where fair Ciprigna sat,
arrived, with lifted face and bended knee,

Adonis spoke: "O deity benign,
for whom a holy ardor warms my breast,
if thou canst placate the malignant stars,
and if my destiny hangs on thy nod,
hear then my prayer: to this unworthy one
bestow the kingdom as thou hast thy heart."

230. At that fair speech the gentle deity,
like starry lamp in the serene of heaven,
unlocked a smile, and then at once held out
the golden crown and with it him adorned.
Ne'er so fair was great Apollo's brow,
when girt with shining rays and kindled flames,
or with a wreath of greenest laurel crowned,
as this youth's brow appeared adorned with gold.

CANTO XVIII

The Death

[Having reached the tragic climax of his tale, the author develops the scene and action of the hunt to the last detail, revealing
some fairly technical knowledge of the gear and the tactics involved in a boar hunt. The ensuing account of the lamentations
of Venus and the nymphs is presented with all of the pyrotechnics of his rhetorical artifice.]

THE HUNT

43. Several times since Venus had gone hence
    Adonis had explored the risky passes
    within that park, protected and reserved,
    and from those sallies had returned unscathed.
    Nor was it out of fear of lance or bow
    that those fierce beasts let him escape unharmed,

but from respect they felt for his fair youth,
and reverence for the goddess of the place.

44. Wherefore, such welling pride grew in his heart,
such confidence, that heedless now and rash,
presuming he no longer need restrict
his forays to that park, he waxed more bold;
at which the cruel destiny, which then
had ample room to execute its ire
through treacheries of both Diane and Mars,
closed in on him, while Venus was far off.

45. Aurora rose, but misty, sorrowful,
and with a pallid and a cloudy face
she showed the world a baleful heralding,
an evil omen of that cruel day.
She wore a veil of Night upon her head,
a garland stripped of leaves and stained with blood,
whereupon the sun was rising dimmed,
and seemed more like the evening than the morn.

46. Adonis, who the day before had raised
a hunting party in that same terrain,
more bands of hunters and of huntresses
invites, to have the hunt range farther out.
The gentle shepherd Clizio is there,
and promises to lend him faithful aid.
Fair Cytherea, in her parting words,
had said, "Adonis I entrust to thee."

47. Soon the most spirited, courageous dogs,
of which a multitude were gathered hence,
through thickest woods and o'er the open plains,
were sped and guided by their masters' hands.
Among them greyhounds came and terriers,
bloodhounds and bulldogs, mastiffs powerful,
the sons of English bitches, Corsican,
Sardinian, and some of bastard breeds.

48. Adonis, driven by audacious folly,
arms himself, prepares the murderous gear.
Over his shoulder he has slung the bow,
and at his side the ill-starred quiver hangs.
The curving horn he fastens at his back,
o'er which enamel gleams on ivory.
But still that ivory, though clear and white,
yields to the lovely hand and candid flank.

49. Besides his bow and arrows, in one hand
he bears a mighty staff, massive and gnarled,
which was the rugged trunk of wild holm-oak,
and at the end ironshod with sharpened point.
With his left hand he leads and manages
one of his hounds, his aid in every trial;
without the one the other ne'er sets forth,
such fine exchange of love and trust they have.

50. This was his favorite hound, that had been bred
out of a Spartan bitch with leopard sire.
Never was there a winged bird so light,
nor Parthian arrow ever half so swift,
nor rushing zephyr that did not seem slow
when it was measured by his speeding flight.
Ne'er with such speed does doe or tiger course,
that matched against that hound seems not to lag.

51. He had a spirit keen, a well-formed frame,
and he could skim the ground so light and quick
that often with his teeth he caught a buck
or speeding stag, thus stopping them in flight.
He had a serpent's head, feet of a cat,
back of a wolf, and panther's dotted hide.
Arrow his name, his course an arrow true,
but sharper than an arrow was his bite.

52. About his neck a collar neatly fit,
a splendid ornament which Venus fair

with her own hands had skillfully adorned
by intricate embroidery in brown silk.
And, without thinking, she had pictured there
in bold design a melancholy tale.
The cruel, fatal hunt of Cephalus
(dire augury) is woven in the work.

53. Thus equipped, his countenance secure,
setting his course where Fate was drawing him,
Adonis started to prepare the traps
for use in that sad, memorable hunt.
By now the eager hounds, their heads bent low,
pursue the distant scent of ferine track,
the greyhounds move by two and two, but still
no baying sound is heard nor blast of horn.

54. Adonis chose a station in the woods,
and held in check the tumult cautiously;
then all through the surrounding woods he drew
long lines of heavy cord, well stretched and tied.
Along these he attached a quantity
of trembling feathers, bright and many hued,
because the feathers, stirring in the wind,
would rouse fear and suspicion in the beasts.

55. That done, he gives the order of the hunt
and designates the guards for every path,
that when the time of the assault arrives
there'll be no need to call aid from elsewhere.
Each guards his post assigned, and every pass
is now closed off where paths lead through a ford.
Keen and intent to man the ambushes,
the well-armed hunters stand on the alert.

56. Now a mighty uproar starts to sound,
the heavens resound with barking and with shouts.
So much the clamor multiplies and spreads,
the woods are deafened and the air is stunned;

and thereabouts, stirred by the leading bands,
the crowns of trees are shaken with the cries,
and Echo answers back, who in those dens
rarely will respond to human voice.

57. Lo, suddenly out rushes from the nests
a host of gentle, harmless animals.
The humble hare keeps shifting course in doubt,
nor does the timid coney take slow steps.
A fleeing herd of ancient deer disperse,
dashing here and there, not knowing why.
The cunning fox alone refrains from flight,
whose aim is the deceiver to deceive.

58. But the too bold Adonis, who believes
his valor to be equal to his charms,
disdains as quite unworthy of his skill
the crowds of little, fleeing animals.
Proudly the handsome lad is seen to move,
and he aspires to test his prowess keen.
Lovely ferocity stamped on his face
has ruffled his sweet smile with haughtiness.

59. Thus the Thessalian youth would spend the day
in hunting to relieve the tedium
and to bring in the horrid hides of bears
and tigers slain to show his biformed tutor.[1]
Thus once perhaps did Carthage see the Trojan
hero [2] coursing through its savage woods,
and with bold front assume his post to wait
the lion charging from the mountain slope.

60. And in such manner I sometimes behold
great Louis lead choice bands of hounds and horse
along the pleasant valleys of the Seine,
to banish sloth by following the chase;
and with the unconquered hand that rules the Gauls,

---

[1] Chiron, the Centaur.   [2] Aeneas.

and that was born to govern warlike tribes,
among most lonely and deserted haunts
for pastime doth assault the unarmed beasts.

61. The woodland scene is with confusion filled,
as one with bow drawn is prepared to shoot,
one man repairs the nets, adjusts the chains,
one loosens ropes, another tightens some.
Others restrain by force the yelping hounds,
and others slip the leash to speed them on.
This one with raucous cry provokes the prey,
another scolds it from a beech tree limb.

62. Adonis all alone scours through the brush,
alone invades the thicket, climbs, descends,
until he comes upon a turbid pool,
the stagnant drainage left by many a shower,
and skirts along the shore, where he was told
a great and fearful boar makes his abode,
because he hopes to find and to destroy
that measureless but animated hulk.

63. "What leads thee to this voluntary grief,
rash youth, is it thy folly or thy fate?
Never the trophy of that pointed tusk
and hairy hide shall you bring from the hunt.
Change, oh, change that obstinate desire;
flee, oh, flee from the approaching death.
The boast of having killed a savage beast
would be too small a prize for such a risk."

64. The grass around him and the flowers seemed
to utter words like these and more besides,
they that were wont to draw strength from his rays
and take their fragrance from his scented breath.
"Turn back, O foolish one, where wilt thou go?"
the nymphs and shepherds urged him from afar.

"Ah, turn thy feet from this accursed pool,"
cried Clizio, his ever faithful friend.

65. "Flee, Adonis, flee the horrid beast;
oh, be not deaf to my most urgent prayer!
I must recall fair Venus to your mind.
Don't make her weep for thee and censure me.
Let not the zealous prodigy of pride
destroy the prodigy of loveliness.
Now may thy genius pardon me that I
advise against thy seeking such a risk."

66. He nothing hears and nothing heeds, but straight
advances where his reckless boldness guides.
He reaches that doomed spot where murderous star
has now prescribed for him the end of life,
there where the minister of mortal ills
lurks to ravage beauty's flower of flowers,
unlucky, infamous, ill-omened woods,
which offer refuge to the rabid boar.

67. Between twin hills that to the sun lift up
their shoulders, dense with briars and bare of flowers,
deep in the bosom of the vale between
there lies a little glade formed like a marsh;
surrounding it are walls of scaly flint,
and through it lies a solitary path;
those rough, grey rocks that bound it, sharp and steep,
permit a single narrow pass, no more.

68. There in the midst of limp and baleful reeds
among deep shadows lies a stagnant pond,
which laps against the filthy, sterile stones
with livid dankness of the putrid waves.
Around the shores there are but few small strips
of level ground (so rugged the terrain),
but one small open space along the path
is there discerned, with slopes or caverns framed.

69. The cattle ne'er approach that dismal shore,
    however tired and panting from great thirst,
    for they refuse to taste the fetid stream,
    or graze the noxious grass along the brink.
    Not only is it shunned by nymphs and fauns,
    abominated by the sun and winds,
    but from the impure, interdicted banks
    even the wolf and owl in horror flee.

70. This is the haunt—I will not say of boar—
    but of the wrath of heaven that nurtured him.
    Silent now the outcry of the scourge
    that ravaged ancient Caledonia.[3]
    Not savage Araby nor Garamant
    e'er held a monster equal to this one.
    Here he crouched, and in the murky pool
    the solitary beast immersed his frame.

71. In the slough which stretches half a mile,
    among the marshy reeds he settles low.
    A gleam of horrid, fierce malevolence
    appears upon his dark and threatening brow.
    His reddish eyes appear like fiery torch,
    like sparks from hammered iron or fresh stirred coals.
    His hide is toughest leather, his rough back
    a hirsute breastplate armed with bristling thorns.

72. From his great snout, slobbered with bloody foam
    protrude long, bony tusks, hook-shaped and sharp,
    whose substance, which is stiff and hard as iron,
    is stronger, sharper far than tempered steel;
    whence, when he chomps and grinds them in his ire,
    he threatens death before inflicting it,
    wherefore 'tis hard to ascertain in truth
    whether the victim dies from wounds or fright.

---

[3] Hercules killed a boar that infested the Caledonian woods.

73. Amazed to see a beast so huge, at once
    Adonis blows a blast upon his horn,
    at which a host of nymphs and followers
    with all their dogs and spears is summoned round,
    who try to drive the grisly beast from out
    the muddy passage of that fenny ditch.
    The woodlands tremble at the mingled cries
    and barking, and the caves are brought to life.

74. Now the proud boar, who harbors in his breast
    the fury of two gods, up rears his head,
    advances boldly, rolling his fierce eyes
    and grinding with his cruel, rabid tusks;
    he snaps off reeds and crashes through the briars,
    trails ivy after him, and crushes thorns,
    and turning furious at the hue and cry,
    he rushes from his den to hunt the woods.

75. As when Aquilon [4] swiftly, foolishly,
    casts off his chains and breaks his barriers,
    and, rising in thick mists o'er Scythia,
    collects the arid and tempestuous clouds,
    while blasting, he puffs out his blackened face,
    he causes trees to tremble, leaves to fall,
    he sweeps across the spacious plains of ocean
    and lashes horribly the rocky shores;

76. just so the ugly beast, at last aroused
    out of the confines of the muddy marsh,
    creates a shattering sound through all the woods,
    shakes the oaks and bends the beech and pine,
    he loosens rocks and he uproots the trunks
    of ancient shrubs, most massive and robust;
    whence, like a stormy hurricane, he spreads
    destruction, striking terror everywhere.

[4] The north wind.

77. He turns his head this way and that, he grunts
    and snorts, more furious than a raging bull,
    and while he makes his passage through the woods,
    he tramples down whatever blocks his path.
    However, he cannot avenge himself
    on those who goad him, for they turn and flee.
    Without once making use of those fierce tusks,
    he wards himself only with frightful eyes.

78. Traversing thickets dense and wooded ground,
    in spite of all he boldly makes his way,
    the double nets and the thick-woven mesh
    he tears to bits and scatters on the ground.
    He comes on with a rush, beats spears aside,
    and furiously he smashes sharpened spits.
    If he but stares or bites, his glance is keen
    as ligntning, and his teeth shoot sparks of fire.

79. He opens up the ranks, attacks the bands,
    nor are there those who dare confront him there.
    His fury wells, and dreadful signs he leaves
    among the throng, a Hebrus filled with blood.
    All objects overcome, he makes his way
    by force, as hunters everywhere take flight,
    and then from various rocky vantage points
    far off they hurl their spears or fire their darts.

80. He passes through the fords among the crowds,
    now broken up, and cares naught for their blows,
    nor is his hide pierced even with a scratch,
    so sturdy is the armor of that brush.
    He has laid waste the dogs that followed him,
    that several now are lying on the plain.
    The cruel tusk leaves many a hound unseamed;
    it quarters some, for others rips the throat.

81. Adonis, who perceives the monstrous beast
    wreaking so great carnage in the field,

is undismayed, and thus with arms in hand
he rushes to encounter the beast's ire.
Here he is, arrived, so far from friends,
here he has the beast so close at hand,
as close, perhaps, as cast from sling or shot
from bow will go, discharged by sturdy arm.

82. He has now drawn his bow and set the dart,
he aims and shoots, and strikes him where he aims;
but so strong is the cuirass of his skin
that though it hits the mark it does not wound,
thus not only is the shot in vain,
but more than ever it provokes his wrath,
and that great fury which had filled his breast
grows more intense and knows no bounds or check.

83. Ferociously he rages, rushes in
and scuffles with the mastiffs of the pack;
the bristles of his snout, shaggy and sharp,
are ruffled and his tufted back as well.
The fires gleaming in his little eyes
appear to steam, he madly twists and snorts;
those horrid lamps all flecked with blood appear
as though they'd dry up rivers or burn fields.

84. Still Adonis' courage does not fail;
he takes a second arrow finer far,
and hopes to turn it crimson in the boar,
because 'twas fired in Aetna by a god.
To his misfortune he has taken it
from lovely Venus's young archer son,
whence in its fiery and malicious heart
were coupled double furies: Ire and Love.

85. The arrow, which thus pierced the monster's flank,
inflamed with human zeal the inhuman soul,
whence, as he turned his glances toward the youth,
who from afar had pierced his unharmed side,

enchanted, and not caring for his hurt,
but, better to behold him, stayed his course,
and, greedy for that beauty so desired—
oh miracle—he irritates the wound.

86. Who then will be amazed that Bibli burned
with infamous desire for a brother?
that Myrrha, she from whom Adonis sprang,
was kindled passionately for her sire?
What marvel is it then that Love inflames
this one or that for one of his own kind,
if in the heart of beast there came to be
a fire so monstrous and so violent?

87. The doughty hunter, seeing that the boar
has turned about and is approaching him,
seeks not to climb for safety beech or elm,
nor to escape within a hidden cave,
but casts aside his bow and turns the point
of spear in the direction of the shore,
and where the pathway intersects the ford,
intrepidly he stands at the defense.

88. First he lets slip brave Arrow's ornate leash,
his finest dog; and once the band is off,
the greyhound, unaffrighted, rushes in
and makes a leap to seize him by the ear.
The boar twists round his snout just when the dog
attacks and digs the curved tusk in his neck.
He slits the throat of the courageous hound
with his foul fang, already stained with blood.

89. Adonis hears his faithful hunter moan
and turns to where he lies in mortal pain,
and as he looks at him, a kind affection,
warm and tender, shows upon his face.
He runs in pity where the dog lies prone,
unhappy to be parted from his lord,

his spirit calls to him for aid, he rubs
him with his snout and pats him with his paw.

90. Adonis grieves so, is so furious
because his tried companion lies in death,
that while he plans to carry out revenge,
daring more than reason governs him.
And, wise or foolish, for what's done he wills
death to him who caused that one to die.
He cares not for his life, assails the swine,
nor questions if alone he can succeed.

91. Desperately he hastes to take revenge,
striving where valor is of no avail,
exposing him to voluntary risk
because of his affection for the dog.
He makes for the ferocious one, then waits,
and brandishing his spear, he then attacks.
His weight on his left foot, he hurls the spear,
and follows the right hand with the right foot.

92. With his soft hand he drives the hardy iron
against the boar with all his youthful strength,
but even a more robust arm and sure
could never penetrate where he has struck.
The sharp steel point, as though encountering
a solid wall or rugged whetstone's flint,
as though the tip had struck an anvil's face,
rebounds without a single drop of red.

93. On seeing that, Adonis finds himself
repentant but too late, takes better thought.
Frightened, he now thinks of some escape
if possible, and he decides to flee.
Because, in staring at the beast close by,
he sees that fierce light on its horrid brow
which streaks the sky when mid the broken clouds
night with a fiery trident sunders them.

THE DEATH OF ADONIS

94. As he flees, the lovesick beast pursues,
    holding the track behind him then, intent
    upon the one who has enamored him,
    and bent on taking him in his embrace;
    then suddenly an unexpected wind
    (I know not if 'twas Mars or Cynthia),
    to bring about his final agony,
    lifted up his robe and bared his thigh.

95. All hot with love the foolish, reckless beast,
    without conceiving what he was about,
    longed to kiss with ugly, cruel face
    that flank which overcame the very snow,
    and thinking to caress the ivory
    he with his tusk impressed his mark therein.
    The blows were loving; Nature never taught
    the creature other amorous acts than these.

96. Adonis, brandishing his spear, resists,
    but that one rushes in and presses him;
    he quickly twists his tusk, the cruel one,
    catches the spear which struck and goaded him,
    and tears it from his hand; not satisfied
    because Adonis is not cast to earth,
    he knocks him down, and then with beastly arms
    he throws himself upon the fallen youth.

97. Striving to lift the garment's hem again,
    he tears the cloth; and flesh being exposed,
    with an assault both amorous and dire,
    he bites the hip beneath the raiment's trim,
    whence it soon appears the pure, white snow
    is all enameled o'er with ruby drops.
    And so the wretched youth lies slashed and gored
    upon the ground close by his well-loved hound.

98. Oh how he gently sighs and languishes,
    oh, what sweet pallor whitens his fair face!
    Not grim, for mid the horror and the blood
    a smile of pleasure lingers on his face.
    There reigns upon his drained and bloody brow
    love enshrined, and triumphs in his eyes,
    and those two stars, though closed and spent, still shine,
    and death on so fair face is beautiful.

99. Thou, Morazzone,[5] who with living hues
    presented him in death on living page,
    portrayed his loving goddess and the streams
    of bitter teardrops shed by her fair eyes,
    breathe thou upon my ink, empty of life,
    the vital air of thy exalted art,
    and may thy brush instruct my failing pen
    to picture him, though dead, still beautiful.

100. For him the gelid fountains burned with ruth,
    tough oaks and pines were moved to sympathy,
    for him the lofty alpine peaks poured down
    lachrymose streamlets from their leafy brows.
    The nymphs wept from their sheltered mountain haunts
    or wailed from out the depths of neighboring gorge.
    Dryads and Napae drown their eyes in tears,
    those who love the woods and these the streams.

101. Clizio rushed up, and with him came
    for succor, but in vain, that tardy crowd
    who recently had vanished suddenly,
    when they took cover from the beast in caves.
    Just so the robber wolf, in dark of night,
    sheltered by the veil of heavy gloom,
    when he has stained his teeth with blood of sheep,
    tail pressed to belly scurries to the woods.

. . . . .

[5] Piero Francesco Mazzuchelli, a painter called "Il Morazzone," 1571–1626.

THE LAMENT OF THE NYMPHS

132. Meanwhile Aurora from her balcony,
     dropping her moist eyes to the fields below,
     beholds the fair Adonis, breathless, dying,
     who still complains with feeble sighs and groans.
     She sees that every nymph accompanies
     with tears the cruel ending of the youth,
     and that they all, repeating his sweet name,
     beat themselves with palms and rend their locks.

133. They cry: "Dead is Adonis. O sad Love,
     why weepst thou not? Adonis fair is dead.
     A fierce and cruel beast with his sharp tooth,
     tooth fierce and cruel, foully murdered him.
     O Nymphs, do you not weep? Lo, suddenly
     Adonis fair, your joy, your happiness
     leaves the flowers moist with his own blood.
     Weep ye Graces, weep you little Loves.

134. "Low lies Adonis, comely youth, Adonis,
     boast of the vales, in lap of grass he lies,
     pallid, crimson-stained. O Muses, now
     forsake your smile, your song. Love, quench thy torch.
     Weep for Adonis, he deserves your plaints,
     torn cruelly by a voracious boar.
     Adonis, our Adonis, lives no more.
     Weep, O ye fountains, shed your tears, O shores.

135. "Let the fair goddess weep for her dear love,
     if from her sphere she spies him here below.
     No more he kisses, no more turns to her
     his sweet and loving glance as he was wont.
     More pitiless than murderous beast her heart
     would she not weep and sigh for dear Adonis.
     Let her distill afflicted eyes in tears.
     Weep, O ye woods, and answer, O ye hills.

136. "Adonis, wretched one, thy face in death
      weary, languid, pourest forth thy soul.
      Double wounds delivered at one stroke,
      Venus her heart, Adonis his fair flank.
      The flank of slain Adonis shows more white
      than is the tooth that bit it and more fair.
      Loudly now redouble your laments.
      Weep, O ye rivers, sigh you gentle winds.

137. "Unhappy hounds, your well-beloved master
      lies on the ground there, lacerated, cold.
      Weep for Adonis, and with barking hoarse
      fill the muted woods and rocky caves.
      Once happy woods, now grieving wretchedly,
      erst gay and clear, now dark and dolorous,
      through destiny, inflexible, malign.
      Weep, O ye stones, reverberate, O woods."

138. Thus, disconsolate, they made their plaint,
      and their lament was blended with deep sighs.
      At so sad spectacle Aurora fair
      showered down her dewy, silver drops,
      as though she wished to lend accompaniment
      to others' torments weeping evermore;
      and stunned by so surprising a mischance,
      she quickly gave to Venus news of it.

139. "Leave, O goddess, leave," to her she said,
      "the spinning of thy orb, which shines no more.
      Dost thou not see down there the horrid scene,
      (descend, what dost thou?) scene of death and grief?
      Now bind no more with roses thy fair locks,
      but rather wear dark cypress, mourning band.
      This is no time to course the circling path,
      while thy sun sets, guide to the other sun."

140. Not so a young pine in the Appenines
      trembles, shaken by old Eurus' ⁶ dance,

      ⁶ The east wind.

as was the lovely goddess moved to hear
the dread announcement of the dire event.
Dazed by the grief that seized her, suddenly
she stopped her course, her circle, and her star.
Stunned and half dead from mortal grief, at first
her plaint was checked and dammed up in her heart.

THE LAMENT OF VENUS

141. But when grief yielded to impulsive wrath,
and could effect escape from out her breast,
at times up to the stars, at times to earth,
she then began to cry out loudly thus:
"What earthly creature had such power and daring
while he who rules the pole [7] was yet alive?
Does my almighty father reign, or do
the impious Titans now hold sovereignty?

142. "Can it be, perhaps, Typheus fierce
has cleft in twain the rocks of Ischia?
Does Alcyoneus, though still oppressed,
now rear his forehead from Vesuvius?
Or does Briarius rise again mid flames
from out the vales of the obscure abyss?
Or has Enceladus, from Aetna fled
to Cyprus, there to see the light once more?

143. "Not yet has there sprung up in woods and streams
a vulgar race of rustic deities.
We are still progeny of that great god
who wields eternal fire in thunderbolts.
Who then presumes to violate my realms?
Is every law of heaven then dissolved?
What slaughters, ah, what evil strifes are these?
Do heavenly spirits harbor such great rage?

[7] Jupiter.

144. "O heavens unjust, not worthy of the stars,
worthy to lodge within your cloisters none
but monsters infamous, akin to that
which 'gainst my love has vented bitter spite.
O wicked tyrants of the eternal realms,
behold, now your desires are gratified.
How wrong is that scorned man who burns incense
or hangs up votive offerings to you!

145. "My love, who dead is deeply mourned on earth,
did never in rebellion 'gainst your power
make bold to drive the stars from out the sky,
erect huge towers, or heave up mountain peaks;
nor ever with a hand unfit for war,
but only used to tame beasts for the field,
did he attempt, with more than human reach,
to snatch your honors or usurp your realms.

146. "Go, seek out Scythian fanes, bloodthirsty Jove,
to satiate thy thirst for human blood.
Ah Juno, what offense, what harm did he
to thee, that bloodless, bloody innocent?
Did he, perhaps, bold and importunate,
seek the embraces of thy greedy spouse?
No, rather humbly, without pride, he lived
a hermit in a solitary cave.

147. "What help for him, alas? Since beauty rare
can never be concealed from envy vile.
Now proud and covetous, you reign above,
triumphing over me with your success."
When these words she had uttered to thin air,
then through the fresh and rosy fields of heaven,
transported by her damasked flock of doves,
with breathless speed she plummets down to earth.

148. Hecuba,[8] perhaps, in such a rage

[8] Wife of Priam, described by Dante as "barking" in her mad ravings.

went barking madly through the streets of Troy,
when she perceived her lovely daughter [9] brought
from Grecian altar drenched in her own blood.
And thus, methinks, in Babylon ran wild
the woman who had tried to reign by fraud,[10]
with hair part bound and partly flying loose,
her one breast covered and the other bare.

149. From far away she heard the woeful voices
of the wretched youths and of the nymphs,
and with her chariot's shaft steeply inclined,
she sped her courser-doves in downward flight.
But when she came to view at closer range
the ruthless work of that ferocious boar,
with that, to earth, distraught and desolate,
she flung herself down from her golden coach.

150. She drops down from the sky and plainly sees
the young Adonis brought to his hard end.
She sees the fair flank lightning-struck and rent
by cruel weapon, sharp and crescent-shaped;
and drooping o'er the shoulder the fair neck,
the mouth is languishing and motionless;
and seeing shut the eyes so beautiful,
she feels a deep wound open in her heart.

151. The pure ray of her eyes, fair and serene,
is covered with a misty cloud of tears.
Alas, what shame, what outrage she inflicts
to cheeks and to her curled and shiny locks!
She rends them and so stains the living May
of her fair face with bright, immortal blood,
and loosening the reins to her warm sighs,
with her injurious hand she beats her breast.

---

[9] Polyxena, who was sacrificed on the tomb of Achilles.
[10] The legend alluded to has not been identified.

152. She throws herself upon the lovely corpse
and like some mad bacchante wildly screams;
she tears her vestments, calling on his name,
regards the wound, and takes him in her arms.
She laves his dusty, bloody locks with tears,
with her soft hands she smooths the tangled strands,
and with her unbound tresses of bright gold
she wipes the tepid rubies from his chest.

153. Her lovely hand, which, weary and forlorn,
brushes off the dust, untangles knots,
in which the snow, tepid and gleaming white
of one and the other presses, tosses free,
and with that motion and that heat she strives
to aid, but still she cannot waken him.
She bends above the pallid youth, she shakes,
she presses him, and with sad words she sues.

154. The youth with muted speech for pity begs,
expressing his appeal through sighs profound.
The other one with eyes alone responds
to him by weeping streams of bitter tears.
"Ah me, what do I see? Is this Adonis?
Who wounded thee? How did it chance, and when?
Who, O my nectar, was the cruel one,
that over all thy sweets spread bitter gall?

155. "What monster vile, alas, what daring hand
seized such a license to effect my grief?
Why did not kindly fate, O my sweet life,
turn sweet again all his asperity?
Ah that a single wound should strike two breasts,
for in thy death my life was stricken too.
That blood of thine is my own blood, that pain
which racks thy body I feel in my soul.

156. "Did I not tell thee: 'Pray do not pursue
the track of savage beasts through treacherous vales,

for like the lightning's flash, that's quickly spent,
thou wilt run swiftly to an early end'?
If only my presages had been false
in auguring such dire calamity,
that now I would not see thy lovely face,
a miserable object stained with blood.

157. "Too keen a follower of the wild beasts,
and of my counsel too incredulous,
much better 'twould have been for thee to stay
within my park, where joy ever abides!
Now the sole trophy of thy daring hunt
is the perdition of my precious flame.
Unlucky beauty, lo, how in a moment
the climax of thy vital course was reached!

158. "Then will those same enamored eyes now go
to waken love within the breast of Death,
those fair white hands and lovely aureate curls
to whiten and to gild the horrid shades?
And will those flowery and fragrant lips
now sow sweet flowers within the dusky tombs?
Will then the splendor of that lovely face
bring paradise to the obscure abyss? . . ."

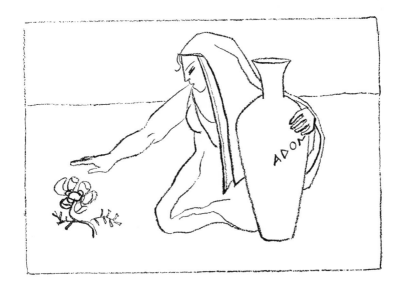

CANTO XIX

The Sepulcher

[The account of the funeral procession affords Marino another opportunity to treat a ceremonial occasion in elaborate and magnificent fashion. The mourners include many of the major and minor deities. (Mars and Diana are absent for obvious reasons.) There are hundreds of troops and numerous bands of damsels, some of them in armor and some in more dainty attire; there are chariots and "floats," flowers and music. Memories of classical literature and the ceremonials of Marino's day have been thoroughly exhausted to present the reader with a grand pageantry.

In contrast, the account of the funeral pyre and the ceremonies accompanying the burning of the body is given in a few stanzas.]

THE FUNERAL PROCESSION

359. Lo, the hollow copper,[1] curved and pierced
loudly resounds with a funereal beat,
and thus it gives the signal to commence
the long procession for the obsequies.
First old Astreus [2] with the Senate comes
among the major ministers of state;
amid these goes Sidonio in arms,
and with Dorisbe, robed in black, Argene.[3]

360. Quadrilles of heralds and of trumpeters
march solemnly before the horrid bier,
and after them there follow two long lines
of cavaliers selected from the best;
some ride on jennets, some on Irish mounts,
whose colors match their armor, black or dun;
now harsh, now faint, in soft and languid tones,
the breath of hollow brasses can be heard.

361. Of unicorns, ruled by the lightest bits,
a hundred pairs, richly caparisoned;
a troop of mounted Amazons comes next,
with breasts uncovered and with brief attire.
Not gilded arrows and gay painted bows
but burnished spears they carry at their side,
their raven tresses loosened to the breeze,
those nut-brown virgins, dark and untamed maids.

362. As many fair ones follow those dark-hued,
to sounds of tabors and of kettledrums.
Conches of incense on their heads are borne,
and urns of limpid crystal in their hands.

---

[1] The tympani.

[2] A high priest who was introduced in Canto XVI.

[3] The love story of Sidonio and Dorisbe was narrated in Canto XIV. Argene was the mother of Dorisbe.

The gowns they wear are drab and unadorned,
the mounts on which they ride are bridled stags,
their spreading antlers draped in mourning cloth,
and all entwined with branches pale and dry.

363. Next came the warriors of Canopus' [4] court
adorned with sanguine bands across the chest,
their squires proceeding, pages following,
and crowned with garlands of night-blooming flowers,
their hue like those which Ethiopia
supplies to us from fervid tropic zone.
Long cotton robes they wore in Moorish style,
and all are like in vigor and in youth.

364. At length a purple chariot, on wheels
of gold and ebony combined, is drawn
by twenty elephants in double rows,
which bears two ladies [5] woefully distressed.
A dwarfish driver rides each elephant,
each crowned with funeral plume upon his head,
their eyes are damp, pallid their countenance,
their mantles shadowy and stained with tears.

365. He who illumines sage intelligence,
eternal treasurer of golden light,[6]
without the laurel wreath to crown his brow,
and with no shining rays, he leads his train.
Pages and handmaids fair accompany him
as lord and leader of all other lights.
Time, with the Seasons, Weeks and Months and Years,
and Night and Day come pacing after him.

366. Upon a cart in shape of mountain rides
the god who over Delphi holds the reign;
and on its double peaks, with laurel crowned,
Parnassus' verdant image is revealed.

[4] City of lower Egypt.
[5] Dorisbe and Argene. mentioned in St. 359.   [6] Apollo.

Thereon a fountain is devised by art,
the which in silver waves and crystal pours;
and by the flood, in image true to life
is figured in relief a flying steed.

367. Nor would exalted Poesy deny
her presence to that solemn company,
and in her train she brought her family,
save Comedy alone, who came not there;
their habits were composed of black entire;
all blackened were the feathers of the swans;
their once white feathers and their purple beaks
had been deep tinctured with the purest ink.

368. The mourning Muses, with their eyes cast down,
languid and tender, and with troubled looks,
their locks with myrtle and with cypress bound,
each bears a golden lyre in her arms.
A hundred poets follow in their train,
each one likewise is crowned with wormwood wreath,
their dolorous and plaintive elegies
resound along the way for all to hear.

369. Mercury desired that with the band
of the blond god his own troop might be joined,
and in like fashion brings in his array
an equal host of fluent orators;
and there too is assembled every type
of artist, liberal or mechanical,
who march before, behind the effigy
of great Minerva, decked in mourning robes.

370. There too was seen the image—such as Rome
adored among a thousand palms of gold
and emerald—of Virtue, her bright hair
with olive and eternal laurel bound.
A host of others on their shoulders bore

a great caduceus,[7] immense in height,
of splendid art, and all of silver save
the serpents, which were of enamel formed.

371. Coming after those, in Thetis'[8] train,
great tabernacles, silver and crystalline,
bear statues of dread monsters of the sea,
whales and orcs, sea calves, leviathans,
and held in sea traps or in double nets
huge cachelots and ancient walruses;
there too are other creatures strange to us,
great hippopotomi and many more.

372. Next are drawn on wheeled contrivances,
created by the most ingenious art
and tireless industry, galleys and ships,
their sails of silver and their shrouds of gold.
With naked bosoms, whiter than pure milk,
come Nereids, their tresses tossing free,
and in their glistening white hands they wave
red coral boughs with many branching stems.

373. The goddess of the sea, with nymphs and youths,
upon a conch-shaped chariot proceeds;
as sirens and as tritons those appear,
her throne is of green stone with seaweed strewn;
and as they go they make a boisterous sound
while with a measured tread they move their feet,
and to the steady beating of sea shells,
their voices echo, tremulous, subdued.

374. One follows now who with large hand bestows
upon the throng gifts of abundant grain.[9]
Her mourning nymphs go spreading golden clouds
of corn from her huge cornucopia.

[7] Emblem of Mercury, a staff with wings and entwined serpents.
[8] A sea goddess who was the mother of Achilles.
[9] Ceres, goddess of grain and harvests.

Others convey upon a spacious board
various viands heaped abundantly;
whatever earth and air and sea produce,
whatever fire can dress appears thereon.

375. Another group transports the fertile horn
of rich abundance, fashioned of fine gold,
whose hollow is adorned with fodder ripe,
and is all brimming o'er with fecund seeds.
Surrounding this a squad of plowmen goes
with proper arms to cultivate that crop,
plows and mattocks, shovels, scythes, and sieves,
and all things else that serve the harvesting.

376. Accompanying Ceres' rustic aids,
baked by the burning sun, custodians
of mead and heath, Chloris with Zephyrus,
Pomona with Vertumnus [10] swell the march;
and these have hampers filled with golden fruits,
those pour out baskets laden with sweet flowers;
the flowing tresses of these deities
are circled with funereal cypress fronds.

377. Next the frolic, jocund god of wine
that foams and sparkles leads his company.
Well-chosen youths luxuriantly arrayed
transport a table with delightful foods.
Each bears a golden cup, with arabesques
designed, with liquid ruby brimming o'er;
and as they march along, from time to time
they sip the foaming cups and offer toasts.

378. Here is Philiscus, with green mitre decked,
a poet famed and Bacchus's high priest,
and all that crew which in those ancient times

[10] Chloris, goddess of flowers, was the wife of Zephyrus, the west wind.
Pomona, goddess of fruits, was the wife of Vertumnus, god who presided
over changes of the seasons.

was called Bacchantes, Macedonians.
Some with smilax, some with lentisk [11] crowned,
have framed with green their cheerful countenance;
and in a frenzy keeping time, some wave
aloft a knife, a thyrsus, or a snake.

379. A carriage with four wheels so exquisite
it makes Aurora's chariot envious,
a dame conducts amid those celebrants,
Nisa, the nurse of him whom Thebes [12] adores;
and it conveys the genial bed on which
his mother [13] once with the great Mover [14] lay;
and bears the crown of that same lord, with vines
and ivy round white fillets intertwined.

380. Behind the car came fifty old Sileni,
inebriate, each on a lazy ass,
forever chanting Epilenian [15] songs
and carrying great, bloated tiger skins;
and pouring wine from those same bulging skins,
they fill huge beakers that they bear in hand,
which overflow with pale juice or with dark,
and spill to strew the path with jeweled drops.

381. On a rich, golden throne Lyaeus [16] sits
resting against a moon-adoring beast.[17]
Eritrean purple is his Spartan robe,
of bright vermilion tinged with violet.
Etched in relief upon the throne appears

[11] An evergreen plant producing an aromatic gum sometimes used as a flavoring in liquors.
[12] Thebes was devoted to the cult of Bacchus.
[13] Semele, mother of Bacchus.   [14] Jupiter, his father.
[15] Epilenia, a Greek festival in honor of Bacchus (Dionysus).
[16] Another name for Bacchus.
[17] The panther, supposed to be put under a spell by the moon. Bacchus is often dressed in a panther skin.

the sad and tragic fate of Pentheus.[18]
A satyr who is seated by the throne
blows on a goat's horn with a raucous sound.

382. Then weeping, one, his red cap twined with mint,
the badge of Bacchus, his immortal sire,
came following the bier, without his staff
in hand, the shaggy-bearded, strong-limbed son.[19]
He straddles one of those grey, long-eared beasts,
and as he goes his head is drooping low.
The veins of his great neck are grossly puffed,
his nose is fiery and bloodshot his eyes.

383. After the tender of Lampsacus' [20] vines,
their lips with mulberry and elder stained,
a flock of biformed creatures, double horned,
a breed of demigod and demigoat,
satyrs and fauns and others of their kind,
rustic divinities, deprived of heaven,
advance propelling a colossal shape
drawn by a hundred ropes and windlasses.

384. That measureless colossus, gilded bronze,
is strangely fashioned in a phallic form,
a hundred cubits long and twenty thick,
so heavy that it makes the carriage groan;
and on the very vertex of the shaft,
where rubies ornament the metal tip,
so bright a star is seen to glisten there
it seems like Lucifer [21] mounting the sky.

385. Never among her columns witnessed Rome
a miracle so rigid and erect,
nor Egypt mid her edifices vast

---

[18] A king of Thebes, who was torn to bits by the women because he opposed the worship of Bacchus.
[19] Priapus, god of fertility.
[20] Principal seat of the cult of Priapus.   [21] The evening star.

could celebrate a greater pyramid.
A chorus of afflicted demoiselles
and wives from Gnidus and Cythera fair,
while singing doleful songs along the way,
shower it with garlands and festoons.

386. Next passed the cortege of that deity
who reigns in Cyprus,[22] with their diverse cares.
At their head a hundred archers came,
a mighty band, with bows and quivers armed,
bearing bucklers which were crescent-shaped
for lightness, and adorned with cuirasses,
in place of helmets gilded coronets.
And all their arms were azure trimmed with gold.

387. Another hundred, following the first,
the right hand heavy with great sword or ax,
of pure, well-polished silver was their gear,
their helms, their targes, and their cuirasses.
Next came the third and final regiment,
with ironshod poles and maces spiked with iron,
and differing in color from the rest,
their armor and their tunics were all black.

388. At their backs there came a hundred rams,
and of like hue a hundred stolid bulls,
all moving at a slow and gentle pace,
their necks submissive and their heads bent low.
Their backs were draped with cloths of damasked silk,
they wore gold collars and headbands of gold,
their horns were garlanded with apple boughs,
and with vermilion bands their eyes were bound.

389. And next there are the priests, an equal host,
with knives and axes for the sacrifice.
With them, in form and habit elegant,

[22] Venus.

a hundred damsels with their faces veiled;
they bear spikenard and leaves of amaranth
and stems of cassia select and pure
upon their shoulders stored in jeweled urns,
as with slow step they tread along the way.

390. Then other maidens blond and fair convey
yet other vessels filled with tears of myrrh,
and of the liquor which is hid therein
each damsel bears at least a thousand drams.
And no less than the first, the second band
is dressed in livery rich and beautiful.
Many wear crimson robes that reach their feet,
others in short, white tunics go attired.

391. Yet other ranks of infantry advance,
wearing no armor but with lances armed.
From Lybian desert and from Nubia
and negroes born in Ethiopia
go bearing ivory tusks and carvings rare
of ebony with purple ornaments.
Many of them are swinging censer pans,
and others carry torches or gold lamps.

392. Although Diane, for reasons we have seen,[23]
did not attend the pompous obsequies,
she nonetheless permitted huntresses
and hunters to accompany the deceased.
One led in hand a lithe and graceful pard
from Riphaein peaks, checked by a splendid leash;
others from the rocky Caspian shores
led tigers, panthers of ferocious breed.

393. A lion one, from sands of Africa,
and one a savage lynx from Thracian woods,
one leads a snow-white Russian bear, and one
a gryphon from the wilds of Scythia.

[23] Diana had conspired to bring about the death of Adonis.

Some with a mastiff or boar hound in chains,
come from Epirus or Hyrcania,
and some with brach or greyhound held in leash,
from Caria or Crete, pass in review.

394. Also come companies of falconers,
with camels, dromedaries, and giraffes
that bear upon their backs a heavy load
of ivory cages with exotic birds,
their plumage strange and various, such that
bright heaven itself has not more lovely hues;
from time to time they let some of these fly,
all free save that their feet are held with cords.

395. Lo, at last, the bier, which is adorned
with emblems and devices all about;
and by armed warriors spaced at intervals
along its sides two funeral palls are stretched,
and in a splendid patterned order set
are kindled brilliant candles everywhere;
and of those gleaming tapers even the wax,
like all the solemn draperies, is black.

396. The nymphs and demoiselles of Ciprigna
surround the catafalque on every side
and lend support to any of those youths
who seem about to fall along the way.
Besides are other handmaidens and squires,
who, grieving sore in aspect and in heart,
bear on their backs, a light, beloved weight,
the couch, the horrid inn of lovely limbs.

397. The last of all, swathed in cloth of black,
fair Venus ends the solemn funeral,
and with her face scarred and disheveled hair
complains against the cruel, envious stars,
from time to time e'en beating with her fists
her pure white bosom and her naked breasts.

      Before, behind, on either side she has
      a host of winged archers, faithful guard.

398. Arrived where she determines to consign
      the lovely corpse to the funereal flames,
      and where the dismal pile has been raised high,
      although unworthy of a gift so fair,
      Venus has the couch placed on the wood
      beside the lofty sepulcher's wide base;
      the fuel being lit and stirred by winds,
      she orders that the pyre be increased.

399. Now over the first branches, scarcely touched,
      the rushing flames are spreading rapidly.
      The jewels on the splendid armor sing,
      the gold begins to sweat, silver to melt.
      The burning brands distill Arabian gums,
      the pungent sap anointing them the while.
      Shrill sounds burst forth at melting in the fire
      of nard, of costum, saffron, cinnamon.

400. A nobler flame ne'er burned upon this earth,
      nor ever richer ashes were composed.
      One poured an urn of white milk on the pyre,
      another foaming cups of dark red wine.
      Still other hands pale honey scattered forth,
      while some cast diverse objects of rare worth.
      Others were sprinkling blood from slaughtered herds,
      to quench the thirst of those same ardent flames.

401. Casting in bows and arrows, nets and snares,
      the tearful little Loves circle about.
      From their wings they pluck the lovely plumes
      and make them food for the voracious fire.
      The three sad Graces, daughters of great Zeus,
      cast in their garlands and their necklaces.
      Venus desires to trim her golden locks
      and offer them as victims to the flames.

402. Thence she begins, according to the rites,
     to make a circuit thrice about the pyre,
     and bending o'er the corpse, to ashes burned,
     salutes those beauties now dissolved in air.
     But since now fiery Vulcan languishes,
     and the beloved bones have turned to dust,
     with her own hands she gathers the remains
     and presses them within a marble urn.

403. Sealed the vase in which is held as much
     beauty as heaven and nature e'er devised,
     Love, who stood in plaintive attitude,
     as if custodian of the precious urn,
     strove to soften with his bitter tears
     the hardness of that greedy sepulcher,
     and with the keen point of his golden dart
     engraved thereon this tender epitaph:

404. "O pilgrim, pause beside this marble urn,
     unless thou hast a heart of marble dure.
     Buried in this stone Adonis lies,
     and burned to ashes Love lies here with him.
     In these cold ashes, in this sepulcher,
     the light is spent indeed, but not the warmth.
     As proof thereof, but lightly touch the stone,
     and without flint a flame will issue thence."

405. Together bound beside the tomb were hung
     the bow, the lance, and all the other arms;
     besides an ivory tusk of the wild boar
     remained as trophy for the marble vault.
     And with like care the dog was then interred,
     and to the honors Phoebus lent his song,
     who on the grave of this slain animal
     in this inscription held his memory:

406. "Here Arrow lies, the dog whose bravery
     brought fear not only to wild beasts on earth

but even terrified the beasts above
that dwell within the heavenly Zodiac.
Pluto, to make his mansion more secure
holds him below to be inferno's guard,
for since bold Hercules invaded hell,
he dares not trust the gates to Cerberus.''

METAMORPHOSIS

[Venus has preserved the heart of Adonis from the ashes. She
speaks as follows:]

415. "What shall I do? If this be granted me,
      I fain would leave upon the earth some mark
      in grateful memory and honored pledge,
      a legacy of our unhappy love.
      If this was not denied the other gods,
      if other mortals merited such grace,
      why then shall I not be allowed the same?
      Oh why will not my idol have this boon?

416. "I then shall bring such honor to my love
      as did Apollo for his murdered youth,[24]
      for surely my dear flame was no less fair
      than was Narcissus or young Hyacinth.
      And since he was the flower of loveliness,
      and since his face and breast were decked with flowers,
      and he was taken in his flowering age,
      let him, changed to a flower, return to life.

417. "Among all flowers, my flower, thine be the prize,
      thou'lt take the scepter even from my rose.
      Thou wilt surpass whatever Chloris showers
      upon the earth, Aurora in the skies.
      Immortal ornament of rosy bowers,
      eternal glory of all Flora's charms,

      [24] Hyacinth.

new splendor of the meadows and the hills,
new trimming for my hair and for my breast."

     .   .   .   .   .

420. When she had spoken thus, by its great gift
that heart began to shower nectar sweet,
which gradually, by miracle divine,
changing its form, opened a lovely flower;
and in the garden's heart she planted it
among the thousand flowers of diverse kinds.
A blood-red flower, 'tis called anemone;
brief is its life, as his delight was brief.

Note on the Revolving Stage of Canto V

The description of the revolving or turntable stage (stanzas 127 ff.), pivoted and set in rotation by a system of cranks and cogs, and permitting a new scene to be set backstage and quickly swung into place, raises the question as to whether it was the creation of Marino's imagination or was derived from a stage he had actually seen or heard described. Despite the many elaborate and ingenious types of stage machinery employed in the sixteenth and seventeenth centuries, there is no record, so far as I have been able to determine, of a turntable stage anywhere in Europe before the nineteenth century. Standard discussions on stage history report that the device was introduced in Germany in imitation of the practice of the Japanese kabuki theater, where it had been employed as early as the eighteenth century.

Marino's modern editor, Giuseppe Ferrero, suggests that Marino may have derived the idea from a passage in Pliny the Elder (*Naturalis Historia* XXXVI, 24) in which he noted the construction in 50 B.C. in Rome of twin theaters set on pivots and rollers so that they could be positioned back to back and used as separate theaters or could be swung around to bring the two stages together and form a complete amphitheater of the banked seats. The fact that Marino alluded to these theaters in a dedicatory letter in *Il Tempio* confirms his interest in the mechanical curiosity, but the actual machinery and the whole concept is fundamentally different from what Marino is describing in the passage under scrutiny.

Another possible source for the idea comes to our attention. It has been reported that Leonardo da Vinci designed a revolving stage for a royal theatrical production at Milan about 1490–95. (For a full presentation of the theory, see Kate Trauman Steinitz, "A Reconstruction of Leonardo da Vinci's Revolving Stage," *Art Quarterly,* XII [1949], 325–38.) To support this claim, three items of evidence are cited: the text of a drama by Bernardo Bellincioni entitled *Paradiso,* for which Leonardo is known to have designed the sets; a brief eyewitness account of that production; and some drawings and notes in one of Leonardo's notebooks for an elaborate stage mountain that could open to reveal a domed cavern. (Leonardo da Vinci, *Codex Arundel* 263, f. 224r, 231v.) The whole thesis breaks down when we examine the drawings referred to in Leonardo's notebook, which show a mountain that would divide and open when its two front sections were swung out and back—a device quite different from a revolving stage.

There are other flaws in the claim for Leonardo: the drawings were obviously not for the production of Bellincioni's *Paradiso,* since the scene in the drawings is clearly labeled "Inferno with Pluto and the Furies." There is no record that the scenery in the drawings was ever constructed. We know that there was a production of *Paradiso* and that the scenery was by Leonardo, and it is, of course, possible that he used the same type of opening mountain for paradise that he drew for his inferno plan, though no mention of this occurs. The only movement which was recorded in connection with the production of *Paradiso* was the movement of some actors in the dome who represented stars.

Nevertheless, the basic objection to the theory is that the movement of the two upright sections of scenery in opposite directions could not function in connection with a revolving or turntable stage as we now employ the term.

Actually as we read Marino's description we find the report of the mechanism is so detailed, so circumstantial, that we entertain a conviction he might possibly have seen such a device or at least heard one described in detail. Nevertheless, since we can find no record of the existence of any revolving stage earlier than Marino, we may tentatively conjecture that he concocted the device out of his imagination.